# Yale French Studies

NUMBER 67

# Concepts of Closure

# Yale French Studies

David F. Hult, *Special editor for this issue*
Liliane Greene, *Managing editor*
*Editorial board:* Peter Brooks (Chairman), Alan Astro,
    Ellen Burt, Paul de Man, Shoshana Felman,
    Richard Goodkin, Karen McPherson, Elissa
    Marder, Charles Porter
*Staff:* Elise Hsieh, Peggy McCracken
*Editorial office:* 315 William L. Harkness Hall.
*Mailing address:* 2504A Yale Station, New Haven,
    Connecticut 06520.
*Sales and subscription office:*
    Yale University Press, 92A Yale Station
    New Haven, Connecticut 06520.
Published twice annually by Yale University Press.

Designed by James J. Johnson and set in Trump
    Medieval Roman by The Composing Room of
    Michigan, Inc.
Printed in the United States of America by The Vail-
    Ballou Press, Binghamton, N.Y.
ISSN 0044-0078
ISBN for this issue 0-300-03224-2

# EDITOR'S PREFACE

Nel suo profondo vidi che s'interna,
  legato con amore in un volume,
  ciò che per l'universo si squaderna.

—Dante Alighieri

In the midst of a carefully handwritten poetic text—itself a transcription of an earlier work—two modest figures are portrayed, each seated at his individual desk and in the process of writing (or composing) still another text. The figures, set into adjacent rectangular boxes, are facing each other; they could almost be mirror images were it not for slight divergences of color, bodily positioning, and the inversion of their writing instruments, stylus and pen-knife. One other significant difference: the figure on the left has covered more than half of his parchment while the one on the right has finished only a couple of indistinguishable characters. Who are these clerical figures?

At first we must assume that these are portraits of the medieval authors Guillaume de Lorris and Jean de Meun, since the illustration is placed at the interval separating the last lines of Guillaume's poetic fragment from the first lines of Jean's continuation. Furthermore, a rubric found just above the illumination provides the following information: "Veez ci commen Maistre Jehan de Meun commence" ["Behold how Master Jean de Meun begins"]. One is tempted to ask how it is that Jean begins, given that both figures are clearly in the middle of their tasks. Does the double portrait, the mirroring of scribal figures, give us the answer? Does one begin as a specular double of that which one emulates? Does one ever really "begin"?

If indeed the illumination purports to tell the "how" of Jean's undertaking, then perhaps the portraits are not to be understood *literally*, that is as mimetic representations of the authors' bodily forms. Perhaps they are allegories for what is then to be taken as the dual operation of writing and continuing—irreducible and complementary factors of *any* text. The apparent simultaneity of the two writers, as though they were working in neighboring cubicles, makes up part of the illusionistic allegory, for we know from elsewhere that Jean will undertake his continuation forty years after the death of Guillaume. The point is, perhaps, that whatever the chronological restrictions might be Jean can still gaze at the text—and perhaps even into the "eyes"—of his predecessor; but, equally suggestive, Guillaume can peer at his continuator. Is literary composition any more (or any less?) than a game of mirrors, of glances, of imitation and projection, of writing and rewriting? Furthermore, is the "how" of the beginning not in turn illusory, since one is always at least figuratively in the midst of one's text? What distinguishes our own pre-text from that of our continuator/interpreter?

Inside/Outside . . . Before/During/After . . . Beginning/End. . . . These are traditional spatial and temporal coordinates used to measure, to circumscribe, indeed to distinguish, events, people and the artistic works they create within a taut historico-geographical framework. They all serve the purpose of conveying a sense of unity, completeness and originality in a world where meanings are fixed and ideas well-formed. Speculation on closure in literature and art represents a contrary movement: it is a response to, and certainly a symptom of, a modern intellectual climate characterized by decenteredness, isolation and absence of meaning (both in the world and in language). The metaphoric thrust of the term "closure" is deceptively simple and has been the object of considerable critical elaboration since Barbara Herrnstein Smith used it, some fifteen years ago, to designate the "study of how poems end." As a spatial description, "closure" initially encompasses all the coordinates appertaining to a circumscribed territory: the "enclosed place" itself; "that which encloses"; "the act of enclosing"; and "the fact of being enclosed." A metaphorical transfer makes the term operate at an abstract level, as applied to logical or perceptual enclosures, a "bringing to a conclusion." But however much the formalistic underpinnings of the term immediately liken "closure" to its quasi-synonym "end," they are to be carefully distinguished. Essentially a verbal form, "closure" (Latin *clausūra*, a participial form of the verb *claudĕre*, "to shut or close") stands in stark contrast to the nominal form of the Germanic word "end." It implies, first and foremost, an *act* (of closing) and thus the intervention of a subject effecting the work's completion. The ground is subtly but no less definitively shifted from that of the work's *essential* unity to its contingency as a discrete object of investigation. "Closure" comes to interrogate not simply predetermined units (those "having" an end) but rather what it is that manages to determine or delimit a given artistic unit, what in fact defines and constitutes its very boundaries. Thus, to make a simple but useful equation: "End" is to "meaning" as "closure" is to "interpretation."

"Closure" thus suggests a line of inquiry which is at least as attentive to openings as it is to closings. And this constitutes the basis of the term's fundamental paradoxicality for, as a discourse on the framing of artistic works, it must necessarily dwell on that which forms the work *from the outside* and which consequently excludes itself. The "discourse on the frame" is largely a questioning of the interpreter's role in the literary process—that "second(ary) figure" who glares at, copies, and circumscribes his predecessor. But what "closure" discovers as well is that the inner movement in the direction of unity or completeness, toward which any literary work must be considered to aspire by virtue of its being an artistic object, is itself a provocative form of *incompleteness calling for a commentative discourse. Inherent in the notion of "closure," then, there would be an antiphilological sense of intersubjectivity, either implicit in the work's structure or simply a consequence of the interpretive act itself. The power of literature resides, perhaps, in the culturally based, multifaceted response it manages to elicit. As the medieval pictorial allegory suggests in such an elegant fashion, the act of writing is a specular, repetitive, profoundly intersubjective one. And one which, conceivably, has no bounds.

Is this scenario a part of the critic's imaginative self-justification (critic-as-artist) or can the closure of the literary work be rethought as a necessary and unshakeable illusion? The response to this question will of course vary depending upon the claims, both explicit and implicit, made by individual works. Changing ideological structures and the evolving attitudes of society with regard to the function of literature will certainly play a part in the scenario. Imposed or invented *material* constraints on the process of writing (such as may result from fragmentation, manuscript transmission, oral composition, and a host of other accidents affecting a written composition) will also enter into an evaluation of closure. And these "other" factors will inevitably nuance the traditional vision of the author's overriding subjectivity and the prestige of his intentionality. The essays gathered together in the present volume—each focused on a specific work—approach the question of closure from a variety of angles and cover a wide range of historical periods, from the Middle Ages to recent writings of the Parisian avant-garde. I have subdivided them into three rough and admittedly arbitrary categories, as they can be seen to reflect distinct stages in an interpretive foreclosure. The first section, "Closure at the Margins of Writing," includes four studies oriented toward literature's play with a nonliterary space, be it a material one affecting the work's realization or a sociopolitical structure which the work purports to encompass. The interests of fiction, ultimately, override the finite concerns of the "real world." The second section, "Experiments in Closure," brings together seven studies showing how works do or do not achieve closure according to some *inner* logic, be it of a formal, stylistic, political or genealogical nature. The final section covers two cases of literary influence, in which intersubjectivity itself becomes internalized as a poetic principle.

Finally a word about the essay which opens the issue and which stands alone outside of confining rubric, that of Eugenio Donato. Far and away the most ambitious of the articles, it is also the most personal and the most difficult to categorize, encompassing as it does a broad philosophical scenario of ends, closures, influences and anticipations which situate theory and literarity in a seemingly untouchable dimension. If we may consider it an irony that this was one of the last pieces completed by Donato before his untimely death, let us see it as a most elegant and appropriate one. This volume is dedicated to his memory.

DAVID HULT

*Hors Texte*

EUGENIO DONATO

# Ending/Closure: On Derrida's Edging of Heidegger

The wasteland grows

—Nietzsche

For that is what we are now; men who have leapt. . . . And where have we leapt? Perhaps into an abyss? No! Rather onto some firm soil. Some? No! But on that soil upon which we live and die, if we are honest with ourselves.

—Heidegger

La proximité de deux langues, ça ne veut rien dire, il y a là toute l'énigme de la traduction.

—Derrida

The task of reading Derrida's relation to Heidegger is, at the present crossroads of critical theory, urgent and necessary yet probably impossible; not only because of its complexity but more pertinently because— between the systematic discussions of Heidegger extending from the earlier *Of Grammatology* and *Margins of Philosophy* to his discussion of Heidegger's reading of Nietzsche in *Eperons* and his later more playful and "literary" references in *La Carte Postale*—there exist some three thousand pages representing lectures and seminars devoted to the German philosopher which to this day remain unpublished.

At the present time, the task of interpreting Derrida's reading of Heidegger would be comparable to that of interpreting Heidegger's reading of Nietzsche without being able to consult the text of the former's lectures at the University of Freiburg, now published in an expanded form under the title *Nietzsche*. The endeavor of reading Derrida's reading of Heidegger belongs to an indefinite future. Nevertheless, paradoxically, in what follows, I should like to underscore the necessity and timeliness of such an impossible task.

Judging from the recent controversies and publications surrounding the notion of "deconstruction," it is safe to assume that such a thing as deconstructive criticism exists and that, whatever deconstructive criticism is, it stems in great part from the works of Derrida—I am using the vague expression "works" rather than the word "theory" because,

3

given the nature of Derrida's philosophical enterprise, one would have to put the word "theory" in between brackets. To leave the word unbracketed would imply an interpretation of Derrida's writings that would considerably simplify their translation into a literary theoretical idiom.

Deconstruction exists today as a specifically American or Anglo-Saxon phenomenon—quite distinct from, say, a continental philosophical idiom inspired by Derrida's and, as such, not only owes as much to De Man, Hillis Miller and Bloom, but is also, strictly speaking, a predominantly literary practice. Broadly characterized as a theory of literary texts and literary criticism, deconstruction is far from being synonymous with Derrida's philosophical—or for that matter literary—aims and practices. Deconstruction is better described as the product of the grafting of a theoretical translation of Derrida's writings onto a number of native literary practices or, as some would no doubt prefer to see it, as the contamination of a native critical idiom by a set of foreign, pernicious philosophical positions and practices. Given the tone of the controversies that have surrounded deconstruction—think of the inane and uninformed pronouncements of a Denis Donoghue in the *New York Review of Books* or a Donald Reiman in the *Times Literary Supplement*[1]—, it is difficult not to imagine that the influence of Derrida on

1. Among the exemplary forms of argument used by the opponents of deconstruction, let me just quote the following two. The first is from Denis Donoghue's "Deconstructing Deconstruction," published in the June 12, 1980 issue of *The New York Review of Books*, and the second is from Donald Reiman's letter to the editor of the February 18, 1983 issue of *The Times Literary Supplement*:

I have only two or three thoughts on the subject. I think Deconstruction appeals to the clerisy of graduate students, who like to feel themselves superior to the laity of common readers, liberated from their shared meanings; liberated, too, from the tedious requirement of meaning as such, the official obligation to suppose that words mean something finite rather than everything or nothing. Deconstruction allows them to think of themselves as forming a cell, the nearest thing the universities can offer in the form of an avant-garde. The wretched side of this is that Deconstruction encourages them to feel superior not only to undergraduates but to the authors they are reading (*The New York Review of Books*, 41).

Paul de Man, in particular, but the entire Yale school in effect, are mystifying literary studies in an effort to cut off students from the reformist and egalitarian values inherent in literary studies in America. By developing an arcane technical terminology and by demanding an exhausting apprenticeship in the reading of their own criticism (as well as in the works of selected European critics and philosophers), they close off from careers in teaching literature students of working-class background and those who began their studies at public (i.e. non-tuition) schools in the American heartland (where the foreign language most

literary criticism is perceived in many an academic hall as the arrival of an intellectual plague. The association of deconstruction with a single institution, and the presumed existence of a Yale school, the publication of *Deconstruction and Criticism*, far from clarifying the issue of the relation of Derrida's writings to literary deconstruction have only muddied the waters to such an extent that, many a subtle difference being erased, a clear, speculative image such as Jonathan Culler's *On Deconstruction* has become possible. That the rare protests against the identification of American literary deconstruction with Derrida's philosophical strategies—such as Rodolphe Gasché's—have not attracted the attention they deserve is itself significant.[2]

The subtitle of Jonathan Culler's book—*Theory and Criticism After Structuralism*—implicitly echoes Frank Lentricchia's book, *After the New Criticism*, which, with its confused genealogies and attempt to situate deconstruction in a continuous history of American criticism, is more interesting as the symptom of a problem rather than because it offers an accurate description or nuanced solution. No doubt Culler sets the story straight and succeeds in giving a clear and succinct, if partial, account of American literary deconstruction. The question I wish to raise is that of some of the implications of this seemingly innocent translation of a continental philosophical problematic into an American literary idiom.

Gasché's essay had cogently argued for the necessity of recognizing a particular philosophical tradition in order to correctly situate the originality of Derrida's enterprise. Specifically, for Gasché, Derrida's notion of a deconstructive philosophical reading has its roots in a reflexive critique of phenomenology. Gasché would place Derrida in a history that would minimally coinvolve the names of Husserl and Merleau-Ponty.[3] Assuming for a moment, and for the sake of argument, that Gasché indeed succeeds in identifying the correct history that subtends

---

widely taught is Spanish), or those who took undergraduate degrees at small colleges, where strong programmes in classical rhetoric, German philosophy, or contemporary French thought are rare and where interest in the relationship of literature to life is paramount (*The Times Literary Supplement*, 159).

2. Rodolphe Gasché, "Deconstruction as Criticism" in *Glyph 6: Textual Studies* (Baltimore: The Johns Hopkins University Press, 1979), 177–215.

3. A recent text by Derrida himself "The time of a thesis: punctuations" in *Philosophy in France Today*, ed. Alan Montefiore (Cambridge: Cambridge University Press, 1983), 34–50 goes a long way towards clarifying part of the intellectual history that subtends his work. Derrida underscores how his interest in Husserl began as a reaction to the use of Husserlian phenomenology by Sartre and Merleau-Ponty. Derrida's statements in fact complicate considerably Gasché's history of deconstruction.

Derrida's enterprise, how could Culler, who devotes roughly 140 pages of his 300 page book to explaining Derrida's position, write: "I will not attempt to discuss the relationship of Derridean deconstruction to the work of Hegel, Nietzsche, Husserl and Heidegger"?[4]

If Derrida had only written the "Introduction" to his translation of Husserl's *The Origin of Geometry* and *Speech and Phenomena*, would we see in him today the philosopher most responsible for philosophical deconstructive reading and, by implication, deconstructive literary criticism? Perhaps. Derrida's comment on the "Introduction" to *The Origin of Geometry*, from the privileged position of the *Grammatology*, singles out the critique of the notion of origin as one of the main themes of his earlier work and, no doubt, a critique of the notion of origin is a by-product of deconstructive readings. Nevertheless, Derrida himself, in the *Grammatology*, that is to say, in the text in which he chooses to massively introduce the term of "deconstruction," characterizes the "Introduction"—or more precisely, his treatment of the theme of origins in the "Introduction"—as a *critique* and not as a deconstruction:

> Quant à cette critique du concept d'origine en général (empirique et/ou transcendentale) nous avons tenté ailleurs d'indiquer le schéma d'une argumentation.

> As for this critique of the concept of origin in general (empirical and/or transcendental), we have attempted elsewhere to indicate the schema of a possible argument.[5]

Again, if we turn to *Speech and Phenomena* and read the extraordinary note to the chapter entitled "le vouloir-dire comme soliloque" ["the will-to-signify as soliloquy"] in which Derrida states his ultimate intention in writing that particular essay, it is not certain that the

4. Jonathan Culler, *On Deconstruction: Theory and Criticism after Structuralism* (Ithaca: Cornell University Press, 1982), 85.
5. Derrida, *De la grammatologie* (Paris: Éditions de Minuit, 1967), 90. All translations throughout this essay are my own. Subsequent quotations from Derrida's writings will be noted in the text as follows:

G:   *De la grammatologie.*
VP:  *La voix et le phénomène: introduction au problème du signe dans la phénoménologie de Husserl* (Paris: Presses Universitaires de France, 1972).
M:   *Marges de la philosophie* (Paris: Les Éditions de Minuit, 1972).
E:   *Éperons: Les styles de Nietzsche* (Venice: Corbe e Fiore, 1976).
F:   "D'un ton apocalyptique adopté naguère en philosophie" in *Les fins de l'homme: à partir du travail de Jacques Derrida* (Paris: Éditions Galilée, 1981).

analysis it offers is strictly speaking "deconstructive" in the sense that the word has in the *Grammatology*. Specifically, the note in part reads:

> En affirmant que la *perception n'existe pas* ou que ce qu'on appelle perception n'est pas originaire, et que d'une certaine manière tout "commence" par la "re-présentation" (proposition qui ne peut évidemment se soutenir que dans la rature de ces deux derniers concepts: elle signifie qu'il n'y a pas de "commencement" et la "re-présentation" dont nous parlons n'est pas la modification d'un "re-" *survenue* à une présentation originaire), en réintroduisant la différence du "signe" au coeur de "l'originaire," il ne s'agit pas de revenir en deçà de la phénoménologie transcendantale, que ce soit vers un "empirisme" ou vers une critique "kantienne" de la prétention à l'intuition originaire. Nous venons ainsi de désigner l'intention première—et l'horizon lointain—du présent essai. [*VP*, 50]

> By affirming that *perception does not exist* or that that which is called perception is not originary, that, in a certain fashion, everything "begins" with "re-presentation" (a proposition that evidently can only be sustained by the erasure of these two concepts: it means that there is no "beginning" and that the "re-presentation" of which we speak is not the modification of a "re-" which comes after or over an originary presentation) and by reintroducing the difference of the sign at the heart of the "originary," we should not take a step back from transcendental phenomenology towards either an "empiricism" or a "Kantian" critique of the pretension to an originary intuition. We have thus indicated the initial intention—and the distant horizon—of the present essay.

Derrida's assertion that perception does not exist, or rather, that perception is not originary but always already a re-presentation, stems from a philosophical critique of a number of concepts which constitute the very ground of Husserlian phenomenology. Specifically, *Speech and Phenomena* constitutes a radical critique of, on the one hand, the "présence du sens à une intuition pleine et originaire" (*VP*, 3) ["presence of meaning to a full and originary intuition."] necessary to the constitution of an ideality which could be "répétée indéfiniment dans l'identité de sa présence" ["repeated indefinitely in the identity of its presence,"] and, on the other, of the possibility or meaning of a *Bedeutung* which is "immédiatement présente à l'acte d'expression" (*VP*, 86) ["immediately present to the act of expression."]

Had Derrida stopped writing after *Speech and Phenomena*, the consequences of his writings would have been crucial for both philosophy and literary criticism inasmuch as both would have had to come to

terms with a new analytics of representation subtended by specific
temporal strictures which would determine its properties and ultimately ground a specific notion of representation which would play a role
similar to that played by the role of presence in phenomenology.

    *Speech and Phenomena* did announce a number of themes which
were going to be central to Derrida's later writings. In *Speech and Phenomena*, Derrida did underscore the metaphysical tenor of Husserl's
valorization of voice over writing. For Derrida, in the text of Husserl, the
materiality of language and the notion of "sign" open for phenomenology a moment of crisis—"Le moment de la crise est toujours
celui du signe" (*VP*, 91) ["The moment of crisis is always that of the
sign."] Again, it is in *Speech and Phenomena* that Derrida introduces
the "non-concept" of *différance*. Finally, it is at the end of *Speech and
Phenomena* that Derrida will introduce the notion of the closure of the
history of metaphysics so central to Derridean deconstruction, and it is
with this notion of closure that he will start engaging his dialogue with
Heidegger and, in particular, with the latter's problematic of the *end* of
metaphysics:

> . . . *à l'intérieur* de la métaphysique de la présence, de la philosophie
> comme savoir de la présence de l'objet, comme être-auprès-de-soi du
> savoir dans la conscience, nous croyons tout simplement au savoir
> absolu comme *clôture* sinon comme fin de l'histoire. Nous y croyons
> littéralement. *Et qu'une telle clôture a eu lieu.* L'histoire de l'être com-
> me présence, comme présence à soi dans le savoir absolu, comme con-
> science (de) soi dans l'infinité de la parousie, cette histoire est close. . . .
> Dans l'ouverture de cette question, *nous ne savons plus.* Ce qui ne veut
> pas dire que nous ne savons rien, mais que nous sommes au-delà du
> savoir absolu (et de son système éthique, esthétique ou religieux) vers
> ce à partir de quoi sa clôture s'annonce et se décide. [*VP*, 115]

Within the interior of the metaphysics of presence, of philosophy as
knowledge of the presence of the object, as the being-close-to-itself of
knowledge in consciousness, we believe, quite simply, in absolute
knowledge as the *closure*, if not the end, of history. We believe in it
literally. We believe that *such a closure has taken place.* The history of
Being as presence, as presence to itself in absolute knowledge, as self-
consciousness within the infinity of *parousia*—that history is closed.
. . . Within the opening of this question, *we no longer know.* This does
not mean to say that we know nothing, but instead that we are beyond
absolute knowledge . . . towards that from which its closure announces itself and decides itself.

    This assertion of the closure of the history of metaphysics leads
Derrida to a suggestive description of his future project: "Pour ce qui

'commence' alors, 'au-delà' du savoir absolu, des pensées inouïes sont réclamées qui se cherchent à travers la mémoire des vieux signes" (*VP*, 115) ["For that which 'begins' then, beyond absolute knowledge, *unheard-of* thoughts are needed that search for themselves across the memory of old signs."]

Yet if this quest for *unheard-of*, that is to say, "unvoiced" thoughts —brought about by a reading and re-writing of old signs—points toward Derrida's *Of Grammatology* and his deconstructive readings/writings, it does not yet constitute deconstruction—and not only because it comes at the end of the essay and constitutes an extension of his critique rather than a deconstructive reading as such. What separates *Speech and Phenomena* from *Of Grammatology* is the fact that, in the former work, the difference between the *closure* of metaphysics and Heidegger's *end* of metaphysics is not yet clearly marked and problematized. It is this not yet problematized relationship between the philosophical before of metaphysics and the "unheard-of thoughts" of its different future that separates *Speech and Phenomena* from *Of Grammatology*.

From the privileged position of the *Grammatology*, the metaphysical "before" of phenomenology and the "after" of deconstruction will be made dependent upon each other:

> Dans la temporalisation originaire et le mouvement du rapport à autrui, tels que Husserl les décrit effectivement, la non-présentation ou la dé-présentation est aussi "originaire" que la présentation. *C'est pourquoi une pensée de la trace ne peut pas plus rompre avec une phénoménologie transcendentale que s'y réduire.* . . . Dans la déconstruction de l'archie, on ne procède pas à une élection. [*G*, 91]

> In the originary temporalization and movement of the relationship to the other, such as Husserl effectively describes them, the non-presentation or the de-presentation is as "originary" as the presentation. *That is why a thought that thinks the trace can neither break with or be reduced to a transcendental phenomenology* . . . . In the deconstruction of the arche, we do not proceed to a choice.

But then this interdependence of deconstruction on phenomenology is itself related to a more problematical relationship between a Heideggerian *end* of metaphysics and a Derridean *closure* of metaphysics. It is in fact only after Derrida introduces the notion of deconstruction in the first chapter of the *Grammatology*, via the problem of reading Heidegger, that he can take a strictly speaking deconstructive, rather than critical, stance towards Husserlian phenomenology and begin to weave his complex "plot for philosophy."

Most readings of Derrida (including Culler's) and of the notion of deconstruction as a tool for a critique of Western "logocentrism" could strictly speaking be derived from Derrida's critique of Husserlian phenomenology and of the analytics of representation that it implies and hardly account for the need to introduce a strategy of deconstructive reading/writing.

*Of Grammatology* has been repeatedly read as a philosophical critique of the implicit presuppositions of the linguistic models of structuralism and semiology which dominated the French intellectual scene in the sixties, and of their scientific pretensions. *Of Grammatology* is supposed to have laid bare their metaphysical presuppositions and to have localized their pertinence to a repeated continuity of a philosophical history which they had pretended to have discarded or superseded.

If *Of Grammatology* was indeed responsible for inaugurating what today we loosely name poststructuralism, and if indeed Derrida's critique of the philosophical presuppositions of the representational system of modern linguistics is one of the salient themes of the work that launched Derrida's reputation outside of French philosophical circles, it is far from certain that it constitutes its most central philosophical concern. Derrida's own description of his intention in writing *Of Grammatology*, stated in the following terms, would locate its finality elsewhere:

> Ainsi, nous rapprochons ce concept de trace de celui qui est au centre des derniers écrits de E. Lévinas. . . . Accordée ici, et non dans la pensée de Levinas, à une intention heideggerienne, cette notion signifie, parfois au-delà du discours heideggerien, l'ébranlement d'une ontologie qui, dans son cours le plus intérieur, a déterminé le sens de l'être comme présence et le sens du langage comme continuité pleine de la parole. Rendre énigmatique ce que l'on croit entendre sous les noms de proximité, d'immédiateté, de présence (le proche, le propre et le pré- de la présence), telle serait donc la dernière intention du présent essai. Cette déconstruction de la présence passe par celle de la conscience, donc par la notion irréductible de trace (*Spur*), telle qu'elle apparaît dans le discours nietzschéen. . . . [*G*, 102–03]

Thus we draw together this concept of trace with that which is at the heart of the latest writings of Emmanuel Levinas. . . . In agreement here—and not in the thought of Levinas—with a Heideggerian intention, this notion means, sometimes beyond Heideggerian discourse, the shaking of an ontology which, in its most intimate course, has determined the meaning of being as presence and the meaning of language as the full continuity of speech. To render enigmatic that which we believe to understand by the names of proximity, immediacy, presence (the close, the proper, and pre- of presence), such would be the ultimate intention of this essay. This deconstruction of presence passes through the deconstruction of consciousness, and therefore through the irreducible notion of the trace (*Spur*) as it appears in the discourse of Nietzsche. . . .

The ultimate intention of the essay, then, has strictly speaking absolutely nothing to do with linguistics, structuralism, or semiology. Derrida's immediate aim, beyond stating the necessity for philosophy to read its tradition, i.e., to read a continuity established by betrayals and translations, is the reading of Heidegger and of his project of an ontology that would situate itself beyond a presumed Nietzschean end of metaphysics.

It is the need to read Heidegger that requires a deconstructive strategy—"style" would perhaps be more exact. If Derrida's statement involves Nietzsche, it is because a deconstructive reading of Heidegger of necessity involves Nietzsche since it is in Nietzsche that Heidegger will locate the *end* of metaphysics—any ulterior metaphysical position for Heidegger being only a localized repetition of a previously exhausted position.

That *Of Grammatology* is meant to define the nature of philosophical discourse *after* Heidegger, and that the critique of a certain linguistic imperialism is only a thematic strategy within this ultimate project, besides Derrida's statement, is evident from the "Exergue" of the *Grammatology,* and particularly from its first chapter, where Derrida for the first time systematically introduces the word "deconstruction" in relation to his proposed reading of a philosophical tradition dominated by the names of Hegel and Heidegger.

The three guiding themes enumerated at the beginning of the "Exergue" to describe the "order" of logocentrism could each be related to Heidegger. The first, namely the necessity of understanding the concept of "writing" "dans un monde où la phonétisation de l'écriture doit dissimuler sa propre histoire en se produisant" (*G,* 11) ["in a world in which the phoneticization of writing must dissimulate its own history in its very production"], refers to the logic of Being as described by Heidegger, a logic in which Being must occult itself in the very production of the history of its metaphysical misreadings. The third deals with the problem of the concept of science and clearly implies the necessity of questioning Heidegger's localization of the presuppositions of science within the aggravated repetition of a previous metaphysical position through their imperviousness to the question of the meaning of

Being. For Derrida, the proliferation of scientific languages, and particularly of the desemanticized syntactic "writing" of mathematics, should point to an area beyond the closure of metaphysics which a traditional philosophical discourse cannot take into account completely.

It is, however, the second guiding theme which is particularly relevant for the rest of the Derridean project. In Derrida's words:

> L'*histoire de la métaphysique* qui, malgré toutes les différences et non seulement de Platon à Hegel (en passant même par Leibniz) mais aussi, hors de ses limites apparentes, des présocratiques à Heidegger, a toujours assigné au logos l'origine de la vérité en général: l'histoire de la vérité, de la vérité de la vérité, a toujours été, à la différence près d'une diversion métaphorique dont il nous faudra rendre compte, l'abaissement de l'écriture et son refoulement hors de la parole "pleine." [G, 11–12]

> The history of metaphysics which, in spite of all differences, and not only from Plato to Hegel (passing even through Leibniz) but also, beyond its apparent boundaries, from the pre-Socratics to Heidegger, has always assigned the origin of truth in general to the logos: the history of truth, of the truth of truth, has always been, with the exception of one metaphorical diversion that we shall have to take into account, the denigration of writing, and its repression outside of the "plenitude" of speech.

Clearly, Derrida's project is to rewrite the "history" of philosophy as it is proposed by Heidegger. Indeed, as is well known, for the latter there exist, so to speak, two distinct "histories" of philosophy: one that starts with Plato and ends with Nietzsche and which constitutes the history of metaphysics properly speaking, then another idiom which precedes and follows the history of metaphysics, namely, that of the pre-Socratics and of Heidegger's own ontology, and which in part depends upon a dialogue with the genuine origin of philosophy as opposed to the false beginning inaugurated by Plato. My only reason for summarizing Heidegger's position in this almost caricatural fashion is to underscore the relevance for Derrida of the distinction between *end* and *closure*. Derrida's *closure* is a reading and a displacement of the Heideggerian notion of *end*. The rewriting of the *end* of metaphysics into its closure necessarily problematizes its concomitant notion of origin. Some thirteen years after the publication of the *Grammatology*, Derrida will return to this question of the complex relationship that endings maintain with origins and insist again on the need to distinguish between *end* and *closure*. In "D'un ton apocalyptique adopté naguère en philosophie"—and this very title is suggestive with regard to any assertion of an *end*—he will write: "La fin a toujours commencé, il faut encore distinguer entre clôture et fin" (*F*, 464) ["The ending has always begun, yet one must distinguish between end and closure."]

The displacement of the concept of *end* to that of the closure of metaphysics, as the preceding quotation clearly indicates, forbids us from thinking of the temporal and spatial patterns involved within such a displacement in terms of any simple, linear or hierarchical notion of history. For the notion of *closure* brought about by a reading of the notion of *end* complicates not only the ordinary notions of a "before" and an "after" that are necessary to any uncritical "history" of philosophy or literary theory, but also problematizes both Heidegger's own notion of the conceptual priority of the pre-Socratics over the Platonic "fall" and his assumed privileged belatedness with regard to Nietzsche—the thinker in whom, for Heidegger, metaphysics runs its full course and exhausts its philosophical content.

If until now I have emphasized the problem of reading as central to an understanding of the relationship of Derrida to Heidegger, making this relationship central to the understanding of Derrida's notion of a deconstructive style of reading underscoring Heidegger's use of his belatedness with respect to Nietzsche and Derrida's more problematical belatedness with respect to Heidegger, it is perhaps because, to a literary critic like myself, the most suggestive way of understanding Derrida's central confrontation with Heidegger comes from the perspective of a Bloomian problematic of influences and misreadings.

The "plot for philosophy" that Derrida writes for philosophy in some ways resembles Bloom's "plot for poetry." Minimally, the belated Heidegger can only become a strong philosopher by misreading his strong antecedent, Nietzsche. Heidegger's reading of Nietzsche as the *end* of metaphysics effectively allows the former, by claiming a continuity with the pre-Socratics, to become the precursor of his own precursor. In other words, the temporality that subtends the notion of *end* in Heidegger is metaleptic.

On the surface, Derrida's gesture of misreading the notion of the *end* of metaphysics as the *closure* of metaphysics seems to redouble the Heideggerian gesture. The very displacement of the Heideggerian necessity of a *destructive* reading into *a style of deconstructive reading*, a displacement which is inseparable from the displacement of the concept of *end* upon that of *closure*, has an immediate consequence— spelled out in the first chapter of the *Grammatology* and systematically worked out in a number of articles that followed its publication—of demonstrating a number of ways in which Heidegger's work is still in nostalgic complicity with the metaphysical system whose end he had proclaimed. It is not my purpose to analyze each specific reading of Heidegger by Derrida. It is enough to recall that Derrida, from the very first chapter of *Grammatology*, clearly states the motifs in Heidegger's thought that place him in the continuity of the very metaphysics he denounces. For instance, to Derrida, Heidegger's recourse to a certain notion of "truth"—even if it concerns the truth of Being—is in continuity with the onto-theology he wishes to supersede:

> Toutes les déterminations métaphysiques de la vérité et même celle à laquelle nous rappelle Heidegger, par-delà l'onto-théologie métaphysique, sont plus ou moins immédiatement inséparables de l'instance du logos ou d'une raison pensée dans la descendance du logos, en quelque sens qu'on l'entende. . . . Or dans ce logos, le lien originaire et essentiel à la *phonè* n'a jamais été rompu. . . . [*G*, 21]

> All the metaphysical determinations of truth, and even the one Heidegger reminds us of, beyond the onto-theology of metaphysics, are more or less immediately inseparable from an instance of the logos, or of a rationality thought within the lineage of the logos, in whatever way it is conceived. . . . Yet, within this logos, the originary and essential tie to the *phonè* has never been broken.

If phonocentrism and logocentrism are inseparable, then both can be shown to determine Heidegger's ontology:

> Le logocentrisme serait donc solidaire de la détermination de l'être de l'étant comme présence. Dans la mesure où un tel logocentrisme n'est pas tout à fait absent de la pensée heideggerienne, il la retient peut-être encore dans cette époque de l'onto-théologie, dans cette philosophie de la présence, c'est-à-dire dans *la* philosophie. Cela signifierait peut-être qu'on ne sort pas de l'époque dont on peut dessiner la clôture. [*G*, 23–24]

> Logocentrism would therefore be responsible for the determination of the being of that-which-is as presence. Inasmuch as such a logocentrism is not completely absent from Heideggerian thought, it perhaps retains that thought within the period of onto-theology, within the philosophy of presence, that is to say, within philosophy itself. This would perhaps mean that we do not go beyond a period whose closure we can sketch.

It is clearly, then, the notion of *closure* which allows Derrida to place Heidegger in a tradition whose *end* determines the possibility of his discourse. The notion of *closure* which reads the Heideggerian notion of *end* is, moreover, inseparable from the displacement—or perhaps I should say the misprision—of another Heideggerian concept; namely, that of an ontico-ontological difference into what Derrida chooses to name *différance*. The most synthetic statement of Derrida which interweaves all of these themes is situated again in the first chapter of the *Grammatology*. This passage deserves to be quoted in its entirety not only because it situates clearly the Derridean reading of the Heideggerian project, but also because it indicates one of the main thrusts of Derrida's own deconstructive motifs:

> En venir à reconnaître, non pas en-deçà mais à l'horizon des chemins heideggeriens, et encore en eux, que le sens de l'être n'est pas un signifié transcendantal ou trans-époqual (fût-il même toujours dissimulé dans l'époque) mais déjà, en un sens proprement *inouï*, une trace signifiante déterminée, c'est affirmer que dans le concept décisif de différence ontico-ontologique, *tout n'est pas à penser d'un seul trait:* étant et être, ontique et ontologique, "ontico-ontologique" seraient, en un style original, *dérivés* au regard de la différence; et par rapport à ce que nous appellerons plus loin la *différance*. . . . [*G*, 38]

> To come to recognize, not within but at the horizon of the Heideggerian paths, and yet in them, that the meaning of being is not a transcendental or transtemporal signified (even if it was always dissimulated within a temporal period), but already, in a properly *unheard of* meaning, a determined signifying trace, amounts to the affirmation that within the decisive concept of an ontico-ontological difference, *all must not be thought of in a single trait;* Being and that-which-is, ontical and ontological, ontico-ontological, would be, in an originary style, *derived* with regard to difference; and by that relationship which later on we will call *différance*.

And the passage will conclude with the statement that it is through the Heideggerian notion of difference and its erasure that "nous pourrons plus tard tenter de faire communiquer la différance et l'écriture" (38) ["we shall later on be able to attempt to put *différance* and writing in relation to each other."] That is to say, it is only through this very notion of *différance* which determines Heidegger's original gesture and its erasure that a deconstructive style of reading can come into existence.

It is, then, by a redoubling of the Heideggerian gesture that the Heideggerian notion of *end* is displaced to include, within the space it determines, that conceptual system that it generates in the first place. The Derridean *closure* is in part the consequence of the necessity for the end to repeat itself and to include that which pretends to overrun its borders. Within this limited horizon, the function of Derrida's *différance* follows the same metaleptic logic of Heidegger's difference. Towards the end of the article "*Différance*," Derrida will in fact be able to affirm that "la différance, d'une certaine et fort étrange manière, [est] plus "vieille" que la différence ontologique ou que la vérité de l'être" (*M*, 23) ["*Différance*, in a certain and rather strange manner, (is) older than either ontological difference or the truth of Being."]

If Derridean *différance* precedes and follows Heideggerian difference, it is because the latter differs from the former inasmuch as neither "before" nor "after" are "absolutes," but are instead effects produced by a system of *closure* that knows itself for what it is, namely, that it differs from difference and, by its repeated gesture, ruins the related notions of origin and end: "Beyond Being and that-which-is, this difference differing (itself) incessantly would trace itself. This *différance* would be the first of the last trace if one could still speak here of origins and of endings" (*M*, 77–78).

We may at this point return to a Bloomian version for a "plot for philosophy" and read Derrida's strong reading of Heidegger as the repetition of Heidegger's strong reading of Nietzsche. Yet that very repetition implies a difference: a difference which, as we have seen, affects the very notion of difference. If Bloom's map is suggestive for an understanding of Heidegger's reading of Nietzsche, it does not completely account for Derrida's reading of Heidegger. If Bloom's model repeats itself from strong poet to strong poet, that repetition is a repetition without a difference/*différance*—however one may wish to spell that word at this point. This is not to suggest that an understanding of Derrida's strategy in reading Heidegger would in any way invalidate Bloom's model. On the contrary, it complicates it to an extent where Bloom's map would describe one specific case of a more general model.

As I said earlier, Heidegger's concept of the end of metaphysics rests upon his reading of Nietzsche. Two questions necessarily come to mind: the first is strictly a Bloomian question, namely: if Heidegger has to undertake a strong belated reading of Nietzsche, what are his specific "dialectics of revisionism"? The other is: what is the function of Nietzsche in Derrida's reading of Heidegger? Each of these questions is too complex to be given, in this context, the attention it deserves. I will, nevertheless, attempt a partial answer, aware that certain generalizations inevitably run the risk of oversimplification.

Minimally, for the Derrida of the *Grammatology*, Nietzsche does not quite exhaust or end metaphysics in the Heideggerian sense. For Derrida, Heidegger, from one perspective, is right; yet it is by and through the Heideggerian reading, and only in that way, that a certain aspect of Nietzsche becomes irreducible to Heidegger's very reading. It is only by abandoning Nietzsche to a Heideggerian reading that one may come to recognize a specific aspect of his work as "post"-Heideggerian, "post" the *end* of metaphysics, and, in a certain sense, also "post" any closure of metaphysics. In Derrida's words:

> Peut-être ne faut-il donc pas soustraire Nietzsche à la lecture heideg-
> gerienne mais au contraire l'y offrir totalement, souscrire sans réserve à
> cette interprétation; d'une *certaine manière* et jusqu'au point où le
> contenu du discours nietzschéen étant à peu près perdu pour la ques-
> tion de l'être, sa forme retrouve son étrangeté absolue, où son texte
> enfin appelle un autre type de lecture, plus fidèle à son type d'écriture.
> [*G*, 32]

> Perhaps we should not withdraw Nietzsche from a Heideggerian read-
> ing but on the contrary abandon him to it completely, subscribing to
> this interpretation without reserve, in a *certain fashion* and up to the
> point where the content of the Nietzschean discourse being almost lost
> for the question of Being, its form regains its absolute strangeness,
> where his text finally calls for another type of reading, more faithful to
> his type of writing.

It is only through the Heideggerian reading that "reading," and there-
fore writing, texts would be for Nietzsche "'originary' operations." But Nietzsche's position with regard to Heidegger—and also to Derrida—is paradoxical. For, in a Bloomian vocabulary, we can say that, on the one hand, Nietzsche is indeed Heidegger's strong precursor who permits the latter to become a strong philosopher by reading in the former a philosophical *end*. Nevertheless, Heidegger, as a strong precursor of Derrida, permits the latter not only to be in his turn a strong philosopher by displacing a problematics of *ending* onto one of *closure*, but Derrida does so by displacing Heidegger's precursor to the position of a successor. Nietzsche is thus both "before" and "after" Heidegger and it is only because Nietzsche is "after" Heidegger that Derrida can also be "after" Heidegger. Ultimately, in fact, a certain Nietzsche is situated possibly even after Derrida, i.e., after the *closure* of metaphysics.

Derrida's reading of Heidegger implies a strategic positioning of Nietzsche that considerably complicates the temporal modes and spa-
tial topology between precursor and successor as well as between the notions of *end* and *closure*, and it is in this complex temporality and topology that Derridean deconstruction and the concept of *text* reside. If every *closure* necessarily inscribes an *end* within itself, it is also true

that every end, by being also a *closure,* cleaves itself to allow a certain part of itself not to be accountable by the mastery implied by an *end.*

The names Nietzsche, Heidegger, and Derrida here stand also for what Derrida would have us recognize as different moments that belong to any literary or philosophical textual practice—inasmuch as every text exists by a redoubled series of readings/writings which depend upon and constitute a unique system in which the temporal and spatial hierarchies of "before" and "after," "inside" and "outside," "form" and "content," etc., are destabilized by their own redoubling within a system that is always simultaneously a reading and a writing.

Given the complexity of this logic, every "reading" would seem to have two possible strategies. The first would inhabit a text from the inside, that is to say, would "tenter la sortie et la déconstruction sans changer de terrain, en répétant l'implicite des concepts fondateurs et de la problématique originelle, en utilisant contre l'édifice les instruments ou les pierres disponibles dans la maison, c'est-à-dire aussi bien dans la langue" (*M,* 162) ["attempt a break and a deconstruction without a change of ground, by repeating what is implicit in the founding concepts and in the originary problematic, by utilizing against the edifice the instruments or stones available in the house, that is to say, in language as well."]

The other alternative would pretend that a reading can place itself in an absolute exteriority. But such an exteriority is always only an apparent effect of a "trompe l'oeil," for "la simple pratique de la langue réinstalle sans cesse le 'nouveau' terrain sur le plus vieux sol" (*M,* 163) ["the simple practice of language ceaselessly reinstalls the new terrain onto the oldest ground."]

The opposition between the two styles of reading being a false one, every reading must "entrelacer les deux motifs" ["interweave the two motifs"] and "parler plusieurs langues et produire plusieurs textes à la fois" ["speak several languages and produce a plurality of texts at the same time."] But, then, Nietzsche and Heidegger are only the names of the *text.*

At this juncture, it is impossible to describe the logic of a *text* in terms of a before and an after, an inside and an outside, etc. The best metaphorical approximation to describe the temporal structure of this logic is perhaps that offered by Derrida himself when punning on the word "veille." He writes:

Doit-on lire Nietzsche, avec Heidegger, comme le dernier des grands métaphysiciens? Doit-on au contraire entendre la question de la vérité de l'être comme le dernier sursaut ensommeillé de l'homme supérieur? Doit-on entendre la veille comme la garde montée auprès de la maison ou comme l'éveil au jour qui vient, à la veille duquel nous sommes? . . . Nous sommes peut-être entre ces deux veilles. . . [M, 163–64]

Should we read Nietzsche, with Heidegger, as the last of the great metaphysicians? Or should we, on the contrary, understand the question of the truth of Being as the last sleeping gasp of the superior man? Should we understand the *eve* as the guard standing watch over the house or as the awakening to the day that comes, at the eve of which we are. . . . We are perhaps between these two eves.

We may turn now to the first question we asked in a Bloomian key; namely, if a deconstructive reading depends upon a model generated by Heidegger's reading of Nietzsche, and of Derrida's reading of Heidegger's reading of Nietzsche, what are the "dialectics of revisionism" of Heidegger's reading of Nietzsche?

The answer to this question is not simple. In his own reading of Nietzsche, Derrida will point to what he calls a "process of propriation"[6] and to a "gambit of the gift" (*coup de don*) as that which in the text of Nietzsche will necessarily escape Heidegger's reading:

Si l'opposition du *donner* et du *posséder* est une sorte de leurre transcendantal produit par la graphique de l'hymen, le procès de propriation échappe à toute dialectique comme à toute décidabilité ontologique. [E, 86]

If the opposition of to *give* and to *take*, of to *possess* and to *be possessed*, is nothing more than a kind of transcendental snare which is produced by the hymen's graphic, the process of propriation would then escape all dialectics as well as any ontological decidability.

Hence, Heidegger's ontological question of the "truth of being" is incapable of reading at least that component of Nietzsche's text which will inscribe, by a necessary reversal, Heidegger's own problematic.

La question du sens ou de la vérité de l'être n'est pas *capable* de la question du propre, de l'échange indécidable du plus en moins, du donner-prendre, du donner-garder, du donner-nuire, du *coup de don*. Elle n'en est pas capable parce qu'elle y est inscrite. [E, 86–87]

---

6. Defined elsewhere in the text as "appropriation, expropriation, prise, prise of possession, gift and exchange, mastery, servitude, etc" (E, 84).

The question of the meaning or of the truth of being is not capable of the question of the proper, of the undecidable exchange of the more into less, of the to give for taking, of the to give for keeping, of the to give for hurting, of the *coup de don*. It is not capable because it is already inscribed in the process of propriation.

The preceding remarks are not meant to exhaust Derrida's reading of Heidegger's Nietzsche in *Eperons*. Derrida, in fact, will suggest that Heidegger himself will eventually, in *Time and Being*, come to recognize the philosophical irreducibility of this "process of propriation" and "submit" (*soumet* is in italics in the text) to it the very question of Being, and comes, in a belated recognition, to accept that the "giving" (*donner, geben*) and the "donation" (*donation, Gabe*) implied in the *es gibt sein* "ne se laissent plus penser dans l'être, dans l'horizon ou à partir du sens de l'être de la vérité" ["no longer allow themselves to be thought within Being, within the horizon, or derived from the meaning of the Being of truth."] In other words, Derrida recognizes in the very text of Heidegger a textual process which remains irreducible to the latter's fundamental ontology.

Be that as it may, inasmuch as the "process of propriation" in Nietzsche's text remains a blind spot for Heidegger—at least in his *Nietzsche*—he has to fail to read it precisely because it is one of the textual components of Nietzsche's writing that reads Heidegger's original philosophical undertaking. Derrida's reading of Heidegger's reading of Nietzsche, then, is not quite reducible to a canonic Bloomian form. If we wish to maintain the Bloomian form of the question, then we must ask what—specifically in the text of Nietzsche—Heidegger refuses to read or chooses to misread. The answer to this question is not provided by Derrida but by Lacoue-Labarthe who, in a series of readings inspired by the questions of Derrida, has attempted to answer precisely the question of what in Nietzsche's text is necessarily erased in Heidegger's reading of his predecessor as the *end* of metaphysics. It would be an impossible task to summarize adequately Lacoue-Labarthe's decisive readings of Heidegger's reading of Nietzsche.[7] In this context, suffice it to say that the axis of Lacoue-Labarthe's texts is a meticulous demonstration that Heidegger's reading aims at a neutralization of the effects of the literary forms, the textual presentation, the *Darstellung*, the fictioning, in short, of the literariness of Nietzsche's texts in general and of *Zarathustra* in particular.

7. See his "Typographie" in *Mimesis désarticulations* (Paris: Aubier-Flammarion, 1975), 165–270, and his *Le Sujet de la philosophie* (Paris: Aubier-Flammarion, 1979).

Heidegger's contempt for what he calls literature, and his stated requirement to separate a poetical idiom, a privileged *Dichtung*, from literature is well known. For Heidegger, the poetic, as distinct from the literary, should be in a privileged proximity to thinking. *Denken* and *Dichtung* belong to each other and are always distinct from the fictional and the literary. To quote one passage among many, Heidegger, in *What is Called Thinking*, writes:

> Homer, Sappho, Pindar, Sophocles, are they literature? No! But that is the way they appear to us, and the only way, even when we are engaged in demonstrating by means of literary history that these works of poetry really are not literature.
>
> Literature is what has been literally written down, and copied, with the intent that it be available to a reading public. In that way literature becomes the object of widely diverging interests, which in turn are once more stimulated by literary means—through literary criticism . . . . The poesy of the Occident and European literature are two radically different forces in our history.[8]

Nietzsche, however, is literary, and literary with a vengeance, and that is the dimension of his work that Heidegger has to neutralize to be able to read his predecessor's writings as the final document of Western metaphysics. For, as Lacoue-Labarthe would have it, if Nietzsche did succeed in speaking "another language," it is because "the concept of *fiction* escapes conceptuality itself" ["le concept de *fiction* échappe à la conceptualité elle-même"] and cannot be "understood within the discourse of truth" ["compris dans le discours de la vérité"].[9] It is, in fact, the problematical nature of the literary dimension of Nietzsche's texts that allows Derrida to place him strategically in a hypothetical future beyond the closure of metaphysics.

The considerable problem raised by Derrida's strategy concerns, of course, the very nature of the specificity of the idioms of philosophy and literature. If, as I suggested earlier, the result of Derrida's reading/ writing strategy for deconstruction is to produce a notion of text in which temporal and spatial oppositions are reinscribed into each other, then, strictly speaking, a stable distinction between philosophical and literary idioms becomes untenable. And if in turn the notion of text liberates literary criticism from any normative function, it also precludes that literary criticism—deconstructive or otherwise—can ever find a

---

8. Heidegger, *What is Called Thinking*, trans. J. Glenn Gray (New York: Harper and Row, 1968), 134–35.

9. Lacoue-Labarthe, *Le Sujet de la philosophie*, 14.

ground for its practice independently from its performative strategies of reading/writing.

As a tentative conclusion to the preceding remarks, I should like, simply, to raise a few further questions. Are we literary critics yet ready to read Derrida? And have we, beyond our traditional and institutional constraints, learned to write in a "plural language"? If one of the many lessons to be learned from Derrida's own practice of reading and writing is that the temporality and topology of a text are such that it is impossible to disentangle its literary and philosophical moments, to neatly display their temporal order and spatial hierarchy, then should we not also admit that any attempt to define a concept of deconstruction based on Derrida's writings is by its very nature a misguided enterprise?

The corpus of writings we call Derrida still remains for us a precursor as well as a successor text, inasmuch as Derrida's philosophical enterprise implies the practice of a literary idiom. In this, perhaps, he is an exemplar. For is not the quest for the literariness of literature, for the "thing" literature which grounds our literary reading/writing as literary critics the very quest, the always/already improbable future, of our impossible practice?

*Closure At The Margins Of Writing*

PAUL ZUMTHOR

# The Impossible Closure of the Oral Text

The idea of closure constitutes one of the recurrent themes of contemporary thought on the text.* In the following pages, I do not intend to follow a similar line of inquiry; instead, I would like to reverse the order of the givens and postulate that closure can no longer be conceivable once one takes into consideration—be it prior to the message, beyond it, or in its innermost reaches—the body which both produces the message and, in so doing, gives it its form.

I am taking the material for the following remarks from the various types of oral poetry (especially song) which have been documented in the last century. Orality implies, obviously, use of the voice. But a voice emanates from a throat, from a chest; hand and arm gestures underscore its intonations; its efficacy, if not its very audibility, is determined by the positioning of torso or of legs. The voice can thus be considered the most subtle part of the body, the least strictly limited in space, less even than a glance. It is a wish-to-speak (*vouloir-dire*) and a desire for existence.† Locus of an absence which, through it, is transformed into presence, the voice modulates the cosmic influxes which traverse us and captures their signals; whence those infinite resonances which make all

*The following article is adapted from a larger study entitled *Introduction à la poésie orale* (Paris: Editions du Seuil, 1983).

†The French expression *vouloir-dire* here used by Zumthor is Jacques Derrida's translation for the German: *Bedeutung/bedeuten* (English: "meaning," "to mean"), which conveys the sense of intentionality lacking in the more common (and more ambiguous, for his purposes) French equivalent *signification*. See Derrida's *La Voix et le phénomène* (Paris: PUF, 1967), 17ff. But whereas in fact the English word "meaning" would be more appropriate for Derrida's discussion, "wish-to-speak" has here been chosen as a translation in order to reflect Zumthor's emphasis on voice in a context of oral poetic creation. Zumthor's quotation of the expression is thus a tacit rereading or revision of Derrida's philosophical position. [Editor's Note]

25

matter sing. It is as a corporeal force that the voice, in so many of our legends, exercised mastery over animals, plants and enchanted stones.

A poem transmitted by the voice is thus, through its very agency, opened onto an exterior toward which it aspires and in which it simultaneously produces an *echo:* the very noise created by my voice. There remains nonetheless an ambiguity: this opening (*ouverture*) sometimes effaces itself. I can "lower my voice." To be sure, every voice listens to itself and also resonates in itself. But is the voice ever alone? Even when listening to a record, I am not strictly limited to my perception of a vocal message. I can vaguely make out another presence, circumstances sketched out, a thousand elements which confirm its outward-turning movement—elements which are perhaps blurred at this instant and yet indissociable from the voice I hear. But there is something further: the poetic work transmitted in performance, unfolded in space, escapes somehow from imprisonment in time. Indeed, insofar as it *is* oral, it is never, in fact, exactly reiterable: the function of the media is of course to mitigate this incapacity. Since a reprise is always possible, it proves exceptional when a work is not the object of several performances: and, by necessity, the work is never the same. From the first to the second, or even to the third hearing of a record, the alterations remain minimal; certain of these alterations (the psychological makeup of the auditor, his particular circumstances at the time of listening) would similarly affect the successive readings of a book; others, such as acoustical conditions, are specific to this medium. In the series of declamations of an epic poem, however, the modifications go so far as to blur, at times, the identity of the work.

In any case, an *illusion of repeatability* constitutes the principal characteristic of oral poetry. It grounds the latter's mode of existence outside of performance while determining its preservation. Such preservation may result from two different practices, contradictory although generally conflated nowadays:

—*archival storage* through writing or electronic recording, which has the effect of fixing all or part of the elements of the work: verbal, sonorous, auditory and even visual if we consider film or video tape.

—or *memorization:* direct as well as—through various mediations—indirect, such as the kind which, having passed through the stage of writing, necessitates an interiorization of the text.

Archival storage stops the current of orality, arrests it at the level of a single performance. Stabilized in this way, the latter relinquishes the source of its vital movement, but at least conserves its capacity for inspiring other performances. Having read a song in a score or heard it on a record, I can sing it myself, have it sung by another, and change it at will. The play of competition will lead me, perhaps, to remake an edition of this work or to record a new interpretation: a sequence of events which poses delicate methodological problems for ethnologists (whose own practices are necessarily inscribed into this scheme).

Memorization, the natural mode of conserving oral poetry, remained the only functioning mode, even in societies with writing, for as long as the latter practice had not become generally accepted: in Europe, this was the case up to the close of the nineteenth century and, in certain regions, to the middle of our own century; but for a large portion of the Third World the situation persists to the present day. Even when it has passed that technological threshold in relation to which its importance rapidly decreases, memorization continues to fulfil its function in the marginal space unaffected by archival storage.

Jack Goody has observed, somewhat emblematically, that oral societies possess storytellers and orchestras, but neither novels nor symphonies. The oral text, by virtue of its mode of conservation, is less easily appropriated than a written one; it constitutes a common good in the social group which fosters its production. In this way it is more concrete than writing: the prefabricated discursive fragments that it conveys are both more numerous and semantically more stable. Within a single text—as it is being transmitted—and from text to text, one observes admixtures, reprises and repetitions which are probably allusive in nature. These are all "exchange phenomena" which give the impression of a circulation of wandering textual elements melding at each instant with others to form provisional compositions. What grants the text its "unity" (if we wish to be so adventurous as to accept this idea) appertains to the level of its movements more than to the realm governed by proportions or measurements: to perceive this type of unity in performance is less a matter of positing a necessary organicity in the text than of situating it among its possible variants.[1]

The complexity of its mode of existence prohibits the study of oral poetry in any perspective which would not take account of rather lengthy time lapses. At the same time, it is expedient to avoid the historicist prejudice which encourages the search for an origin containing all subsequent developments in seminal form. I would approach the question from the other direction and stress the equivocity of the work's

1. Jack Goody, *The Domestication of the Savage Mind* (New York: Cambridge University Press, 1977), 72; Paul Zumthor, "Intertextualité et mouvance," *Littérature*, 41 (1981), 15–16.

temporal status, which cannot be situated in an abstract time frame (an external measure of becoming) and yet is inconceivable outside of a concretely and interiorly lived time.

As a direct consequence, its spatial status is no less equivocal. Indeed, out of a space which is specific to each performance and which constitutes its dimension of reality, another space is engendered, an extrinsic one, owing to the multiplicity of successive performances. Hardly noticeable when these performances are played out in the same locale, the effect of this exteriorization can become considerable when a large-scale geographic shift is produced.

In Europe and Asia we have access to documents whose number and reliability are sufficient to place the traditions of many works in a chronological framework. The earliest versions of the *Rig Veda*, whose transmission among the Brahmans is still oral (despite the existence of written versions), must have been contemporary to Homer. This case is, of course, both extreme and unique. On a more modest scale, a certain number of French "popular songs" are attested as of the Middle Ages. Several have spread to Québec: out of a total of 355 "chansons en laisse," C. Laforte has found two of them dating from the thirteenth century, one from the fourteenth, eleven from the fifteenth, and so forth. Of the three hundred English and Scottish ballads drawn from the Child collection by H. Sargent and G. Kittredge, a dozen can be dated from the thirteenth, fifteenth and sixteenth centuries, but how many others are, unbeknownst to us, just as old?[2] In Africa, in Oceania, and amongst the Amerindians, the absence of comparable evidence does not prevent us from positing the antiquity of certain poems or poem cycles. Thus, several songs of the Mauris exalt the land they inhabited before settling in New Zealand, perhaps in the fourteenth century. The Mandingo epic's Soundiata, a historical personage, died in 1255: how long did it take for the poem still sung today by griots like Mamadou Kouyate to be formulated?

The geographic dispersion of oral poetry is often no more clearly documented. It happens that extremely similar forms associated with nearly identical themes are found in the traditions of peoples whose

2. Ruth H. Finnegan, *Oral Poetry: Its Nature, Significance and Social Context* (Cambridge/New York: Cambridge University Press, 1977), 135, 150–51; Henri Davenson [Henri-Irénée Marrou], *Le Livre des chansons* (Neuchâtel: La Baconnière, 1944), 116–18; Conrad Laforte, *Survivances médiévales dans la chanson folklorique: Poétique de la chanson en laisse* (Québec: Les Presses de l'Université Laval, 1981), 8; Helen Child Sargent and George Lyman Kittredge, *English and Scottish Popular Ballads edited from the Collection of Francis James Child* (Boston/New York: Houghton Mifflin and Co., 1904), xiii–xiv.

habitats are distant and who are historically without contact. Are we dealing with a fortuitous cultural interference due to the adventure of some solitary navigator? Or might these be independent creations, pointing to the existence of a universal model? As it turns out, these questions concern only a small number of isolated cases. Most of the confirmed instances of poetic dispersion have been traced along specific itineraries which are well-known for other reasons: namely, migration, commerce and pilgrimage trails. On occasion, the history of an individual or group furnishes an ostensibly plausible explanation which, upon close scrutiny, leaves itself open to considerable doubt.[3] For instance, nothing is less mysterious than the clustering of popular European poetry on the American continent along the inroads traced by Spanish, Portuguese, French and English fleets from the sixteenth through the eighteenth centuries . . . and yet this also occurred in Madeira (where someone in our century discovered an unknown version of the *Cid*), as well as among Sephardic Jews exiled in Morocco at the end of the fifteenth century. Ballads collected in England or in Scotland in the eighteenth and nineteenth centuries were recovered around 1930 by C. J. Sharp—straight from the mouths of Appalachian mountain men in the remote areas of Kentucky, Virginia and the Carolinas. Certain of the ballads have been reported in Australia.[4] Imported, these poems can be maintained for a long time in only a slightly altered form. But the need which insured their survival in small immigrant communities works on them from the inside and, in the end, transforms them. Around these relics are reconstituted new traditions which, while maintaining certain of their originary traits, develop along a profoundly foreign rhythm with divergent tendencies: thus, the Appalachian hillbilly song was spun out from the English ballad.

A stroke of good fortune occasionally allows a small group of immigrants, established in an allophonic milieu, to conserve its cohesiveness, its language and some of its oral poetry. Such scattered islets, endlessly threatened by submersion, dot the map of migration zones across the world. Recordings have been made of songs in French or in Walloon dialect still current among elder members of select rural families in an area of Wisconsin which Belgian immigrants opened to agriculture around 1860. This group, although dispersed in isolated farms, nonetheless maintained some social unity up to the 1940s. Most

3. Finnegan, 153–54.

4. Finnegan, 136–37; Ramón Menéndez Pidal, *Romancero hispanico (hispano-portugués, americano y sefardí): Teoría e historia*, 2d ed. (1953; Madrid: Espasa-Calpe, 1968), 2, 203–38 and 306–65.

of their songs had been cabaret successes in Liège and its environs from 1830 to 1850. Today's singers, often not knowing French (but still speaking a modified Walloon), have preserved the songs' original forms with almost total purity.[5] Once in a while a fortuitous discovery reveals the itinerary of an isolated work, transmitted by some roustabout, which might in other circumstances have engendered a lasting tradition in the land of exile. Thus, M. Da Costa Fontes, while interviewing Portuguese workers emigrated to Toronto, transcribed a *romance* related to the 1864 Paraguayan war (1864–70) as it came from the lips of a seventy-seven-year-old woman, originally from the Azores—in all likelihood brought to the Azores by another migrant who had returned from southern Brazil![6]

Aside from a displacement of peoples, an osmosis can also cause exchanges between neighboring sectors of a homogeneous geographic and cultural area: versions of the Tibetan *Ge-sar* are sung in Mongolia and in certain Chinese cantons; the Chilean "new song" of the 1960s came close to winning over all of Latin America. . . . While linguistic barriers are not enough to stop this movement, the lexical, syntactic and, above all, rhythmic kinship of the languages in contact facilitate it. Thus, for centuries, the circulation of oral poetry among the diverse Scandinavian linguistic zones was intense, and sometimes even came into contact with Scotland.

A comparable phenomenon of lesser proportions (might it have resulted from the influence of written traditions in these territories?) maintained a unity among the Western Romance languages in popular circles up to the beginning of the nineteenth century. The song *Donna Lombarda*, based on an ancient legendary theme, and probably composed in the environs of sixteenth-century Turin in the Piedmont dialect, has been recorded in half a dozen other Italian dialects, in a French version encountered in the Massif Central as well as in Québec, in Spanish . . . and even in Albanian. *Gentils Gallants de France*, part of a longstanding tradition, is common to France and Spain—although, admittedly, there are notable variants. The dramatic *romance* of *Bernal Francés*, whose hero was one of the conquerors of Granada in 1492, radiated throughout the Spanish world, as far as Argentina and in the Judeo-Spanish communities of Turkey; but we also possess versions in Catalan, French and the Piedmont dialect, none of which alters the

5. Françoise Lempereur, *Les Wallons d'Amérique du Nord: Etude principalement consacrée aux Wallons établis au Wisconsin* (Gembloux: J. Duculot, 1976).

6. Manuel da Costa Fontes, ed., *Romanceiro português do Canadá* ([Coimbra]: Por ordem da universidade, 1979), no. 489.

metrical structure of the original.[7] Translation into a new language can result in mistakes which contribute to the thematic drift. A Spanish *romance* composed at the end of the nineteenth century (and perhaps inspired by *Bernal Francés*) recounts the tragic death of the wife of Alphonse XII in 1878. As it happens, in a Portuguese version found in Brazil, the name *Alfonso Doce* was understood as "Gentle Alphonse," which strikingly modifies the balance and meaning of this sad story![8] How many European adaptations of American rock'n'roll lyrics have preserved the raw violence of the latter, not to mention their allusive power?

In this twofold peregrination, how (and to what extent) does the work, in changing, remain the same? The controversial notion of "tradition" attempts to address this question. For the ethnologists of the present-day contextualist school, the term refers to a scientific construction more than to a cultural product and the discourse one uses to speak of it proceeds from an ideology which functions according to categories developed in our own social sphere. In fact, it is quite easy (in observing the mechanisms of imitation by which a society comforts and perpetuates itself) to delineate *some* traditions; it is less easy to define *the* tradition. Here I am more interested in considering, from a relatively distant and elevated stance, that density of social time which, at every moment of existence, tends to neutralize the contradictions existing between the present and the past, not to mention the present and the future. These contradictions are perhaps denied in one place while elsewhere they are proudly defended, expressed in a purely verbal fashion or through decisive acts, deliberately or unconsciously. These diverse ways of collectively reliving the conflicting layers of time could serve as possible criteria for a typology of cultures . . . and of poetries. "Traditions," manifold responses to the challenge thrown out to us by the evanescence of all that our language names: seen as the outgrowth of an instinctive and ultimately primitive perception of our fragility, traditions correspond to the role of physical labor in man's transformation of nature. Collectively, the social group refers to the universe as its terminus and guarantor, and interiorizes this reference as it consents to the norm thus objectified—that is, what must be known and how it can be known. So long as the individual does not reflect upon this effort, thought and language, close to their archetypes, readapt themselves

7. Davenson, 204–06; Menéndez Pidal, 2, 320–23 and 361–62.

8. A. Moreno and I. Fonseca dos Santos, "Création et transmission de la poésie orale: La chanson d'Alfonso XII" *Arquivos do Centro cultural portugues* [Paris] (1980), 411–52.

incessantly in a pure temporal duration, with malleability and without much constraint. Reflection opens the doors of history and introduces a risk connected to the status of the group's cultural heritage. Nowadays, perhaps, the cultural behavior of a class of young people left to their own devices is none other than the manifestation of their desire (were it only possible!) to go back through the doors in the opposite direction. . . . It is within this network of perceptions, customs, and ideas, that "oral traditions" are developed and lost. Language, the bond of the collectivity, procures the sole possibility of *making known* the name and conduct of its ancestors, as well as of the group's day-to-day raison d'être. But speech, the interiorization of history, is not unfolded in time as a sequence of events would be; it follows upon itself dialectically in a constant reorientation of existential choices, affecting the totality of our being-in-the-world each time it resonates. Be it to confirm or to contest, the voice that I hear throws its fragile, sonorous footbridge between two unpronounced voices, murmuring inside us, too deeply ensconced to break through to the public domain: the voice that our ancestors speak within us, and the other voice which rejects their influence. Thus, we are propelled forward and, simultaneously, remain bound.

What results from this is, according to Jack Goody (and yet refuted by J. Vansina), a homeostatic equilibrium between a society and its oral traditions; at a given point in its historical trajectory, that which no longer corresponds to a current need in these discourses becomes the object of a "structural amnesia," and either survives as an empty form, or disappears. If an overly strong cultural trauma ensues, the society in question will spend several generations reconstituting a general economy of the collective speech: thus, medieval Europe after Gutenberg, Africa in its period of colonization . . . or our Western World in its confrontation with the computer. Instability and functional ambiguity are the major traits of what H. Scheub calls "images": that is, complex mental, linguistic and bodily forms whose performance makes up the corpus of our traditions.[9] It is less a case of these traditions existing in and of themselves than of their being engendered in the memory of those who have lived through them and who base their lives on them: a cumulative knowledge that the group, as a group, has of itself, and which it invests in language according to thematic or formulaic rules.

    9.  Jack Goody and Ian Watt, "The Consequences of Literacy," in *Literacy in Traditional Societies*, ed. Jack Goody (Cambridge: Cambridge University Press, 1968), 27–68; J. Vansina, "Once upon a time: Oral Tradition as History in Africa," *Daedalus*, 100 (1971), 457; H. Scheub, "Oral Narration Process and the Use of Models," *New Literary History*, VI (1975), 353–77.

These rules and the modalities of their use differ according to culture-type. Archaic societies possess a greater capacity for absorbing individual contributions and blending them into more or less constraining customs, the enlargement of the network of communications and the diffusion of writing, coupled with the subsequent establishment of a regime assuring writing its preeminence, contribute to the weakening of people's memories and to an acceleration in the rhythms of transmission: a contradiction henceforth inscribed in the language itself and in its relation to the body. Thus we find the emergence of new social roles: the intellectual, the poet, the "author." . . .

Nevertheless, compared to the other elements which ground the consciousness ("conscience") of the community, oral poetry does not rely on what is called a "long-term memory." With the exception of certain strongly ritualized mythic forms, the discourse of oral poetry is much less durable than it was thought even a short while ago. Its dynamic quality dissimulates the fragility of its linguistic, vocal, and gestural elements, all of which fatally partake in what I have called elsewhere *mouvance,* a term which I used to designate the oral poem's radical instability.\* But *mouvance* is only conceivable and per-ceivable in performance, just as a speech can only be in situation. When, for my own pleasure, I hum one of the songs stored in my memory, I assimilate it for a second to my living consciousness; then, it falls back into silence. The fervent rock or reggae fan participates in what he experiences as tradition (or as fashion, which comes down to the same thing). But this participation is revealed through an intensity in the pleasure associated with a *specific* performance, relative to a *specific* expectation of detailed circumstances. Tradition is probably none other than the conditioning fostered by this expectation and made habitual for an unspecifiable period of time.

Indeed, what the voice of the poet reveals to me is a twofold identity. One identity is brought about by presence in, literally, a "common place" where glances are exchanged; but another identity results from a convergence of varieties of knowledge and the ancient, universally accepted evidence of the *senses.* Woodie Guthrie used to say that he want-

---

\*Zumthor discusses *mouvance* and the medieval text in his *Essai de poétique médiévale* (Paris: Seuil, 1972), 65–75, which also provides the following concise definition of *mouvance:* "that character of a work which—to the extent that we can consider something to be a work before the era of the printed book—results from a quasi abstraction, insofar as those concrete texts which constitute the work's real existence present through the play of variants and reworkings something like a ceaseless vibration and a fundamental instability" (507). [Editor's note]

ed to be "the man who tells you what you already know." Iouri Lotman has recently shown how this "esthetic of identity"—proper to pre-modern art forms, to oral poetry, and today, to texts transmitted by the media—functions through the assimilation of stereotypes which have, notwithstanding, never become automatic, floating in the unstable medium of lived experience.[10] In it and for it, the ordinary voices of the community weave a continuous, horizontal succession of threads, out of which that of the poet, forming a unique vertical continuity in a temporal dimension all its own, emerges and distinguishes itself.

In this way comparable to individual and group memory, vocal poetry makes a homogeneous consciousness out of dispersed percep-tions. The songs are always given in advance, in the immobile presence of memory, Blanchot once said. Menendez Pidal spoke of *latency*. In the context of the epic, he understood it to mean the undetermined histor-ical space where the event engenders the myth, and the myth emerges in poetry. I would extend the notion of latency to poetry itself, ready at each instant, like my body's voice, to spill over from the probable to the certain, from the expected to the actual, at the center of that circle which unites us. In this perspective, it is no longer a past which influ-ences and informs me when I sing; it is I who give form to the past . . . just as each writer, it is said, creates his precursors. Each new poem projects itself on those which have preceded it, reorganizes their totality and confers upon them another coherence.

The performance of a poetic work thus finds the plenitude of its meaning in the relation which ties it to those preceding, and those to follow. In fact, its creative power results from the work's *mouvance*. To be sure, several genres of oral poetry require a strict memorization of the text and proscribe any variation: Polynesian dance songs, genealogical poems of Rwanda, Amerindian rituals, and perhaps the most ancient Japanese poetry. All appear tied to a particular conception of knowledge and its transmission. In this case, then, it is a matter of "zero *mou-vance*," which has its own particular significance. In our society, habits acquired under the influence of writing encourage impressarios to pro-gram the details of their shows in an exacting way during rehearsals; whatever the ultimate intention might be, this technique contributes to the collapse of effects attributable to *mouvance*. Although weakened by such programming, these effects do not disappear because of it. Since Schlegel, the Romantic tradition has considered the written literary work in its oneness, as the end point of an evolutionary genesis. It could

10. Iouri Lotman, *La Structure du texte artistique*, trans. Anne Fournier [et al.], under the direction of Henri Meschonnic (Paris: Gallimard, 1973), 56–57 and 396–99.

be maintained that such is equally the case with the oral work, but in its *multiplicity* revealed through the totality of performances. As such, it is never finished; it is, as D. Hymes puts it, "context sensitive." In speech no less than in the State, writing engenders the law, establishes constraint with order. At the heart of a society saturated with writing, oral poetry (resisting the ambient pressure better than our daily discourse) tends, because it is oral, to shirk the law and to bend only to the most supple formulas, whence its *mouvance.*

Viewed in this way, an "authentic" text does not exist. From one performance to another, one slides from nuance to nuance, or even to an abrupt mutation. In this zone of gradations, where is one to trace a demarcation line between what is still the "work" and what has already gone past it? Folklorists and ethnologists have periodically pondered the question as did Davenson long ago, with regard to French songs like *La Pernette* and *Mon Père avait cinq cents moutons.* The interpreter is often himself unaware of the modifications he brings to an object that he considers to be of common currency and at the same time immutable. The notion of plagiarism would have no more meaning in this context than that of author's rights. Among singers in our society, the fact that plagiarists are tracked down and authors are roundly accepted is a marginal influence of writing. This right remains a highly practical one at that, for it exclusively concerns those "roles" implicated in the written version of a song: the lyricist and the composer. In order to gain access to a comparable status, the interpreter must inscribe his voice on a record.

The well-documented tradition of English ballads has furnished an excellent practice field for researchers. Accordingly, attempts have been made to measure certain parameters of variability therein. According to W. Anders, the breadth of variation depends on four factors: the amount of time separating the performances, the length of the text, the extent of the interpreter's repertoire and his familiarity with the work in question. Truisms? All that really counts is the probability of various types of movement. I have made a rapid calculation based on two hundred ballads from the Child collection, using the Sargent-Kittredge notes. Six pieces (3 percent) include from 20 to 28 different documented versions; 28 (14 percent) from 10 to 19; 52 (26 percent) from 5 to 9; and 85 (42.5 percent) from 2 to 4. These figures are valid only as indicators, rather approximate at that.[11] More important than the number of variations is

11. Wolfhart Anders, *Balladensänger und mündliche Komposition: Untersuchungen zur englischen Traditionsballade* (Munich: W. Fink, 1974), 223; David D. Buchan, *The Ballad and the Folk* (London/Boston: Routledge and K. Paul, 1972), 170–71; Tristram Potter Coffin, *The British Traditional Ballad in North America*, rev. ed.

their breadth. Ruth Finnegan observed that in Africa, dance and work songs demonstrate a considerable stability; this is true, in general, for poetry of peoples in contact with writing, like the Swahili and the Hausa. Davenson, on the other hand, drew up as an example a line-by-line table of the four known versions of the French St. Nicholas chant *Il était trois petits enfants*—versions admittedly copied down at diverse periods (from the sixteenth to the twentieth centuries) and in diverse regions. They differ in melody, stanzaic form, length, in the names and qualities of the characters (with the exception of the saint), their number and role (there is sometimes a butcher's wife, sometimes not), and in the instruments used in their action! What remains is the common narrative scheme, explicitly referred to Nicholas and reducible to certain well-recognizable functions and *actants*. Here we have, properly speaking, a "work"; it actually exists, at once as a memorial pre-text locked in memory and as a multiplicity of concrete texts which it is capable of engendering.[12] Most children's songs move in a poetic space just as broad; text and melody vary from one generation to the next (as long as school has not appropriated them, that is), and one would hardly want to speak of "evolution" in this case. In the Rumanian ballads, according to A. Fochi, formal variations of all kinds can influence as much as fifty-four percent of the text. The songs which R. Jackson recorded in Texas prisons have, as fixed elements, scarcely more than a title, a refrain, and some isolated stanzas. The singers can nonetheless continue to identify them, in the midst of a poetic tradition which is perpetually in a state of becoming. This textual and musical fecundity intrinsic to a particular vocal work can, in the passage of history, far outstrip the creative period of new works. Thus between the 1880s (when F. J. Child assembled his five volumes of English ballads) and 1904 (the date of Sargent and Kittredge's collection) many versions of texts already known were collected, but not a single new ballad.

I am grouping under the term *variant* differences of every kind and degree by which the *mouvance* of the text is manifested in the performative act. I distinguish two types (which are brought together, in fact, in the functioning of the work) according to whether the differences are realized in the performances of different interpreters or in those of the same interpreter.

---

with supplement by Roger D. Renwick, Publications of the American Folklore Society, Bibliographical and Special Series, 2 (Austin: University of Texas Press, 1977), 2–15; Sargent-Kittredge, 671–74.

12. Ruth H. Finnegan, *Oral Literature in Africa* (Oxford, 1970; rpt. Nairobi: Oxford University Press, 1976), 106; Davenson, 265–67.

The first type presupposes the intervention of personal differences, training, age, but it occasionally includes social constraints imposing a certain style or a particular tone on a given class of individuals: for example, in the heyday of Ma Rainey and Bessie Smith, the differences between female and male blues singers; or, in the beginnings of jazz, between black and white interpreters. The variants of the second type result either from qualitative changes due to circumstances or, contrariwise, from an express desire not to repeat oneself. Once in a while the intention is more subtle: the desire to modulate the response according to the expectation of a given audience. The passage of time plays no uncertain role and greatly increases the impact of these effects. A. Gilferding, who collected Russian *bylinas* in the Lake Onega region between 1860 and 1880, noted that a singer never executed a poem in the same way twice. P. Rybnikov, traveling through the region twenty or thirty years later, observed such differences in the performances of informants already recorded by his predecessor that he hesitated to identify several of the works. Thus, the ballad of *Ilya of Murom*, in the two versions provided by the famous singer Trophime Ryabinine, is twice as long in one of these versions as in the other.[13] The Rumanian ballads have been the object of many studies on variants. To take one example, in an excellent study which examines the eleven known versions of the poem *Mogoş Vornicul*, Rosa Knorringa is led beyond the rather fuzzy limits of the work; it is at the level of the tradition as such that she defines a specific intertextuality which constitutes the work and grants it its unity.[14]

Many attempts have been made to classify the diverse types of variants from a poetic perspective. Those which, inspired by Formalist studies, limit themselves to the verbal apparatus of the tradition seem to me of little utility here. I would give preference to classifications based on the respective economies of textual, melodic and rhythmic modifications: the traditional French songs have been analyzed from this point of view many times. Autonomous but correlated variations in the text and in the melody have been noted. Melodies are depleted and renewed more quickly than texts. Their borders are still more uncertain: motifs and entire musical phrases are dissociated and migrate toward other contexts to be recomposed at the core of the tradition, in the manner of epic formulas. It has even been said that the melody of

13. C. M. Bowra, *Heroic Poetry* (1961; London: MacMillan, 1978), 217.
14. Rosa Knorringa, *Fonction phatique et tradition orale: Constantes et transformations dans un chant narratif roumain, Mogoş Vornicul* (Amsterdam: Rodopi, 1978), 66–112.

oral tradition only exists in its variants. If by chance, the work is transferred into a region culturally distanced from its milieu of origin, a more profound transformation is produced, the purpose of which is to adapt it to another musical system: such was the European chant commemorating the death of the aviator Chavez, which a Peruvian Indian once sang along the intervals of his five-tone range . . . likewise for blues, which paid a rather high musical price for its wide diffusion: the loss of "blue notes."[15] As another possibility, the same melody can carry many songs, even at times crossing over from one song to the other in the course of its history; conversely, a unique and very nearly stable text can be sung to several melodies. For *La Belle barbière* (Number 44 of Davenson), no fewer than 14 have been collected; for the *Beau Déon* (Number 6), there are 28! It would seem that the rhythm of a single verse line is most durable; by contrast, the stanzaic form, generally linked to the melody, is scarcely more stable.

Musical variants are ordinarily accompanied by textual variants, less as a direct consequence than by virtue of the inventive freedom which predominates in performance—and which in our own time, the mechanization of transmission has not totally abolished. When the text's authority (imposed by a ritual procedure or based on the model of writing) prohibits its modification, the musical interpretation offers the only possible margin of play. Bob Dylan's fans insist that the singer never once interpreted a song twice in the same way, and that on each concert tour he varies his melodies.

From among the textual variants, those which touch upon vocabulary or syntactic sequences can be diversely motivated:

—by the desire to adapt the work to the particular context of the performance, either by suppressing what might be incongruous or misunderstood or, conversely, by accentuating the incongruities or provocations contained therein.

—by the need to smooth out the semantic difficulties raised by the text, especially if it is traditional and of ancient origin: for instance, archaic words, ambiguities due to the obliteration of outdated cultural contexts, the apparent arbitrariness of proper

15. Davenson, 82–89; Conrad Laforte, *Poétiques de la chanson traditionnelle française, ou classification de la chanson folklorique française* (Québec: Presses de l'Université Laval, 1976), 34–35; Marguerite and Raoul d'Harcourt, *Chansons folkloriques françaises au Canada: Leur Langue musicale* (Québec: Presses de l'Université Laval, 1956); James L. Collier, *The Making of Jazz: A Comprehensive History* (Boston: Houghton Mifflin Co., 1978), 123–25.

names; whence, an incessant reinterpretation, replete with misunderstandings of the original context.

—finally, by the demands of versification, whose rhythms or sonorities, altered in the course of time, sometimes require delicate readjustments, especially in languages using rhyme.

Other textual variants touch upon the disposition of discursive masses and the ordering of parts. These are probably more beholden to the profoundly dynamic nature which animates every operation of the voice: that forward thrust ("élancée") of speech which scorns pre-established programming, an elan which no "poetic art" of any kind has ever managed to quell without some difficulty. This tendency is as clearly revealed in the distribution of microtextual schemas and the rhythm of formulaic recurrence as it is in the organization of subunits: introduction, suppression and exchange of refrains or of stanzas. The examination of vast poetic sectors such as those of French, English or Mexican folkloric songs suggests that oral poetic unity (the level at which an identity can be recognized) resides in the stanza rather than in the song itself. *Mouvance* would thus involve two stages: stanzaic unity and assemblage of these unities. If the poem tells a story, this instability is projected on the narrative structures; accordingly one finds additions, suppressions and displacements of episodes or of characters, not unlike those encountered in the epic. The same mobility, the same slipperiness in style and composition, the same ephemeral stanzas and tonal altera-tions have accompanied the oral existence of Jean Cuttat's beautiful poem *Noël d'Ajoie.* Composed in 1960 and recorded on tape, this long *romance* was incessantly declaimed in the cafés and public meetings of the Swiss Jura during fifteen years of political battles, gradually being invested with the functions of a national hymn and a song of liberation. An unverifiable number of versions are still circulating, although the author published in 1974 what he wished to be the definitive text. From version to version, motifs emerge or disappear, the tone changes from the epic to the intimate, the general theme is plied in directions which risk being contradictory. It is, *in fine,* the work's very function in the social group which is more or less modified.

Corresponding to the wandering motifs are stanzas and migratory verses, often flotsam from forgotten songs, not only available but aspir-ing to be reintroduced in new combinations. The French song *La Per-nette* (Number 3 of Davenson) numbers in its tradition no fewer than four different beginnings and three endings, each of which can be found in some other song. A similar brew occurs in the English ballads and in children's songs; one might take as a concrete example the Italian folkloric song where the swooning lover contemplates the ocean in one version, a mountain in another . . . or in Russian *bylinas,* where Peter the Great, Ivan the Terrible and Ilya of Murom blithely exchange names and heroic memories. This explains why there are frequently global modifications touching upon the text's allusive capacities. A certain English ballad recorded at a twenty year interval from the lips of a young girl who had become a shepherd's wife appears under versions which are identical as to their narrative elements but the second of which eliminates any detail having to do with food, drink, and love.[16] More generally, one could point to the technique of *contrafacture* practiced all over Europe during the Middle Ages, of which several examples remain famous. The sequence *Laetabundus* of the twelfth century was "counterfeited" at least fifty times, in all languages and registers. Davenson's 122d listing—perhaps originally a Noël—parodied in a 1627 vaudeville which alluded in successive stanzas to Alexander, Moses, Gideon and other heroes, not only received diverse onomastic variants, but by the substitution of terms or motifs gave birth as early as the seventeenth century to Bacchic songs (it is in this form that I became aware of it around 1950), to contemporizing songs (one of which, in 1792, paid homage to the guillotine!), and to several other Noëls. Number 138, invoked by lovers of "pure poetry" at the time of Abbé Brémond ("*Orléans, Beaugency*"), an Orléanais carillon air of the sixteenth century, then reduced to an enumeration of toponyms, was recast in the seventeenth century in order to glorify the General of Vendôme, supplemented in the eighteenth century with a stanza evoking the slowness of nocturnal hours, and in the nineteenth century with the well-known stanza on the Dauphin Charles, which so artificially connects this little text to the legend of Joan of Arc.[17]

Thus the oral poetic work, surrendered to the hazards of time, floats in the indetermination of a meaning which it incessantly undoes and recreates. The oral text calls for an interpretation which would itself be in movement. The energy which underlies the text and tinkers ("*bricoler*") with its forms recovers at each performance the lived experience and integrates the latter into its material. The questions which the world asks of it do not themselves cease to be modified: for better or worse, the work modifies its responses. In Bangui, I heard a song sung on the occasion of Bokassa's escape which had been composed twenty

16. Buchan, 115–16.
17. Davenson, 530–32 and 579–80; d'Harcourt, 55.

years earlier in honor of the death of President Boganda. Few words needed to be changed for the serious chant to be made into a parody. Alteration of the text is not even indispensable, provided the historical context has changed. As Lionel Gossman once remarked, Schiller's *The Brigands*, produced by Piscator in the revolutionary Berlin of 1926, as compared to a performance in the overfed Mannheim of 1957, cannot be considered one and the same play.[18] Were the Russian recruiters' songs the same around 1930 and again under the Czarist regime, when a stint in the army lasted twenty years? Contemporary songs brought over to Europe from America often become insipid, even when the musical component is kept unaltered; they tend toward a sort of commemoration rather than a rupture in the value system, which was an important feature of the original. This is probably a consequence of imitation, but more particularly of the difference in national mentalities and manners, which serves to weaken the immediacy of the connotations.

Inscribed in this *mouvance* of the poetic function are the "returns to sources," whose riches have been so much more widely exploited in the history of oral poetry in the last two centuries than in the written poetry of the period—as if the voice yielded to these sorts of nostalgia more naturally than the hand. A return to emotive themes, to the commonplaces, to the hidden artifices of a "popular" poetry, drawn from the vast romantic melting pot: peasant singers and workers of the late nineteenth century, like Gaston Couté, or boulevardiers from between the Wars, such as Charles Trenet in his heyday; Even Boris Vian (in such sentimental popular songs as *Cueille la vie* or *L'Ecole de l'amour*) periodically sought artistic consolation in a return to this common current—at the risk of some blandness. A parallel movement in Québec brought together for a time a Gilles Vigneault, a Louise Forestier, with the Charlebois of a dislocated America. What results is a return to a folklore felt to be original, an infinitely fertile matrix of songs—as Québec was still able to demonstrate for some twenty-odd years with Mère Bolduc and Abbé Gadbois; or Chile, which rediscovered around 1960 the rhythms of *Cachimbo*, the Argentina of Atahualpa Yupanqui or the Italy of Giovanna Marini. . . . All of these suggest a reversion, beyond centuries of musical culture, to the timbres of speech and the carnal inflections of the voice. In the United States, where learned European music had dug shallower roots, the "folk renaissance" of the 1940s drew from the mixed wealth of Anglo-Saxon, Irish, Mediterranean and

18. Lionel Gossman, "Literary Education and Democracy," *MLN*, 86 (1971), 774–75 and 778.

African popular traditions which had been strewn across the continent by successive influxes of immigrants. Linked to pacifist campaigns at the time of Vietnam, but indifferent to ideologies, folk music—fragile, slightly tender—dreamed of another life and unanimous recognition in a song whose secret it thought it had uncovered. But then, Bill Haley wedded it to blues, opened it up to Black rhythms and launched rock 'n' roll in 1954. The idyll was over; but it suddenly became apparent that many types of folklore from a long-lost world were resurging, unrecognizable and yet sure of themselves, bubbling over with life and salutary violence, in a rejuvenating bath of youth. Through this blind quest for an illusory, lost paradise, the contemporary art of the voice has recovered, in its own manner and style, that which grounds the social value of oral poetry: a value which had been suffocated in "classical" centuries of our writing. At the heart of the collectivity, this singing voice, this voice so ancient and profound, signifies the Law of a body, but of a body reconciled.

Translated by Jean McGarry

RENÉE RIESE HUBERT

# The *Tableau-Poème:* Open work

The modern work of art is essentially open, proposing a dialectic between the work and its interpreter. It refuses to impose a reading (whether pictorial or textual) which is unique and closed. Umberto Eco quotes a line from Paul Valéry: "Il n'y a pas de vrai sens d'un texte" ["There is no true meaning of a text"]. Eco stresses the multiplicity of possible readings, the ambiguities which arise from a work of art according to the varying sensibility, education, cultural background, and intelligence of the reader.[1] This openness seems even more inevitable in the case of the *tableau-poème* in which text and image combine while remaining separated at least in part. Text and image, despite their difference, tend toward a hypothetical unity. The interaction of the visual and the verbal, each refusing to dissolve completely into the other, creates the particular nature of the work. Forms which can never be entirely compatible are added on top of each other, undergoing successive metamorphoses. The theories of Umberto Eco lend themselves to the study of the *tableau-poème* (whether or not the critic had envisioned this application), for they take into account the importance of typography, blank space, and layout—in short, a post-Mallarmé sense of poetry's spatial dimensions. Moreover, the notion of textual permutation which Eco invokes in his discussion of Mallarmé's *Le Livre* might describe the activity or flexibility which is required to read the work of a painter who is seeking to integrate the poetic and the pictorial and to discover what is dynamic in their structure.

In our comparative reading of a few *tableaux-poèmes,* the dialectic simultaneity of art and poetry enclosed in each work engages us in an interplay (*jeu*) of readings where frequently the visual spectacle is at

1. Umberto Eco, *L'Oeuvre ouverte* (Paris: Seuil, 1965), 23.

43

stake (*enjeu*). It is rare that these works propose a definitive movement from text to image, or vice versa. The possibility of a single meaning, initial or final, seems excluded. I postulate that the dialectic attains an equilibrium, but not a complete fusion, or even a closure.

The order we shall follow may appear arbitrary. We shall progress towards *tableaux-poèmes* which increasingly resemble the image of a page on which letters appear, hence an order based on the written, if not literary, word. The *tableaux-poèmes* of Joan Miró seem to be situated at the antipodes of an arrangement which would simulate the textual. The writing, sketched by hand, apparently with speed and spontaneity, arises from an extreme form of the gestural. Margaret Rowell, in her preface to a Miró catalogue entitled "Magnetic Fields," analyses a number of *tableaux-poèmes* in terms of the greatly reduced, even epigrammatic, format of the texts.[2] She locates precise sources for Miró's texts and on several occasions makes use of the calligram or the illustrator's art as guides in her analysis of the *tableaux-poèmes.* In "Le Corps de ma brune," text and image are said to evoke verbally and graphically the flight or trajectory of a bird, a quality which would indeed liken the work to a calligram. The metaphors which Miró inscribes in his *tableaux-poèmes* are rather typical surrealist images dealing with metamorphosis.

Miró is himself a poet; his texts, together with his own illustrations, were published in *Les Cahiers d'Art.*[3] *Le Lézard aux plumes d'or* is a confrontation between poet and painter whose dimensions surpass those of the *tableaux-poèmes.*[4] I propose to discuss two *tableaux-poèmes* from different periods. "Oh! un de ces messieurs qui a fait tout ça!" (1925) offers a text which, apart from the painting, would hardly be considered a poem. This banal exclamation becomes poetic only within the painting itself. What begins as purely undefined ends up as suggestive, decidedly vague. Our reading directs us implicitly towards the image which would represent the imprecise, implied event. As Uwe Schneede has suggested, the relation between text and image has nothing to do with a commentary, since the image is neither a paraphrase nor an illustration of the text.[5] The rapport seems rather to be an erotic one, the text alluding to a male, while the undulating lines of the image, in a schematic but nevertheless expressive way, suggest female torsos, locks

2. Margaret Rowell, "Magnetic Fields: The Poetics" in *Joan Miró, Magnetic Fields* (New York: Guggenheim Foundation, 1972), 54.

3. *Les Cahiers d'art,* nos. 20–21, 1945–46, 269–300.

4. Joan Miró, *Le Lézard aux plumes d'or,* atelier Mourlot, Broder, Paris, 1971.

5. Uwe Schneede, *Surrealism* (New York: Abrams, 1973), 78.

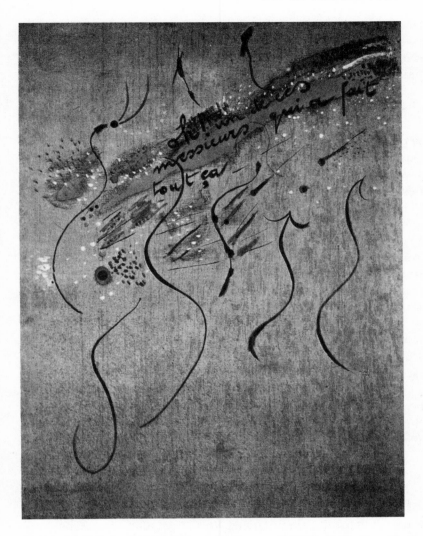

*Mirò. "Oh! un de ces messieurs a fait tout ça!" 1925. Collection Aimé
Maeght, Paris. © by ADAGP, Paris 1984.*

of hair. The multiplication of lines, their suggestive, essentially fluctuating quality, unbounded by the contour of any body, present an impersonal, undefined aspect which corresponds to the "tout ça" ["all
that"] of the text. On the narrative level the painter-poet leaves an
opening for the reader-viewer, the interference between the masculine
and the feminine—namely, the literary and the pictorial—playing as
much upon absence as upon presence.

All that suggests physical gesture, the rapidity of the strokes, the speed which gives Miró's painting certain graffitilike characteristics, as Schneede has remarked, creates other similarities between writing and the visual. The undulating lines, many of which are also vectors, are subject to manipulation by invisible magnetic forces. Thus they evoke surrealist eroticism and its links to magnetic fields, allowing Miró, in particular, to pass from the intimate to the cosmic. The vectors, insofar as they prevail over the well-defined, static contours, propose the erotic as a dynamic force rather than as a simple representation, thereby linking up with the text which is also necessarily a sign. The black, undulating lines betray a strong resemblance to writing, to letters traced out by hand. They suggest the coming-into-being of letters, that is, the advent of writing. A blank area lies at the center of the painting, representing the sky with brush strokes as distinct as the strokes of a pen in writing. Miró sets up an interference between text and image in various ways, excluding, so far as it is possible, the anecdotal. He allows the reader-viewer the choice of constructing his own narrative or of being totally indifferent to that aspect. We have said that the text extends a misleading invitation to view the image as an explanation, or a type of closure. But the text, a double exclamation, in no less an underhanded way, itself constitutes a critical fragment. The "author," both painter and poet, disguises himself in it even as he produces a self-reference to himself— Miró's ironic way of making himself both absent and present just like the plastic pictorial and verbal elements of his *tableau-poème.* By his intrusion, the painter-poet participates in the essence of his painting, an opening through which the masculine and the feminine, the text and the image, refer the reader-viewer to some space beyond the painting.

In 1952 Miró published in the journal *XX^e siècle* a lithograph whose text is considerably more extensive as compared to the image.[6] Like so many of Miró's texts and images, the poem suggests a trajectory towards the far-off, the cosmic. Coming back to the paradox of presence and absence uncovered in our last analysis, we notice that the bird which is flying off constitutes a departure towards a land of intangible substances where down ("duvet") grows, a departure which becomes an encircling or closure of the distant, the cosmic. This distancing corresponds at the same time to a drawing together. The "collines encerclées d'or" [ "hills circled with gold"] suggest the simultaneity of the sky and the earth, as well as of plant and animal life. The visual configuration of the page does not conform to the verbal indications of the poetic image. Unlike

6. Cf. *Miró Lithographe,* vol. 1, Tudor Company, 1972, 222 (for both reproduction and information).

"Oh! un de ces messieurs qui a fait tout ça!", the writing is not inscribed within a delimited space, nor according to a given direction. Writing and figures alternate across the entire surface. Writing, having lost its normal spatial continuity, comes out in bits, requiring from the reader-viewer descents, climbs, crossings, twists and turns. In places it seems totally freed from any attachment to the page; it dances, unfettered; each letter, each word, is deformed, stretching and breathing. The size of the letters, the capitals, the supplementary loops are no longer subject to a geometric regularity. The further along we read, the more our habits are disturbed, the more we acquire the freedom to resume our thrust without seeking to attain a goal. From the beginning Miró incites the reader to plunge rather than advance straightforwardly. Jumps begin to multiply, textual continuity on the page is increasingly disrupted, syntactic and spatial orders diverge. The reader must move from "est" on the left to "or" at the extreme right. The encircled last word suggests an ascending curve, a reversal with respect to the initial descent. But the isolation of words creates a discontinuity and a paradox with respect to their meaning. In one way, the words move further away from each other as compared to ordinary textual arrangement, and thus find themselves perhaps subordinated to invisible and unknown forces; but seen from another angle, certain words intersect with precise figures, or are situated within their context. The word "or" lies close to a star, the word "zone" is near a zone, that is, a black circle. We might note that the star does not reproduce the color "gold" found in the text. The central figure, colored red, green, blue, and yellow, allows for multiple interpretations; as a poetic as well as a visual entity it establishes new links to the text. We can recognize one of the painter's typical fantastic characters, schematized in the extreme, face and torso combined into one. It is undoubtedly a silhouette of the bird whose feathers rise up between the words "duvet" ["down"] and "poussent" ["grow"]. While writing is introduced into the sphere of the figures, figures enter the sphere of the writing; the star and the black zone are likened to punctuation marks, the dashes of color and the brush strokes, to the strokes of a written text. The face is closed in upon signs, eyes and mouths which repeat letters of the alphabet. Even though the image of the bird seems relatively static and even strangely placed in relation to the text, which concerns a bird taking flight, Miró has succeeded in conveying the mobile force and élan through the writing. The reader-viewer is induced to circulate in a space belonging alternately to painting and to writing. As a result of continually renewed passages from one to the other, any closure seems excluded.

In "Recherche calligraphique sur 'Une Saison en enfer'" (1914),

Robert Delaunay is preoccupied, not with the type of gestural dynamism found in Miró, but above all with the cognitive aspects of his art.
The painter has chosen a text situated at the heart of the very same
problematic with which he is preoccupied; thus a visual translation
would amount to a self-affirmation as much as to a homage to the poet
Rimbaud. In the text used for the "Recherche calligraphique," Rimbaud
alludes to his theory of vowels, which is of course also a theory of colors.
Delaunay highlights a paragraph of "Une Saison" without taking into
account the fact that the poet recapitulates his creed there, so as to
dissociate himself from it or even to abandon it. The vowels, in the order
of the alphabet and not in the sonnet's rearranged order, divide the page
diagonally. The movement from "A" to "u" requires a descent. Only
the names of the colors—black, white, red, blue, green—are not in
calligraphy since the vowels are cloaked in these same colors. The arc
unfolds from a rather broad, colored cloud which becomes progressively
smaller towards the bottom. The rest of the poetic text in Delaunay's
pictorial construct is subordinated to the figuration of the vowels
which, by virtue of their presentation of the initial, primary colors as the
painting's basic givens, form the axis of the painting. A somewhat unequal triangle, the letter "A," constitutes in all its blackness the generating force. While he faithfully transcribes the poet's text, Delaunay
does not produce a regular "written" or calligraphied page. Except in the
letter "A," the painter avoids black, the usual color of writing and
printing. The title is inscribed horizontally, but the rest of the text
refuses any linearity or parallelism. Such a structure offers an interpretation of Rimbaud's text—suggesting the idea of a new alphabet,
of a linguistic invention, of a certain delirium, but not of a total over-
throw—which an ordinary page could never communicate. The colored
axis of the vowels necessarily subverts linearity. Our habitual reading
practices are disrupted as the syntactic and pictorial orders diverge. An
opening, a break in the middle of the page produces groups of ascending
and descending lines. The calligraphied letters remain essentially pictorial elements, lines which acquire strength and autonomy through
the addition of colors, light and either opacity or transparency. Their
order no longer corresponds to that of the spectrum, the rainbow. "Je
réservais la traduction" ["I reserved the translation"]—these words also
apply to the limits Delaunay has imposed on himself. Gestural irregularity, very different from that of Miró, manifests itself in the size and
shape of the letters—bare, deformed, rigid—and the chain which links
them. Added to this are the shifts caused by the colors; first the vowels,
then the consonants, form luminous and colorful bundles, their shade

*Robert Delaunay, "L'Alchimie du verbe," 1914. Bibliothèque Nationale. ©
by ADAGP, Paris 1984.*

fluctuating sometimes from light to dark between the top and bottom of
the letter. Insofar as these fluctuations animate the writing with rhythmic vibrations, they maintain a connection with Rimbaud's poetic
language.

Robert Delaunay, by transforming the word into light, creates a
spectacle of rhythmic simultaneity, as he himself says in *Notes historiques sur la peinture.* "La clarté sera couleur, proportion, ces proportions
sont composées de diverses mesures simultanées dans une action."[7]
Within this pursuit of measures which forever remain uneven, Delaunay is able to make the successive nature of a poetic text secondary
by means of color constellations, thus granting the text's elements a
simultaneity which refuses any closure or fusion in which the text
would be overwhelmed by the image.

The *tableaux-poèmes* of Max Ernst combine the gestural élan of

7. Robert Delaunay, "Notes historiques sur la peinture" in his *Cahiers inédits.*
(Paris: S.E.V.P.W., 1957), 147.

Miró and the noetic concerns of Delaunay. In "Tableau-poème" (1923), the poetic text is inscribed in its entirety upon the surface of the painting, transforming the canvas into a page. At the same time the words, occupying squares, divide the surface into colored zones which can be likened to miniature canvasses. Arranged along parallel lines, the words conform to no rigorous order, for they are mysteriously projected into a three-dimensional space proper to painting. In places, the letters themselves take on volume. Writing and painting, each appropriating the spatial characteristics of the other, affirm their conventional properties even as they violate them. The written text promotes spatial construction and intensifies its perspective. The painting, by surpassing not only two, but three dimensions, multiplies its planes: the receding street adds depth, whereas the two trumpets project into the foreground.

The painting is certainly not reduced to serving as a mere container for the writing. The viewer recognizes in it both a landscape and a still life. The receding street is bordered on both sides by houses whose facades form a wall, suggesting the layout of another page. For lack of a true upper limit, the writing lends its shape to the roofs. Monumental letters assume the construction of both the text and the image. At the center, the intertwining of two nightingales creates a sign, a point from which all the writing germinates. Once they have become visible, the birds dispel night from which, according to any poet worthy of the name, they are inseparable. In more ways than one, the landscape abolishes its reference to nature and fragments its own spatiality. The still life, with its bulbs, trumpets and pears, makes use of conventional elements only to parody the genre to which it belongs. The arrangement of the objects no longer imparts contour and solidity to space. The pears, rather than offering a vision of beauty and harmony, rather than engaging the viewer to discover their ordered structure, are shriveling. A white, rectangular surface, which we can consider to be the smallest common denominator between a cloth and a page, seems void of any function at all because of its incapacity to serve as a background for the objects. Despite, or perhaps even on account of, the dispersions at work, the *tableau-poème* generates an extraordinary dynamism.

This text, which functions so creatively on the pictorial level, is characterized by its descriptive qualities. Paradoxically, it imitates its own creation in the pictorial domain. The poem, simultaneously verbal and visual, engages the reader in a back and forth movement between the original and its representation. In its reference to the still life, to the landscape, to the nightingale, and to the streets, it alludes to painting without really doing it justice, as if to reveal the inadequacy of verbal

*Max Ernst, "Tableau-poème," 1923. Collection Urvater, Brussels. With the
kind permission of Mr. John Cavaliero on behalf of Mrs. Dorothea T. Ernst.*

representation. This text, which parodies certain of Baudelaire's prose
poems, especially "L'Invitation au voyage," confers the most active role
upon the still life. This is why the text's meaning deviates from its
original premise as well as from the painting, which it simultaneously
inscribes and describes—a device which perforce fences it in.

In "Qui est ce grand malade," Ernst seems to have eliminated the
presence of the page to a much greater extent than in the *tableau-poème*

we have just read. The writing, sometimes individual handwritten letters, sometimes intertwined letters, is not applied to a flat surface. Its
visibility and readability vary. Some words can be seen from the front,
making them easier to read, while others can be seen only in profile, not
as composed of individual letters, but as parallel lines linked together to
form a kind of receding wall, which approaches only to veer away. This
writing, which cannot be read along a flat surface but which in places
traces a path jutting outward, extends along a third dimension, sometimes projected towards the viewer, sometimes eluding his gaze. The
perspective of the letters, the visibility of which varyingly increases and
diminishes, never coincides with the figural perspective. By reading the
written text according to one perspective we displace spatial perception
toward a domain which is not normally its own. In places the writing
recalls those illuminated signs in which advertising images and slogans
continually replace one another. The curve traced by the letters simu-
lates a circulatory movement. To transcribe this text onto a page would
be to weaken it, for its spatial organization suggests that we are confronted not simply with a text, but with the text's temporal and spatial
resistance to being deciphered.

This spatial deciphering depends not only on whether we see the
text from the front or in profile, but also on how close or far away it is,
and on the color and size of the letters. In places, especially in the upper
left, the writing takes on a certain relief, becoming sculptural, and
thereby occupying a third dimension. In the lower left, the colors en-
croach upon the letters and spill into the empty areas. The letters in
these spaces thus become windows or painted frames, as in the first
*tableau-poème.* They move away from writing and closer to painting
proper, or rather, the writing itself is always in a state of transition.

If we look at the written text as a whole, a text which bears some
resemblance to Ernst's dadaist poems, we have some difficulty grasping
it as a totality. Aside from the differences of direction, size, calligraphy,
color and perspective, the parts of the poem seem disconnected, as if
they belonged to independent spaces controlled by forces lacking a common center and origin. The reader is unable to reconstruct the page; he
can no longer read from left to right as usual, for the text is bound by the
spatial laws of painting which have no relation to those of writing. A
constant tension dominates this *tableau-poème.* In this way the poem
as a poem does not allow us to reach an end. At the beginning, the letters
seem to arise out of an obscurity as would a creation whose origin we
could never grasp, and which would remain open upon the unknown.
On both sides of a column which divides the painting, we read the word

"qui," but we do not know if this repetition occurs after the first question: "Qui est ce grand malade," or at the end, because the normal reading order is not obligatory. The poem possesses neither beginning nor end; it consists rather of a continual movement of the eyes between a big circle, another smaller circle and some straight, incomplete lines.

The letters, far from being directly applied to the top of the image, extend its directions or spatial projections so as to participate in a vertical division of the *tableau-poème*. What is the relation between figuration and writing? Between figuration and text? On either side of the column there is a pair of mannequins, one behind the other, one embracing the other, in close proximity to a few steps of a staircase. Certain resemblances between the forms are made clear: the column, no less than the mannequins, evokes human figures. Divided horizontally and truncated by the stairs, the column restores the linearity of the absent page. Visibility is subjected to the same laws as this fluctuating legibility. Recessed black areas resist any identification and emit no familiar signs. The absent faces belonging to anonymous bodies surrender no secrets. The couple fluctuating between the immobility of stone and the vitality of dance intensifies the enigma. The text twice poses the question of identification, only to confirm the presence of mystery, of irreducible ambiguity. This question without an answer is but another trap, provoking us to seek a deeper understanding beyond our reach. After the initial question a series of possible replies is proposed, all the more fanciful since they exclude any simple meaning, as well as any type of clarification. The sequence of names, which allude to identities, does not produce any discernable metaphoric or semantic relationships. It seems as if a text which is assimilated to painting must be resolute in its avoidance of verbal explanation, or simply reject it altogether.

Mirò manipulates the text and figures in order to intensify and multiply the interferences between them, in order to create his own verbal as well as pictorial language. Ernst plays with alleged comparisons, that is, with false attribution, and multiplies the paradoxes through the resemblances themselves. Klee, like Ernst and Mirò, is a poet, but in one of his most famous *tableaux-poèmes* he limits himself to borrowing a fragment from the *Song of Songs*. He renders this eminently lyric text visible within the frame of his painting. How does he effect the linking of the visible and the readable? How does he situate the verbal text with respect to the visual? What discontinuities, what openings does he allow to remain? The poetic intensity, the biblical rhetoric, the identity between divine and human love expressed in the quotation hardly lend themselves to a visual rendering. Indeed, Klee is

*Paul Klee, "Er küsse mich," 1921. Angela Rosengart Collection, Luzern. ©
by COSMOPRESS, Genève & ADAGP, Paris 1984.*

careful to avoid a mimetic translation of the text. This watercolor represents a page; the sheet of paper is divided by parallel lines on which
typographic characters, drawn by hand, are inscribed. Klee recreates the
spatial configuration of a page, by all appearances even its frame, its
closure; he incorporates, like Mirò, the gestural. This *tableau-poème*
representing a page is not at all unique in Klee's work. "Une page des
archives de la ville" reproduces an alleged document. On parallel lines it
presents both a diagram made of letters and an ideogram recounting the
history of the town, as well as its geography and architecture. Through
this ambiguity the painter transforms the canvas simultaneously into a
page and a wall, into a text and an image. It is not simply that they
coincide spatially, but that the signs function doubly, as text and as
image. In this work Klee even seems to be distancing himself from the
open work. In "Er küsse mich," the page functions at the same time as a
landscape, a landscape which is hardly schematized by repetition and a
reduction to signs. The biblical text, revelation in the strong sense of the
word, is inscribed across the sky, the celestial landscape; the two are
thus intimately united. Klee proposes a return to the origin, to the
productive act. The sky becomes the first page; poetry and painting,
language and landscape, are thus born in the same creative act. Thanks

to this dynamism, the page of a book can never be taken for a copy or an imitation. Text and image meet through their simultaneous presence in the same space, through the presence of the gestural in both the brush strokes and the irregular lines of writing, and also through their common reference to divine creation, a creation which absorbs all differences into a unity. Without a doubt, this painted sky does not convey a sense of infinity, of space, of ether. It is composed of different colors of varying opacity or transparency—painter's colors. The handwritten text offers no resistance to the reader, as it does in Ernst. To see and to read become inseparable; viewer and reader are constituted by the same act, for creation occurs in a single gesture and not by degrees or transitions according to which nature would precede perception, as silence would language. Art, being neither reaction nor synthesis, pretends to the absolute.

But the absence of stages does not mean the eclipse of progression or the absence of time in Klee's vision. As we have noted, the blue of the sky is not uniform, the space between the lines varies with the colors. Following the lines of text according to the direction in which one normally reads, the eye moves from dark areas to lighter areas, from transparency to opacity, from an ethereal blue to greyish tints, and finally, to yellows and oranges. The eye encounters the darkness which precedes all genesis, and the flux which accompanies it. A look at the whole sky suggests the coexistence of diurnal and nocturnal regions, of stars and their radiance, sometimes present, sometimes eclipsed. Thus the sky reveals the simultaneity of day and night for the viewer interested purely in spectacle. For the viewer, wishing to decipher the image, transition points are available, presenting the dawn at certain intervals following the course of the night. And it is through this duality that Klee allows a certain gap to subsist between text and image, despite the fact that the bright areas of the image coincide with words which evoke intense sources of luminosity. The vision of the sky, this page by Klee, exists somewhat outside time and eternity, for in the lighter areas there is a manifest shimmering effect: allusions to other layers, to slippages, reverberations; a slight instability, a refusal. This sky, these lines of paint, will never absorb the text to the point of impairing its visibility.

We have seen in the majority of *tableaux-poèmes* a juxtaposition of figures and writing which, while retaining a relative autonomy, are each in a process of transgression with respect to the other. Writing tends towards painting, for its gestural and calligraphic qualities distinguish it from typography and printing. It approaches painting by refusing to adhere to straight, parallel lines affixed to the page, and by simulating a reading effect in motion. The canvas and its figures approach the readable by reproducing the forms of typographic characters or the rhythm of their directions. The text, always inscribed within the frame of the painting, never in its margins, challenges our reading habits and lays a trap for us, requiring turnabouts and substituting spatial depth or a multiplicity of planes for a flat surface. All closure is excluded; the *tableau-poème* engages us in the play of its duality and tensions. Our activity must be double, to participate in a play of transgressions which can end only hypothetically with the complete assimilation of the readable and the visible, with their union. The *tableau-poème* confirms the theories of Eco, for it invites us to take part in the painter's work—an ideal field for an infinite series of readings—to which we can apply without reservation the following words of Eco: "un type d'oeuvres qui, bien que matériellement achevées, restent ouvertes à une continuelle germination de relations internes."[8] ["A type of work which, although finished in its material aspects, remains open to a continual germination of internal relations."]

Translated by Kathryn Aschheim

8. Umberto Eco, op.cit., 35.

THOMAS M. GREENE

# The End of Discourse in Machiavelli's "Prince"

### I.

Machiavelli was a writer preoccupied with the gravity of endings, oppressed even with the pathos of human terminations, but he was capable of discriminating between what might be called their degrees of decorum.

> Egli è cosa verissima come tutte le cose del mondo hanno il termine della vita loro; ma quelle vanno tutto il corso che è loro ordinato dal cielo, generalmente, che non disordinano il corpo loro, ma tengonlo in modo ordinato.

> There is nothing more true than that all the things of this world have a limit to their existence; but those only run the entire course ordained for them by Heaven that do not allow their body to become disorganized, but keep it unchanged in the manner ordained.[1]

This sentence moves, not uncharacteristically, from a universal fatality to a sense of human obligation to perpetuate things (most notably, political regimes and institutions) through their natural or prescribed

---

1. Quotations in Italian from *Il principe* and the *Discorsi* are taken from Niccolò Machiavelli, *Opere*, ed. Ezio Raimondi (Milan: Mursia, 1969). This passage from the *Discorsi* appears on page 253. Future page references to Raimondi will appear parenthetically after the quotation.

Quotations in English from *The Prince* are taken from the translation by George Bull (New York: Penguin Classics, 1980). Quotations from the *Discourses* are taken from *The Prince and the Discourses*, intro. Max Lerner (New York: Modern Library, 1950). The passage quoted appears on p. 397. The parenthetical page references will refer to these English editions. I have however taken the liberty throughout of substituting the Italian word *virtù* for its supposed English equivalent, since the argument of this essay depends upon the reader's recognition of this term.

57

career. Things which attain their destined end expire decorously as things do not which are botched by human misjudgment, neglected or aborted irresponsibly. Few things in fact do attain that decorum for Machiavelli; part of the oppression of human affairs lies in the interruptions, the truncations of natural curves, in the human impotence or malignity that produces amputated history. It is the unique achievement of the Roman republic, as analyzed in the *Discourses on Livy*, to have sustained its own natural course for so many centuries, but the more common pattern is the uneven, jarring, indecorous rhythm of *The Prince, The History of Florence*, the *capitolo* "Di Fortuna." In *The Prince* endings tend to be violent, disastrous, and simultaneous with fresh beginnings which are themselves shallowly founded and insecurely extended. The kind of harmonious change which dovetails each new structural addition (chapter 2) appears in the context of the entire work as a rare exception.

The treatise indeed would have no reason for being were this not the case. It assumes and addresses the indecorum of contemporaneous Italy. It *assumes* the political muddle like a weight to be carried and disposed of, and in so doing it abjures the false decorum of *belles lettres*. The dedicatory epistle repudiates rhetoric; the clipped opening chapter repudiates the graces of humanist elegance; from the beginning, the book refuses to be literature, that most refined corrupter of communal discipline (*History*, 5, 1). *The Prince* signals its willed estrangement from the cultural processes it claims to analyze. It will not enjoy the ritual comforts of the products of high culture, including the factitious ending, the dialogue that fabricates consensus, the generous unrealities and bland conclusions of fiction that passes for description. It will remain outside all that, so that any closure it succeeds in attaining will be the hard won closure of the intelligence embedded in that actual history which frustrates natural endings. "Unlike writing, life never finishes" wrote Robert Lowell. Machiavelli's authorial stance as his book opens seems to reject that *textual* conclusiveness and to promise only whatever *analytic* conclusiveness can be wrung from the perennially continuous. This honesty of method is the honesty which would leave the *Discourses* essentially unfinished and the last sentence of the *History* opening onto the ruin that continued to engulf Italy endlessly.

But the reader who begins *The Prince* is not discouraged from presuming that a decorous analytic closure lies within its author's power. What the reader first encounters are the curt distinctions of a new, embracing political science. All states are either republics or principalities. Principalities are either hereditary or acquired. If acquired, they are either entirely new or grafted. We appear to enter upon a total system, a Thomism of statecraft which within its modest length will find a place for all possible political conditions and define their constituent elements from a position outside and above them. Yet as the chapters follow devoted to successive individual cases, the reader receives rather the opposite impression: he or she is down on the ground of history, watching the author clear away limited areas of general truth, moving not inward from universal principles but outward from concrete events. This is the first shadow cast upon the presumption of analytic closure. The author's goal is to clear away a conceptual space uncluttered by prejudice or ethics or loyalty or myth, a space where the pure intelligence can operate freely to discover the laws of political behavior and precepts for political success. But this enterprise has no basis in axiomatic first truths; it is rigorously, bravely inductive.

The faculty engaged in clearing this space is elsewhere termed *discorso* by Machiavelli (*Discourses*, 1, Proemio, 73), a term which might be glossed as the power of rational analysis. It begins with concrete experience and history, such as the débacle of Louis XII's Italian wars discussed in chapter 3, and its actual power can be measured in the tightness of the correspondence between example and generalization. The generalizations in chapter 3, "Composite Principalities," are based upon the negative examples of Louis's failures, but the failures have prescriptive value: they can be used to produce rules for success. Louis can be said to have made five errors, which historical analysis can isolate from his experience and others'. In the future a ruler who wishes to graft a new member upon an established state, as Louis did, can be taught how to proceed effectively. This is a small clearing of conceptual order, since it involves only one particular situation among many hypothetical situations confronting a prince. But in theory this clearing can be duplicated in the analyses of all other situations. When this has been accomplished, then a legitimate analytic closure would be reached.

In chapter 3, little is said of individual *virtù*, because *virtù* is an explosive, improvisatory, antisystematic capacity for which the emergent political science has no need nor indeed any place. It appears in the brief opening chapter as a kind of enabling talent which would permit the apprentice ruler to attain a position where scientific precept would be useful to him. But *virtù* only begins to emerge as a significant force in a chapter devoted to legendary legislator-founders, and then later, more dangerously, in Cesare Borgia's sanguinary epic. *Virtù* in these earlier chapters is not contained by analysis, but it does not threaten seriously to blunt analytic reason, *discorso*. It might be said merely to complicate that close correspondence between precept and event which is essential to the writer's method. Thus governments set up overnight "are destroyed in the first bad spell . . . unless those who have suddenly become princes are of such *virtù* that overnight they can learn how to preserve what fortune has suddenly tossed into their laps" (54).

> Se già quelli tali . . . che sì de repente sono diventati principi, non sono di tanta virtù, che quello che la fortuna ha messo loro in grembo e' sappino subito prepararsi a conservarlo. [19]

Already in this passage exceptions have to be made for genius, and in the very negative, concessive formulation the text admits an energy which gathers power from its semidismissal. Contrary to custom, contrary to precept, a wayward dynamism enters the text, is created by the text which seems to dismiss it. But it does not here threaten the very logic of the argument.

The conceptual space cleared by intellectual power is however progressively perceived as hemmed in by all the immense body of history that resists generalization. Every law is vulnerable to the exceptions, the qualifications and inconsistencies of political experience, just as the intellectual power is vulnerable to any internal inconsistencies or faulty logic. Because there are no transcendental principles, because the analytic movement always works from the specific case outward, *The Prince* reluctantly reveals its radically *conative* dimension; it is obliged to strive against the complexities that hedge its clearings. Its language betrays the traces of an academic *disputatio:* "If you advance this objection, then I reply thus. . . ." "*Disputerò* come questi principati si possino governare" (7) ["I shall debate how these principalities can be governed" (33)]; the verb adumbrates an adversarial relationship. To extend the circumscribed area of truth requires a felt effort, a courage, a risk, as well as a violence upon convention and morality. Given the resistances, it becomes hard to believe that the extensions outward will come to control all the delimiting space. One suspects that something will always remain to be appropriated. Closure at best, it seems, will fence in a finite territory against the uncharted space always lying outside.

II.

Machiavelli's effort to clear a conceptual space resembles the prince's effort to clear a politico-geographical space on which to impose his will and his order. The metaphor commonly applied to the prince's activity, the imposition of form on matter, can equally be applied to the writer's activity. The writer employs a conceptual violence, a sacrifice of myth, of ethics, of "literature," and this violence is vulnerable to conventional judgment as is the physical violence of the ideally ruthless ruler. The writer of *The Prince*, like his creature, has to wrestle with Fortune, who can jumble *post hoc* analysis as she frustrates *ante hoc* calculation. Each space, the conceptual and concrete political, is threatened by an inherent principle of disorder which must be allowed for and which to a degree can be combated. Thus the hero of the book, the timeless hero with a hundred faces who battles and plots and kills to impose his discipline on a recalcitrant polity, is doubled by the thinker who in defining him has risked a murderous sacrifice of pieties in order to discipline the wayward details of history.

The common effort in which writer and statesman meet is termed "imitation." Imitation for Machiavelli as for many other Renaissance preceptors is an extension of reading, and in his specific extension writing and action come together. This duality is first suggested in chapter 6 of *The Prince*, and perhaps it is no accident that in this opening paragraph the word *virtù*, employed three times, makes its first important appearance in the treatise, as though through the pedagogy of imitation that antisystematic energy could be contained.

> Non si maravigli alcuno se nel parlare che io farò de' principati al tutto nuovi e di principe e di stato, io addurrò grandissimi esempli; perché . . . debbe uno uomo prudente entrare sempre per vie battute da uomini grandi, e quelli che sono stati eccellentissimi imitare, acciò che, se la sua virtù non vi arriva, almeno ne renda qualche odore; e fare come gli arcieri prudenti, a' quali, parendo el loco dove disegnano ferire troppo lontano, e conoscendo fino a quanto va la virtù del loro arco, pongono la mira assai più alta che il loco destinato, non per aggiugnere con la loro freccia a tanta altezza, ma per potere, con lo aiuto di sì alta mira, pervenire al disegno loro. [16–17]

> No one should be surprised if, in discussing states where both the prince and the constitution are new, I shall give the loftiest examples. . . . So a prudent man should always follow in the footsteps of great men and imitate those who have been outstanding. If his own *virtù* fails to compare with theirs, at least it has an air of greatness about it. He should behave like those archers who, if they are skilful, when the target seems too distant, know the capabilities (*virtù*) of their bow and aim a good deal higher than the objective, not in order to shoot so high but so that by aiming high they can reach the target. [49]

The writer implies that the prudent prince should imitate *him* in his own scrutiny of the most illustrious (ancient) examples; the writer and the prince are properly ranged side by side as they both put to use the book of the past. A later restatement of this theme will underscore the inseparability of reading and action.

> Quanto allo esercizio della mente, debbe il principe leggere le istorie, e in quelle considerare le azioni delli uomini eccelenti; vedere come si sono governati nelle guerre; esaminare le cagioni delle vittorie e perdite loro, per potere queste fuggire e quelle imitare. [39]

> As for intellectual training, the prince should read history, studying the actions of eminent men to see how they conducted themselves during war and to discover the reasons for their victories or their defeats, so that he can avoid the latter and imitate the former. [89–90]

The prince in other words should do what in fact Machiavelli is doing in the composition of this treatise. In the prince's conduct we can judge his skill as reader, the skill which renders this particular treatise unique. The wise prince will join Machiavelli in rejecting history as mere *belles lettres;* he will scorn humanist reading for the creative, dynamic reading of history which acts upon the concrete present.

The fullest discussion of imitation appears in the "Proemio" to Book 1 of the *Discourses.* The neglect of the past by modern rulers, Machiavelli charges, is due to the lack of real knowledge of history (*vera cognizione delle storie*), which is read only for the pleasure afforded by its variety rather than for the purpose of active imitation, wrongly judged to be not only difficult but impossible. Machiavelli will study Livy so that his readers will be able to derive from it that utility in which true knowledge of history must be found. The author writes to perform (*operare*) things desirable for the common good, and the content of his labor will be those achievements filled with *virtù*, those "virtuosissime operazioni" wrought (*operate*) by ancient kingdoms and republics. The *Discourses* comprise an imitative *operazione* designed to inspire ulterior imitative *operazioni* on the part of the active "virtuous" reader-ruler. Thus this Proemio draws a distinction implicit in *The Prince* between the humanist/dilettante, the merely verbal imitator, and the true reader/knower/active imitator. The result of this distinction is to lump Machiavelli together with his ideal hero and his ideal reader, active imitators all.

This is the positive version of what Machiavelli is doing in writing as he does, but even in these optimistic formulations one discerns shadows of doubt. There is clearly doubt in the simile of the archer quoted above, who aims above his target in order to reach it. This tacit admis-

sion that the summits of ancient achievement will always prove superi-
or to the modern reveals the intrinsic flaw in Machiavelli's imitative
project. The affirmation of the unchanging character of man, made in
the same Proemio in Book 1 of the *Discourses*, has to be balanced
against the contrast between ancient *virtù* and modern vice which, he
writes elsewhere, is "clearer than the sun" (Proemio to Book 2). Machiavelli's historicism and his doctrine of imitation have to be accom-
modated to these antithetical perceptions, each often repeated but never fully reconciled. If the ruler/imitator is inherently corrupted, then his
"reading" will be continuously vitiated and the thought of the writ-
er/imitator wasted. The rejection of textual, fictive, mythical conclusions for analytic, prescriptive, operative conclusions may entail a final
result in botched and vicious parodies.

This likelihood is increased since modern decadence confronts
both thinker and ruler with the common challenge of *extension*. There
is a risk, we learn from the *Asino d'oro* (*Golden Ass*), in the extension of
power beyond the walls of the city state. The appetite for extending
dominion is there represented as self-destructive, whereas German cit-
ies, content with no more than a band of six miles surrounding them,
live in security.

> A la nostra città non fe' paura
>   Arrigo già con tutta la sua possa,
>   Quando i confini avea presso alle mura;
> E or ch'ella ha sua potenza promossa
>   Intorno, e diventata è grande e vasta,
>   Teme ogni cosa, non che gente grossa.

> Formerly [the emperor] Henry VII with all his might aroused no fear in
> our city, when her boundaries were near the walls, but now that she has
> extended her power round about and become large and vast, she fears
> everything, not only the strong.[2]

Florence's spatial expansion is a cause of insecurity although, as the
*Discourses* suggest, a city like Rome might feel a compulsion to expand
in order to preserve internal equilibrium. A still more serious challenge
lies in temporal extension. Because Fortune operates in time, time itself
is dangerous. A legislator may found a healthy state but his laws and
institutions may be subverted before they have time to root themselves.
If a state attempts to reform itself (Florence in 1502 under the Soderini

---

2. *Tutte le opere di Niccolò Machiavelli*, ed. F. Flora and C. Cordié (Milan: Mon-
dadori, 1950), 2, 768–69. Translation by the writer.

republic), it may be crushed before it has time to conclude (Florence, 1512, after the return of the Medici). But if Fortune favors the state with victory and prosperity, these may lead in time to softness and corruption (*History*, 5, 1). The paradigmatic story of Borgia is the story of a clever antagonist of time, who staves off ruin for a while through a protracted series of expedients. Even Cosimo de' Medici, the most successful single figure of the *History*, sees his public and private affairs "going to ruin" at the end of his life (7, 6). Real duration in Machiavelli represents a (perhaps unknowing) concession to myth, since the true founders of enduring states—Moses, Theseus, Romulus, Cyrus—were all to some degree legendary. The modern archer cannot shoot so high; he must aim for narrower expansions, indecorous endings, briefer extensions, aborted reigns, precarious continuities.

This vulnerability of political extension affects the security of the thinker's conceptual extension. The potential collapse of a political order involves the viability of the cognitive order, since the cognitive discourse first presented itself as counsel for successful action. As the implicit distance widens between model and realistic goal, as the demeaning decline of culture stands revealed, then the double *operazioni* of imitation appear less and less plausible. The extension of the conceptual clearing assumes a fund of relevant nonmythical examples to be drawn upon to meet each problem of praxis. But this fund in *The Prince* proves to be shallow. The situation of Machiavelli as innovative thinker can be compared most readily to the situation of that prince who is a newcomer in a *principatus novus*. Of such a prince's task it can be said that "nothing is more difficult to arrange, more doubtful of success, and more dangerous to carry through" (51). To achieve something like decorous closure under these circumstances may require the surrender of hope for a single extended clearing; it may require one to settle for random patches of relative order, clusters of insight connected arbitrarily. The closing chapters of *The Prince* will be decisive in determining whether in fact it does adumbrate a calculus capable of scientific coherence.

III.

This determination proves to be negative: analysis leading to precept is progressively abandoned in the last third of the book. Scientific pretensions are quietly withdrawn as the semblance of conclusive law fades from the text. In this progressive capitulation, a few stages can be roughly distinguished. Quite early one can trace a disturbing gap between example and precept: in the failures of the exemplary figures Cesare Borgia and Oliverotto da Fermo, in the blurred distinction between Borgia and Agothocles, in the success of Scipio whose leniency should in principle have proven fatal, in the success of French armies employing those mercenaries which are allegedly the root cause of Italian military disgrace. As the analysis proceeds one can follow the increasing effort of the precept to disengage itself from the entangling texts of recorded history and remembered history. *This* text begins with gestures ostensibly grounding precepts in past experience and then goes on essentially to unground them, to demonstrate as it were in spite of itself the difficult struggle of the precept to stem directly from experience.

This struggle is rendered still more arduous by the progressive recalcitrance of the precept to remain simple, pure, clear-cut. The famous chapter 17 ("Cruelty and compassion; and whether it is better to be loved than feared, or the reverse") has been noticed chiefly for its ethical brutality, but for our purposes it can serve to exemplify the intensifying discursive qualification. Brutal this chapter may be, but the harshness emerges from an undergrowth of distinctions, reversals, exceptions, and modifications. The text is finding it increasingly necessary to complicate generalizations, turning back on its own discourse to raise objections or modify rules. One can work through chapter 17 noting the complications in purely lexical terms, in the frequency of expressions like "nevertheless," "but," "however," "on the other hand" (*"nondimanco," "pertanto," "ma," "pure," "dall'una parte," "dall'altra"*). Not every usage involves a qualification of the argument, but taken together they underscore the difficulty of reaching firm guidelines in the shifting morass of human affairs. The conceptual clearing becomes more visibly overgrown.

In the chapters that follow, the ability to elicit unqualified rules from history will grow feebler. The long chapter 19 ("The need to avoid contempt and hatred") presents a new stage in the deterioration of analysis, a stage which substitutes contradiction for qualification and which in effect offers an alternative to precept. Two cases of contradiction can suffice. First instance: Machiavelli's lifelong support of the standing militia in preference to mercenary armies, support which is expressed elsewhere in *The Prince* (chap. 12), is subverted in chapter 19 by his analysis of the Roman army's destructive role in the empire and his congratulation of modern rulers on their freedom from this threat. Second instance: the confusing discussion of conspiracies argues that "there have been many conspiracies but few of them have achieved their end" (103) ["si vede molte essere state le coniure e poche avere avuto buon fine" (47–48)]. A survey of the factors that cause their failures and which should deter a potential conspirator leads to the surprising assertion that "it is unthinkaole that anyone should be so rash as to conspire" (104) ["è impossibile che alcuno sia sì temerario che coniuri" (48)], an assertion that denies the facts and denies what immediately precedes it. The contradiction remains if both generalizations are restricted to those regimes which have won popular support. This is the case of the one example offered: the Canneschi family conspired against and assassinated Annibale Bentivogli, prince of Bologna. But the Bolognese so loved the dynasty that they killed the Canneschi, then found a bastard scion of the Bentivogli and allowed him to rule until the rightful heir had time to come of age. Thus I conclude, writes Machiavelli, "that when a prince has the good will of the people he should not worry about conspiracies" (105) ["uno principe debbe tenere delle coniure poco conto, quando el popolo gli sia benivolo" (48)]. This will not comfort Annibale, who perhaps should have worried about conspiracies somewhat more than he did. In his case men *were* rash enough to conspire and they succeeded in doing him in.

The alternative which in effect replaces the crumbling analytic precept in chapter 19 has maintained a vigorous presence through most of the treatise but is only now explicitly permitted to dominate the argument. This is the undefined, perhaps undefinable gift of *virtù*, whose mysterious significance in this book can only be grasped by triangulating contexts, and whose contexts themselves are richly, perversely various. What we learn from this chapter is that politics cannot be mastered as a science but intuited as an art beyond the reach of rules. Politics becomes an arena for flair, instinct, genius, which no treatise can circumscribe and whose description can never be closed because it cannot, properly speaking, be begun. Why did the emperor Severus, a "new prince," keep his throne, when all the other emperors of his era who, like him, had recourse to undue cruelty were killed?

> In Severo fu tanta virtù che, mantenendosi e soldati amici, ancora che i populi fussino da lui gravati, possé sempre regnare felicemente; perché quelle sua virtù lo facevano nel conspetto de' soldati e de' populi sì mirabile che questi rimanevano *quodam modo* attoniti e stupidi, e quelli reverenti e satisfatti. [50]

> Severus was a man of such *virtù* that, keeping the soldiers friendly, even though the people were oppressed by him, he reigned successfully to the end; this was because his *virtù* so impressed the soldiers and the people that the latter were continuously left astonished and stupefied and the former stayed respectful and content. [109]

The narrative that follows fails to distinguish persuasively Severus' conduct from the others'; the basis of his success was simply his *virtù*, which the text cannot really concretize. The *virtù* remains an absolute, impervious to description or even to understanding.

> A Caracalla, Commodo e Massimino [fu] cosa perniziosa imitare Severo, per non avere auta tanta virtù che bastassi a seguitare le vestigie sua. [53]

> It was fatal for Caracalla, Commodus, and Maximinus to imitate Serverus, since they lacked the *virtù* to follow in his footsteps. [114]

We seem on the brink of a tautology wherein *virtù* obtains success and success results from *virtù*. The close of this long chapter can add little to this semantic circle.

The following chapter 20 foregrounds a factor which will complete the subversion of a prescriptive political science—the factor of the unique set of circumstances, the unpredictable, asystematic *kairos*. Should the prince disarm his subjects, deliberately antagonize them, foster divisions among them, build fortresses?

> Di tutte queste cose non si possi dare determinata sentenzia se non si viene a' particulari di quelli stati dove si avessi a pigliare alcuna simile deliberazione. [54]

> It is impossible to give a final verdict on any of these policies, unless one examines the particular circumstances of the states in which such decisions have had to be taken. [114]

Despite this impossibility Machiavelli states his intention to discuss each question in general terms, but each discussion tends to appeal finally to "i particulari," "i tempi." The appeal implicitly calls into question the analysis and the counsel of the preceding chapters, since these have been presented as transcending concrete occasions and as generally valid. Here rather in the dominance of circumstances lies the vindication of that instinctive *virtù* which will seize upon the essentials of each concrete occasion and manipulate them with daring and imagination. Just as the writer ends his treatment of the fortresses by commending those who build them and those who do not, so his choice of able advisors is a choice beyond rules: "Good advice, whomever it comes from, depends on the shrewdness of the prince who seeks it, and not the shrewdness of the prince on good advice." (127) ["Li buoni consigli, da qualunque venghino, conviene naschino dalla prudenzia del principe, e non la prudenzia del principe da' buoni consigli" (61)]. The closing sentence of chapter 24, the last ostensibly analytic chapter, seems to offer the only version of closure the book is now capable of.

> Quelle difese solamente sono buone, sono certe, sono durabili, che dependano da te proprio e dalla virtù tua. [63]

> The only sound, sure, and enduring methods of defense are those based on your own actions and *virtù*. [129]

The activity of the prince is now fundamentally improvisatory. All courses of action are risky in the nature of things ("l'ordine delle cose"). The prince as we last view him is profoundly lonely, extemporizing stratagems and precautions to extend his hazardous rule, unable to count on his people, his allies, his advisers, or on ancient models of achievement. He must adapt himself ceaselessly, restlessly, to the caprice of changing circumstance, as the penultimate chapter 25 affirms, but to do this is to be extravagantly, inhumanly volatile.

> Se uno che si governa con respetti e pazienzia, e tempi e le cose girono in modo che il governo suo sia buono, e' viene felicitando; ma se li tempi e le cose si mutano, e' rovina, perché non muta modo di procedere. Né si truova uomo sí prudente che si sappi accomodare a questo. [64]

> If a man behaves with patience and circumspection and the time and circumstances are such that this method is called for, he will prosper; but if time and circumstances change he will be ruined because he does not change his policy. Nor do we find any man shrewd enough to know how to adapt his policy in this way. [132]

The lonely ruler, shifting his balance and his policy, remaking his own character as he remakes his style, listening for each whisper of change in the times, will nonetheless falter in the end from a tragic insufficiency of pliancy.

This failure of the prince betokens the failure of the analyst whose admission of circumstance has caused his conceptual space definitively to implode. Stage by stage, he has withdrawn from dogmatism to qualification to contradiction to a surrender before pure contingency. The text, unable to perpetuate its order, unable to validate imitation, acts out its own version of the prince's failure. The analyst has been unequal to the volatility of his own subject and if, in his penultimate chapter, he leaves open, or tries to, the struggle between Fortune and *virtù*, his own rational power seems defeated by Fortune. Counsel based on experience is impracticable; success lies in the harmonizing of conduct with occasion; and this book, by maintaining ostensibly its function as manual, has evidently denied itself any meaningful statement. The final conclusion, given this collapse of system, would appear to be necessarily confessional or duplicitous. The only real question, apparently, is how much failure to admit.

## IV.

The final twenty-sixth chapter of *The Prince* ("Exhortation to liberate Italy from the barbarians") may have been written well after the others, as though the writer were dissatisfied with his original close. It radically alters the rhetorical mode from deliberation to apocalypse. A desperate urgency, heretofore barely discernible, produces calls for a redeemer like Moses, Cyrus, and Theseus, and the very prostrate condition of Italy, personified pathetically, becomes an argument for her future salvation. Stylistic restraint gives way to oratorical melodrama, and the scorn for myth gives way to the invocation of a savior. In this last chapter the repressed visionary in the author returns to life, the visionary of the *capitoli* and the *Asino d'oro*. The strained hope of the vision results in ironies beyond his control: irony in the evocation of "unheard of wonders" (*estraordinarii, sanza esemplo*), in the predicted defeat of the Swiss and Spanish infantry by newly trained Italians, in the identification of the Medici with the hypothetical redeemer, in the concluding quotation from Petrarch, 150 years old, predicting a speedy victory of native *virtù* over the barbarians. The desperate urgency of this chapter apparently derives from the ruinous military situation, but one wonders whether the deeper cause is not the deterioration of the writer's enterprise. If in fact he had established with calm logic the prescriptive science his book had seemed to promise, there would be no need for miracles and messiahs. This conclusion could not properly be called either confessional or duplicitous, but it does not seem free from a degree of self-deception.

To say this however is not seriously to deal with the problematic question of the book's closure, nor to determine ultimately what we are left with. One way to respond to these questions would be to point to the text's increasing dependance on a single signifier, *virtù*, which possesses at once too much and too little significance. The meanings of this word as derived from context "go round in an endless series of incompatibilities," according to one critic,[3] and from this circular plethora of

3. Sydney Anglo, *Machiavelli: A Dissection* (London: Gollancz, 1969), 236.

meaning, stable meaning might plausibly be seen to leak away. Thus it might be argued that Machiavelli's book is progressively usurped by a signifier which is essentially vacant, pretending to denote a referent which cannot be shown to exist. Historical analysis and political analysis would stand revealed as dependent on a term which is radically blurred, so that the text as a whole could be said to reach an impasse or to move around endlessly in that vortex of incompatibilities. This account would postulate then a helpless closure of decentered or hollow statement, feebly circling around its weakness.

An alternative account would recognize in the messianic close an admission that the book had begun by misrepresenting its own character and that it truly belongs to that flow of cultural production it had initially wanted to repudiate. The close restores the book to cultural discourse, "literary" discourse, as against that ulterior, detached, purely analytic discourse it had seemed to claim for itself. The "Exhortation" reveals a mode of imitation which breaks down the segregation of rhetorician and activist, which accepts models from poetry as well as from praxis. The ruler/reader is no longer situated side by side with the writer, engaged in a common *operazione,* but rather opposite the writer, the object of his exhortation. In this view of *The Prince,* the presumption of scientific, systematic closure would be regarded as a distraction which the book gradually, then dramatically dispels. The text could thus be understood as acting out the discovery of its authentic goal, which is the goal of "literature" and all culture, namely the fabrication of a vulnerable construct. The prince Machiavelli fabricates, the conniver with a hundred faces, belongs to the realm of the mythical which the text has never exorcised, and the prince's *virtù* retains that potent and volatile opacity which is the property of imaginative fictions.

The construct of *The Prince* is of course ungrounded like all cultural constructs. It achieves the shaky validity of an extemporized invention which is exposed, precarious, *bricolé,* conative. If the signifier *virtù* is vulnerable through its simultaneous superfluity/emptiness of meaning, then like other problematic signifiers it calls for the intervention of the reader to drain and fill it, to penetrate its opacity and grasp the emergent integrity of its "incompatibilities." If in the politico-geographic realm the fragmentation of Italy invites a redeemer, in the textual realm the fragmented meanings invite more plausibly the intrusion of the reader's synthesizing and flexible understanding. The invulnerable construct, if such a monster could be conceived, the construct lacking this text's polysemous density, would be condemned to sterility. *Virtù* as a signifier is incontestably imprecise, but it makes demonstrably a sombre, obsessive aggression upon the mind which could not be propelled either by pure precision or pure vacancy. *Something* is there in the text, something not wholly unstable, that sort of thing we look to culture to provide. As a scientific concept, *virtù* blurs; as an otherwise unnamable, explosive, newly isolated property of experience, it can be received as seminal. Machiavelli's book does open up a clearing of space, not so much for analysis as for the historical imagination, a space of suggestive uncertainty surrounding a word, and this space becomes a constitutive element of the text, perhaps the most valuable element.

From this view of the book, *The Prince* reaches its close when, having discovered its own mystery and mythicality, it comes at last to admit and proclaim them. This mythical dimension does not cancel out the play of analytic intelligence which has governed earlier chapters. It does not discredit the effort to generalize political action and to read performatively all history as a text. But it does seal the analogy between writer and ruler more firmly, since the writer like his most prestigious models is a prophet, a *profeto*. His book can end decorously when he accepts the role of prophet, and if his crudest concluding prophecy invites irony, we can find in the body of his work a prophetic vision of bitter dignity, a composite image of brilliant, beleaguered fury which cannot effectively be deconstructed. He dismisses in a famous aphorism the role of unarmed prophet: "All armed prophets have conquered, and unarmed prophets have come to grief" (52) ["Tutti e profeti armati vinsono, e gli disarmati ruinorno" (18).] This dismissal does not really affect his own role. As a prophet, Machiavelli is not totally disarmed: he is armed with that fury of *virtù*. Closure then is not a matter of completing a design; it fulfills no ideal proportions; it does not allow an intellectual order to expand to its outermost limits. Closure in this case constitutes rather a recognition that the text belongs in the sphere of other texts, the sphere of human society—improvisatory, groundless, metamorphic, fictive—the sphere of tragic conation where it finally places and joins its hero.

WILDA C. ANDERSON

# Diderot's Laboratory of Sensibility

The affinity theory dominated French chemistry almost from the moment that Geoffroy presented his affinity tables to the Académie des Sciences in 1718. It remained dominant at least until the major changes brought about by Lavoisier at the end of the century. It is even possible to argue that its influence extended well beyond—and in spite of—him, into the nineteenth century, through the work of chemists like Berthollet.[1] But one may also show, in the work of contemporary authors whose intellectual goals and professional interests were about as distant from each other as was possible, that this theory could produce a multiplicity of models applicable to very different domains. In Diderot's *D'Alembert's Dream* and Pierre Joseph Macquer's *Dictionary of Chemistry*, these models furnished their authors with more than just a way to talk about the material world. They also permitted them to create the conditions necessary to provoke a new type of scientific thought.

The choice of Macquer and Diderot is not arbitrary. Diderot had extended contact with the chemistry of affinities not only through the courses of G. F. Rouelle at the Jardin du Roi, but also through his work with Rouelle and Venel on the chemistry articles for the *Encyclopedia*. Macquer is generally recognized as one of the most important spokesmen for the chemistry of affinities. He too studied with Rouelle, and officially took over his chair at the Jardin du Roi in 1777. But he is above all known for his books. He wrote two treatises on chemistry and then in 1766 brought out his famous *Dictionary of Chemistry*. The second edition of this work, dating from 1778, proposed a compromise theory, in fact quite brilliant in its own right, which attempted to incorporate

1. See Jean-Claude Guédon, "Chimie et matérialisme, la stratégie anti-newtonienne de Diderot," *Dix-huitième siècle*, no. 11 (1979), 185–200.

Lavoisier's discoveries into the theory of chemical affinities supported by the phlogistians.

For Macquer, chemistry *is* the science of affinities. He postulates that "this great effect is so general that it can be considered to be both the cause of all combinations and the tool we use to make sense out of them."[2] In other words, the affinity theory furnishes Macquer with a description to represent chemical reactions and an interpretive theory which permits him to make observations and to explain them. For many of these same reasons, as we shall discuss later, he found that the ideal format to present a coherent treatise of chemistry was the alphabetical cross-referenced structure used in his *Dictionary of Chemistry*.

The logical place to start to look for the theory and epistemology proper to Macquer's chemistry is in the article entitled "Affinity" in the *Dictionary*. The organization of this article is simple but eloquent. For the first ten pages, Macquer outlines a theory of the scalar combinations of chemical principles derived from the hierarchy that Geoffroy had instituted in his "Tables of Affinities" in 1718.[3] The basic assumption of this theory was as follows: matter can be analyzed, in other words, broken down into smaller components, either quantitatively or qualitatively. To be able to carry out either of these two very different kinds of decomposition, it is necessary to overcome the *affinity* that the parts have for each other. Macquer defines affinity as both a tendency and a force:

> AFFINITY. One must understand by affinity, the tendency that the parts of the body have, whether constituent (heterogeneous) or integrating (homogeneous), each towards the other, and the force that causes them to adhere together when they are united. [57]

At its simplest level, the concept of affinity is clearly an analogy, in the domain of chemistry, of the image associated with Newton's universal attraction. It is a sort of microcosmic gravity,[4] the force inherent in masses to move towards each other (57). But from the beginning of Macquer's argument, the primary empirical observation that leads to the postulation of this force is the attraction that can be seen to exist between two bodies of the same substance, especially drops of liquids.

---

2. P. J. Macquer, "Affinité," in his *Dictionnaire de chymie*, 2d edition (Paris: Lacombe, 1778), 1, 57. Further references to this work will be noted in the text. This and all further translations are my own.

3. Etienne-François Geoffroy, "Tables des affinités," *Mémoires de l'Académie Royale des Sciences pour l'année 1718* (Paris), 202–12.

4. See, for example, the famous suggestions made by Isaac Newton in the "Queries to the Optics," in *Newton's Philosophy of Nature*, H. S. Thayer, ed. (New York: Hafner, 1953), Question #31, 160.

Affinity, unlike gravity, is not considered by Macquer to be a the-oretically derived force.[5] It exists. It is an essential property of matter, a factual *given* that does not need to be justified and which is not open to challenge: "This great effect is perhaps a property as essential to matter as its extension and its impenetrability and about which we cannot say anything other than that it is thus" (57). In the case of two drops of water that dissolve into one drop on contact with each other, Macquer's asser-tion that the existence of affinity is a fact is in itself not very interesting in chemical terms. It becomes crucial, however, when Macquer extrap-olates to cover all chemical reactions, whether between the same sub-stance (what I would call mechanical affinities of aggregation) or be-tween unlike substances (which are more justifiably called chemical affinities): "The affinity existing between the principal parts or the constituents [of a compound] is demonstrated by the detail of all the phenomena of Chemistry" (57). Macquer moves from the behavior of like substances to posit a false analogy with the behavior of both simple and complex combinations of heterogeneous substances. Moreover, rather than drawing conclusions from experimental data, Macquer pre-sents his theory wholesale and only then supports it, using *definitions of terms* based on his assumptions rather than experimental observations.

> I believe that one can distinguish several sorts of affinities: not that I think that there are several different kinds; for it is *quite certain* that it is only a single and same property of matter which is modified diversely according to the diverse circumstances.
>
> The simple affinity producing the union and cohesion of [two] heterogeneous parts is called affinity of composition. The result of this union is a new body which is . . . a compound of the two. We can call Complex Affinity the one in which there are more than two bodies acting on each other. When two principles are united together in a compound, and a third one arrives in their environment, phenomena of decomposition or of composition are observed, which differ according to the affinities that the three bodies have for each other. [58–59]

Macquer posits that *qualitative* differences in the behavior of unlike simple substances, or principles, as he calls them, can be understood as a function of the varying inherent *quantities* of affinity that they have for

5. For example, in the "General Scholium," *Principia*, Book 3 and in the "Letter to Richard Bentley" of January 17, 1692/3, Newton says: "You sometimes speak of gravity as essential and inherent to matter. Pray do not ascribe that notion to me, for the cause of gravity is what I do not pretend to know and therefore I would take more time to consider of it." *Newton's Philosophy of Nature*, 53.

each other. This intensity of attraction cannot be measured directly, but is only assumed or postulated in order for Macquer to continue to explain the selective behavior of increasingly complex systems. By the time he reaches compounds acting on compounds, Macquer's description is dependent on the theory; the principles that are separating out from each other and recomposing into different compounds are never seen in their isolated states. Their existences—and especially their identities—are only deductions from the theory of affinity. This theory has several possible consequences, which Macquer states as follows:

> The last remark to be made about the simple affinity of composition furnishes us with a very general fundamental law of widespread usefulness in recognizing, even without their decomposition, the principles of which bodies are composed. Here is that remark: it is that *all compound bodies have properties which are similar to those of the principles out of which they are formed.* Thus, for example, the union of two principles, of which one is fixed and the other volatile, forms a compound which has a degree of fixity or of volatility that is an average of those of its principles.
>
> It is the same with all other properties, such as heaviness, opacity, transparence, ductility, fluidity, etc., and even in the case of the affinities; the result is that, *supposing that one knows perfectly the properties of the principles in a compound, it is possible, by examining the properties of the compound, to recognize the principles in it even when the [material] analysis would be impossible.* [61, my emphasis]

This is, of course, Macquer's justification for his statement that "this great effect [affinity] is so general that it can be considered to be both the cause of all combinations and *the tool that we use to make sense out of them.*" It is easy to sort out the assumptions that made this statement possible.

But we must first define our next term: the chemical principle. Chemical principles are not elements in a modern sense—in other words, simple undecomposable substances defined by the internal structure of their constituent particles or atoms. They are substances which support a specific group of identifying properties or qualities. The presence of a particular principle in a compound is recognizable by the presence of its characteristics in that compound, and the intensity of these qualities is an indication of the quantity of the principle present. The principles in a heterogeneous compound maintain their integrity in the various compositions and decompositions that their affinities bring about, and this integrity is "read" by the experimenter who notices that the characteristic properties of each principle exist in the new compound. But the integrity of a principle is directly visible only if affinity operates as postulated, and affinity can be understood as an analytic selection mechanism only if principles can be assumed to keep their characteristics intact in composition. Neither the definition of "affinity" nor the definition of "principle," therefore, can exist without the support of the other; they are mutually defining terms.

Behind these two definitions, supporting them but nonetheless relying on them, is an implied definition of both the chemical and mental procedures of analysis. The definition of "analysis" that Macquer gives in his dictionary is reducible to the standard eighteenth-century concept of analysis as the systematic decomposition of an object into its constituent parts and the elaboration of the links between them. This is the definition that we find in Condillac, d'Alembert, and others. But the standard derivation uses a static visual field as the model of an object to be analyzed. The object of *chemical* analysis is not as easily characterizable. Even if one takes as object a single compound, a simple description of its most striking characteristics and the relationships between these characteristics is not a chemical analysis. A chemical analysis attempts to distinguish the actual substances that make up the compound, and to describe the relationships between them. Ideally, this information should be acquired materially through physical and not mental decomposition. But often, the compound can only be decomposed in the presence of another compound, and that at the same moment that a *re*-composition with part of the second compound is effected. Only the judgment of the researcher can derive the intervening states indirectly.

Where the intersection of chemical and philosophical analysis lies is clear, as well as what the implications of this intersection are: "supposing that one knows perfectly the properties of the principles in a compound, it is possible, by examining the properties of the compound, to recognize the principles in it even when the [material] analysis would be impossible." Chemical principles are merely the mentally accomplished materializations of observed qualities.[6] The mental analysis has priority over the material analysis of the laboratory; the goal of the chemist is in the long run to be able to *name* the constituent parts and their relationships rather than merely to be able to separate them physically. The privilege accorded to the process of reading compounds to carry out a mental analysis provides us with insight into Macquer's

6. Ludwik Fleck argues the importance of this kind of hypothetical entity in *The Genesis and Development of a Scientific Fact* (Chicago: Chicago U. Press, 1979), especially 58.

fascination with the dictionary format. The equivalents of the "principles" are the word entries in the *Dictionary* which should—if the *Dictionary* has been perfectly constructed—mirror in a one-to-one relationship the substances and procedures of the material world. The entries are representations of a world analyzed, sorted out and deployed before the eyes of the reader. The complementary mental synthesis is performed by the chemist, in his armchair, as he reads the dictionary. The mental equivalent of the physical force of affinity is the working out of the "cross-references" that combine one term to another to form names for compounds, descriptions of events, and even the network of relationships that constitutes a chemical theory for the philosopher.[7]

We hope to have suggested that the terms "affinity" and "analysis" provide, for Macquer, more than just a workable theory of chemical combinations. The relationships between them form the philosophical basis from which both a picture of the chemical world and a corresponding description of the nature of chemical research are generated. Both are dependent on their isomorphism with the analytical theory of naming, the system of representation that is embodied in the format of the *Dictionary of Chemistry*. The theory of affinity, as Macquer elaborates it, serves not only as a way to answer chemical questions, but even as a philosophical method. It prescribes patterns of reasoning that determine how the chemist can conceive of and how he can read the data of his laboratory experiments. In summary, *analysis* tells one to take apart, to decompose a compound into its constituent *principles*. *Affinity* provides the interpretation-system that shows how to read where one principle begins and where another leaves off: affinity is not only the name for a force that draws substances together; selective affinity is also the reaction process through which repeatable sets of visible qualities or properties separate each other out of compounds. Together they enable the chemist to mentally attribute a substantive existence, and then a name, to a selected set of qualities. Affinity ties together both

7. Guédon, 190: "La chimie des affinités change de problématique et devient une *science des réactions*. Le chimiste abandonne le projet de comprendre *l'intimité de la matière* pour s'attacher plutôt à la *circulation des corps*. D'autre part, il faut vérifier que les transformations d'un corps en un autre, lorsqu'elles se font en plusieurs étapes et que plusieurs "routes" sont possibles, mènent à des résultats non-contradictoires." [The chemistry of affinities undergoes a change in its problematic and becomes a *science of reactions*. The chemist abandons his project of understanding the intimate nature of matter in order to focus, instead, on the circulation of bodies (*circulation des corps*). Furthermore, it is necessary to verify that when the transformations from one body to another occur in several stages and along several possible "paths," they lead to non-contradictory results.]

experimental procedures and the reading of them. It is the operator through which the linguistic and chemical domains close on each other: the chemist seems to be working at the same time in the realm of names and the realm of things.

Bachelard will say (talking about the alchemists), that "a science which allows images is, more than any other, victim of its metaphors."[8] But unlike the alchemists, the image of which Macquer is a victim is not a simple metaphor, but the structure of the analytical system translated by analogy into the concept of affinity, of cross-reference, or of grammatical syntax. Macquer wanted to develop a language of scientific practice that would carefully maintain both a distinction and a parallel between what comes from the world and what comes from the mind. He hoped that this would allow him to move on the several levels of analysis at once (the physical, linguistic, and that of observation), or to move from one level of analysis to another, while remaining securely inside the same language. But we must emphasize that in any case, language was always to be privileged over the other types of analysis, because Macquer shared the Condillacean definition of language as the paradigm of all types of analysis. The *Dictionary of Chemistry* was intended to be the tangible presence of language, waiting to be organized into an infinite number of equally valid "sentences," systems, or representations of compounds. Thus, as a formal move away from the traditional, linearly argued treatise structure, the dictionary format was to be the final alignment of the rhetorical presentation of the theory of chemistry with the physical, grammatical, and mental procedures of analysis.

Keeping this very schematic description of a particularly Enlightenment chemistry in mind, let us try to see what it allows us to say about one of the more disquietingly difficult-to-define texts of the same period, *D'Alembert's Dream*. I would like to argue that this work, which is often described as "interdisciplinary," is nothing of the sort when replaced in its own epistemological context. Let us begin by baldly looking for analogues in Diderot's text of the structures we have described in that of Macquer. The strategy is less naive than it would seem, for analogy is itself one of Diderot's favorite tools. It is built into the *Encyclopedia* through the system of cross-references and is for Diderot the material of which scientific hypothesis is made, by which the artisan in his *Thoughts Concerning the Interpretation of Nature* "sniffs out un-

8. Gaston Bachelard, *La Formation de l'esprit scientifique* (Paris: Vrin, 1975), 38.

known procedures, new experiments and unseen results."⁹ Analogy is
in fact the operation that we must describe in some depth. But first, how
does Diderot himself describe it? In the *Exchange*, the first of the three
texts that make up *D'Alembert's Dream*, Diderot teases d'Alembert
with a metaphor of the mind as a harpsichord.

> Analogy, in the most complex cases, is nothing more than a rule-of-
> three which is executed in the sensible [feeling] instrument. It is a
> fourth cord, harmonic and proportional to three others whose reso-
> nance [with it] the animal always listens for in himself, but which does
> not always come about in nature. That this may be so matters little to
> the poet; it is nonetheless true. For the philosopher, however, the case
> is otherwise. *He* must question nature who, often providing him with a
> phenomenon completely different from the one he had expected,
> shows him that the analogy he had used had seduced him.¹⁰

First we will follow Diderot's plan by trying to find the cords that
resonate, and then we will see just how well this seduction has worked.

One of the most striking examples occurs barely into *D'Alembert's
Dream* itself, where Mlle de l'Espinasse is reading to Dr. Bordeu the
monologue that d'Alembert spoke as he was dreaming. The passage is
long but important. It begins with what by now will be a familiar image.

> Just as a drop of mercury melts into another drop of mercury, one
> sensible and living molecule melts into another sensible and living
> molecule. First there were two drops; after the contact there is only
> one. Sensibility becomes common to the common mass. And indeed
> why not? The contact of two homogeneous molecules, perfectly homo-
> geneous, forms a continuity . . . and it is a case of union, of cohesion, of
> combination, of the most complete identity that can possibly be imag-
> ined. Yes, philosopher, if these molecules are elementary and simple;
> but if these are aggregates, if they are compounds? The combination
> will be made none the less, and as a result you will [still] have the
> identity, the continuity. And then the typical (*habituelles*) action and
> reaction. It is certain that the contact of two *living* molecules is some-
> thing entirely different from the contiguity of two inert masses. A very
> pure gold wire, I remember, is a comparison that he made for me; a
> homogeneous network, a tissue of sensible matter, an assimilating
> contact; active sensibility here, inert sensibility there, which is com-

9. Denis Diderot, "Pensées sur l'interprétation de la nature," Pensée 30 in his
*Oeuvres complètes*, ed. J. Assézat (Paris: Garnier, 1875), 24.
10. Denis Diderot, "Le Rêve de d'Alembert" [1767], *Oeuvres philosophiques*, ed.
Vernier (Paris: Garnier, 1964), 280. Further references will be cited in the text.

municated like movement, without taking into account, as he said so well, that there must be a difference between the contact of two sensible molecules and the contact of two molecules which aren't. And this difference? What might it be? An action, a reaction, perfectly habitual . . . and this action and this reaction have a very particular character. Everything concerts together, then, to produce a kind of unity which exists only in the animal . . . in faith, if this isn't the truth, it certainly resembles it very much. [289–90]

We hear again the same problematic opposition between the aggregates of like or of unlike substances that Macquer used to generate his model of affinity. Diderot and Macquer both move quickly over the sticking point: that the aggregation of two bodies of *like* homogeneous substance is not at all the same as the combination of two qualitatively *different* substances into one unique and continuous whole. For Macquer, the elision is made so as to move from a discussion of the melting of one drop of water into another to the explanation of the intimate but unexplained forces that combine chemically different substances into new, but easily identifiable and resolvable compounds. In Diderot, before we are even told what is being compounded together, we are told that there is an essential difference between mere contiguity (or amalgamation) and continuity (or the process of forming enduring new identities which are more than just the sum of their parts). But what is being aggregated? Molecules . . . formed out of the combination of matter and with a peculiar substance that Diderot calls "sensibility," which seems simply to mean the capacity shared by all matter to sense what is around it. What distinguishes brute matter from living beings? There is no clean distinction, but in living beings, the sensibility component is in an active rather than in an inert state. This is reminiscent of the phlogiston theories which carried their full meaning in chemical contexts such as the one that Macquer develops. It is useful to elaborate here for a moment. Fire can exist in two distinct states: free, when it is directly perceivable, or fixed in a compound. In this latter case, fire becomes "phlogiston," only perceivable through a series of chemical decompositions and recompositions in which *metaphorical analogues* of the observable properties of fire are followed from compound to compound. And after all, what is there to prevent Diderot from conceiving of sensibility in analogous terms? What would a compound of matter and sensibility look like? More exactly, what would a series of decompositions and recompositions of living beings with their sensibility look like? Diderot gives us at least two answers to this last question. The first is provided by the explicit content of the "scientific" argument concerning the nature of sensibility that we follow through the three conversations that make up *D'Alembert's Dream*. The second answer has to be read in counterpoint, as a fugue with the first. The conversation between the various characters itself *demonstrates* several different kinds of decompositions and recompositions of the various minds, of the mentalities or of the sensibilities of the four persons speaking. Diderot even puts each of his characters in different states of "composition" with his own sensibility, sometimes inert and sometimes active.

There is a third answer to our question concerning the nature of a compound of matter and sensibility, an answer which is in some senses a result of the first two. There is an obvious continuity of effect between the content of the argument worked out in the dialogues and the effects being demonstrated. In some ways, the two demonstrations are analogous, but they are more than just a theoretical argument and its "experimental" demonstration. We must above all avoid reading Diderot's description of the actions of his characters as an ironic commentary on their understanding of the subject matter. In fact, the "actions" in one chain of "argument" bring about the actions in the other, *and vice versa*. This linking together begins slowly, but accelerates.

In the first dialogue, the *Exchange Between Diderot and d'Alembert*, we start out with two speaking voices who are engaged in what seems to be a discussion, a pure debate, between two disembodied minds. But towards the end, the voice "d'Alembert" reveals indirectly that it belongs to a material body: "Good-bye, my friend, and good night." The discussion has tired him out, he wants to go home. The voice "Diderot" answers him: "You make jokes, but you will dream on your pillow of this discussion, and if it doesn't become conscious there, too bad for you, because you will be forced to adopt hypotheses which are just as ridiculous, only in a different way." D'Alembert shoots back: "You are wrong; I will go to bed a skeptic and a skeptic I will arise" (281).

It is of course Diderot who is right, and d'Alembert who does not understand the real implication of Diderot's words: he is not going to try to convince d'Alembert using a logical argument; he will work on his mind indirectly using the *physical* state of the dream.

What is a dream? It is like a state of solution, where the barriers between minds weaken, where the conscious identity of the person is also weakened or even suspended.

MLLE DE L'ESPINASSE: All right, but sleep?
BORDEU: Is a state of the animal in which there is no longer an ensemble. All subordination and cooperation between the parts cease. The master is abandoned to the discretion of his servants and to the frantic

energy of his own activity . . . in a waking state, the network of fibers [that makes up the nervous system] is subject to impressions received from exterior objects. But in sleep, it is the exercise of his own sensibility that brings about everything that happens in him. There is no distraction in the dream, hence its vivacity. . . . [360–61]

This is precisely the state in which d'Alembert spends the greatest part of the central dialogue. The dream state is a physical condition of the living body, brought about by "an erithism, a passing attack of disease," in this example by the words of Diderot, which institute a physical state in d'Alembert that looks so much like a disease that Mlle de l'Espinasse calls in the doctor.

What is being demonstrated here is the necessary consequence of defining sensibility as a material condition which is so similar to regular matter that it can enter into compounds with other material substances, act on them and undergo reactions with them in—not an analogous—but an identical way. In other words, sensibility is not thought here by Diderot to be metaphorically similar to matter, but to form one component of the universe of substances (276).

Diderot's positions in *The Dream* thus deny the dualism of body and mind. The words of Diderot produce a series of "chemical" reactions between the compounds identified by the names of "d'Alembert," "Mlle de l'Espinasse," and "Dr. Bordeu." Moreover, Diderot stated, in a well-known letter to Duclos,[11] that "the animal is the laboratory in which sensibility goes from being inert to being active." Assume for a moment that the *Exchange* is the theoretical justification for an experiment in this laboratory of sensibility, that the *Dream* is the reaction itself, and that the *Continuation of the Exchange* (the third dialogue) demonstrates the results. What do we obtain?

Let us concentrate on the long passage already quoted at length. Diderot and d'Alembert function as two living molecules put into contact during—and in fact by—the *Exchange*. They stay contiguous but they do not melt into each other. At the end of the *Exchange,* the molecule "Diderot" predicts to the molecule "d'Alembert" that he will enter into a dream state that will allow the words of Diderot to penetrate into the mind of d'Alembert. The monologue of d'Alembert with a dreamed Diderot, the text of the dream that Mlle de l'Espinasse reads to us, is in fact the continuation of this first discussion. Sometimes it is almost impossible to distinguish between the words of the dreaming d'Alembert and those of the dreamed Diderot; sometimes the voices are

11. Cited in Guédon, "Matérialisme," 198.

so mixed together that they produce the effect of an aggregate voice. This is precisely the image that opens *The Dream*, an image which recurs throughout the three dialogues:

> MLLE DE L'ESPINASSE: He [d'Alembert] continued. . . . "Well then, philosopher, so you can conceive of polyps of all kinds, even human polyps? But nature shows us none." [296]

Bordeu, in his commentary on the text Mlle de l'Espinasse is reading to him, gives only two or three rare and monstrous examples of human polyps—such as siamese twins—in order to prove that his research shows d'Alembert to be wrong. The finesse of Diderot, on the other hand, is to present d'Alembert's own dream as being itself already a polyp and even, for the consequences of this dream are curious, to show that the conversation between Mlle de l'Espinasse and Doctor Bordeu that is provoked by the reading of the dream text produces a similar phenomenon. Mlle de l'Espinasse wrote down everything that d'Alembert said, thinking that the mad speech of d'Alembert would reveal the state of physical disease to the doctor and allow him to "cure" his patient. However, it was discourse in the first place that provoked the "diseased" physical state in d'Alembert and not the contrary. If there is disease, it is to be found first in the region of thought, and its mere evocation will bring about a whole series of contaminations. The first occurs when the doctor cannot quite manage to distinguish clearly the two voices inside the dream text. Then he confuses the words of Mlle de l'Espinasse with the text of the dream. Finally, the doctor and Mlle de l'Espinasse talk at the same time, each one finishing the other's sentences, predicting the other's thoughts; they end up speaking by ellipsis and allusion and cut short their discussion when each one realizes that the other has already reached the final point of an argument. "Let us reason together" seems to be the answer to the question that d'Alembert had asked at the very beginning of his dream: what happens if two living "molecules" are mixed together? Posit that sensibilities have been "compounded," and that this compounding produces and is produced by a conversation: "an action, an habitual reaction . . . and this action and reaction have a particular character. . . . Everything works together to produce a kind of unity which exists only in the animal" (290). The product of this reaction is a tiny "thought-collective," as the immunobiologist Ludwik Fleck would have said in the thirties.[12] Our

12. Fleck, 39.

interlocutors have not lost their own identities, but they have managed to construct a larger one which includes them all . . . all four of them.

However, this situation does not exist merely at the level of words. It also shows up in the physical states of bodies. These physical states, which are after all sensibility phenomena, can also be transmitted . . . even without the help of words.

> MLLE DE L'ESPINASSE: (she begins by quoting the sleeping d'Alembert) "Mlle de l'Espinasse, where are you?" "—Here I am." His face became flushed. I tried to take his pulse, but I don't know where he had hidden his hand. He seemed to undergo a convulsion. His mouth was open, his breathing hurried; he let out a deep sigh, then a weaker but even deeper sigh; he turned his face to the pillow and fell asleep. I looked at him with attention, and I was quite moved without knowing why. My heart was beating, but not out of fear. . . . [300]

The "seduction" that takes place here will be mirrored throughout the conversation between Mlle de l'Espinasse and Doctor Bordeu. This seduction reflects, or is the material version of, the attractive resonance established between the two people by their discourse. Their thoughts mingle more and more, and their bodies will try to get into the act as well (314, 323, 348). But at the end, the seduction fails. Mlle de l'Espinasse allows Doctor Bordeu to escape—a Doctor Bordeu who, the more he talks about desire, the mixing of species, and of sexuality, the more he becomes nervous about the slippage of his own identity. As soon as he realizes this, he escapes—as quickly as he can.

*The Dream* opens with two quite distinct interlocutors who are talking to each other, then four whose identities are mingled in the process of discussion, and finally this compound body dissolves back out into its components under the action of too much discussion, which brings about too much sensibility. We find ourselves again with two distinct interlocutors taking leave of each other. And through these four speakers the words of Diderot, whispered into d'Alembert's ear to start off the *Dream*, have travelled, have united the speakers, and have finally dispersed them.

But what is the *lactus* (a technical term from the chemistry of Rouelle), i.e., what is the particular quality in a mixture that causes it to have a certain affinity for another body?[13] What is this "means of union, of appropriation," as Diderot defines it in the *Exchange*, which permits compounds of the sort that we have just seen? Where does the force come from that holds the different substances in a compound body

13. Guédon, 199.

together? If we try to push the analogy between Diderot's epistemology and the one that supports the chemistry of principles, can we find an equivalent for the affinity of the chemists, in other words something that will do for sensibility and matter what affinity did for the chemical elements?

If there is any possible equivalent, we would first have to see what a body built of sensations would be like.

> DIDEROT: And on what is this awareness of himself based?
> D'ALEMBERT: On the memory of past actions.
> DIDEROT: And without this memory?
> D'ALEMBERT: Without this memory he would have no "himself," since, feeling his existence only in the very moment of sense-impression, he would have no history of his life. His life would be an interrupted series of sensations that nothing would tie together.
> DIDEROT: Marvelous. And what is memory? Where does it come from?
> D'ALEMBERT: From a certain type of organization which waxes, wanes, and sometimes disappears altogether. [270–71]

If a sensation is analogous to a substance, then the compound form of pure sensations would be memory. And what about the *selective* nature of affinity, which chooses, or selects out, or organizes? Let us listen again to Mlle de l'Espinasse: "I would say that, everybody having his own set of eyes, everyone sees and describes differently. I would say that each idea calls up others" (368). We are in the realm of the association of ideas, of sensations that are called out by resonance, by affinity, with other ideas or sensations. It is of course here that we rediscover the function of analogy for Diderot. This analogy is obviously at one and the same time the organization in a material body that produces "resonances" that provoke in turn sensibility compounds like memory or conversation and the organization that allows them to be deciphered. Therefore, I could force on Diderot a slightly rigid equivalent of the epistemological matrix used by Macquer in order to work within, and to understand, the chemical world. The result would be the following table:

| | Interpretive Process | Natural Process | Things or Entities To Be Combined |
|---|---|---|---|
| Macquer | Analysis | Affinity | Chemical Principles |
| Diderot | Analogy | Association of Ideas | Sensations and Substances |

We immediately see at least one striking difference between the two schemes. In the chemical laboratory, one considers compound bodies as being by themselves more or less stable structures. If we wish to undertake a series of experiments—in Macquer's terms, a series of decompositions and recompositions determined by the laws of affinity in which we can follow the circulation of the various substances—we are obliged to act upon the bodies, to put them into contact with each other, to heat them, to dissolve them. We introduce from the outside the dynamic aspect that begins the reaction. This dynamic aspect is in fact the instrument that the experimenter uses to manipulate his experimental system. It is precisely *from the outside* that the experimenter wants to act, in order to assure himself of a stable and noncontingent position from which to make his observations. For Macquer, the affinity which allowed the chemist to link the world of words—his "outside" domain—with the physical world, only put words and things into a state of metaphoric complementarity. Words are not things. Each defines and supports the other, but the metaphoric relationship remains just that: it emphasizes the distinction between the two domains while linking them only for the interpretation of the experimental system.

On the other hand, in the laboratory constituted by the man-machines of *D'Alembert's Dream,* the two domains are not complementary. They are identical. There *is* no "outside" to this experiment. The instigator of any "experiment" is himself immediately swept into the series of mixtures and decompositions that result. The dynamism does not need to be artificially maintained from the outside: it is inherent to the system. It comes from sensibility, which is after all defined as a state of physical instability, a tendency to react, to transform itself, or . . . *to think.* But sensibility is nonetheless itself contingent: "sensibility [is a] general property of matter, or [a] product of its organization" (276). On the one hand organization is history, it is the physical residue of all of the events which an object has undergone. Sensibility is continually being patterned into an object by its interactions with the world. But these reactions are on the other hand determined by the operation of the analogies, the "resonances," which themselves are the mental and material memories of prior reactions. There is no such thing as a "free" association of ideas. There is only that predetermined association of ideas, that concretization of the memory, that network of analogies in a body which we will call its affinities. Human compounds are naturally unstable. There is a continual flux of events, and every event brings about a change in organization. The affinities are "determined" at any one point in the life of an object by its past history, but they are in no way predictable, because they are not the manifestation of a common or universal structure. They are nothing but the concretization of an historical process that is of course different for every object.

> D'ALEMBERT: And why, if the same dispersed elements came together [at a different time] to unite into one object, would they not yield the same results?
> DIDEROT: It is because everything is tied to everything else in nature, so that he who supposes a new phenomenon or tries to bring back a moment that has gone by, recreates a new world. [269]

Whence the disquieting consequences for the nature of the Diderotian process of scientific investigation. In spite of their apparent similarities, and even though they both at first seem to be derived from the same anti-Newtonian chemical theories, the epistemologies of Diderot and Macquer not only diverge, but end up opposing each other in practical terms. Where Macquer sees a utopian vision of a world in which research concerning the most intimate structure of matter can be carried out through words, Diderot's system denies any possibility for establishing any durable knowledge, much less absolute knowledge, outside the system of reference established by the closed experimental context. The choice remains: either one stands outside the system and accepts merely to watch what happens without intervening to ask direct questions, or else one must be drawn into the system by the effects of the experiment. The very act of asking a question is itself a thought and therefore forms a sensibility phenomenon, which inevitably enters into "action and reaction" with the world under observation. Asking a direct question of nature about its organization is tantamount to changing the nature of the object studied. To undertake a scientific experiment it is necessary to assume not only material closure (in other words a closed system, like a sealed flask), but also epistemological closure. In Macquer's *Dictionary*, the system guarantees both sorts of closure, and in fact the closure of one system guarantees the closure of its metaphoric analogue. But in Diderot's universe, to undertake any experiment at all is to immediately change *both* the material and conceptual givens of the problem. There is not only a lack of stability; there is also the impossibility of even provisionally fixed knowledge.

> MLLE DE L'ESPINASSE (quoting d'Alembert's dream): "In this immense ocean of matter, not one molecule that resembles another molecule, not one molecule that resembles itself for an instant: *Rerum novus nascitur ordo*, such is its eternal inscription. . . ." Then he added with a sigh: "O, the vanity of our thoughts! O, the poverty of our glory and our

labors! O misery! O the pettiness of our views! There is nothing solid except to drink, eat, live, love and sleep. . . ." [300]

From one perspective, Diderot does little more than reinforce the noninterventionist point of view that he had proposed more for moral than for epistemological reasons in the *Thoughts on the Interpretation of Nature*. From another point of view, the consequences of this position allow us to make a first (provisional) division between a scientific usage (Macquer's) and a literary usage (Diderot's) of what appeared at first to be the same epistemological structure. But in fact, if we look a second time at the twin matrices, we see that we are not in the presence of two uses of the same model. There was no choice: Macquer did not say, "I opt for a scientific discourse," while Diderot said, "I prefer to write literature." There are two separate systems, and for either author the act of speaking necessarily brings about a position with respect to knowledge that is opposed to that of the other author. In Macquer's system, there *is* the possibility of writing science. There is even (as I have tried to show elsewhere and have only suggested here),[14] the possibility of a scientific discourse that, through the system of cross-references embodied in the *Dictionary of Chemistry*, provides itself with the power of poetic analogy in order to create new ideas, to propose new perspectives or to suggest new experiments. But in Diderot's system, as materialist as it is—and paradoxically, above all because of its materialism, in which thought is material just like any other substance—the possibility of a stable structure of knowledge and thus of a scientific discourse, does not exist. Where knowledge is by definition unstable, one can only write literature. From this standpoint, *The Dream* is not an interdisciplinary work after all.

What is this literature? What does it mean to write literature in a world in which even thoughts are material? What would this literature look like? First of all, it would of course look like *D'Alembert's Dream*. Not only do we find the analogical, interrupted and changing discussion that is the explicit content of this work. "We are not composing, we are chatting," says Mlle de l'Espinasse to Doctor Bordeu when he complains about the lack of logic in their conversation. There is above all the experiment on d'Alembert that is activated by Diderot at the end of the *Exchange* and whose results we observe, we the readers, from the outside. We can now define this experiment as a nonscientific experiment (if by scientific we wish to indicate a procedure that attempts to reveal stable or noncontingent truths). We are involved with a poetic experi-

14. "Figurative Language and the Scientific Ideal. . . ." *Neophilologus* 65: 1 (1981).

ment . . . but what we call "poetic" is explicitly defined in materialist terms:

MLLE DE L'ESPINASSE: What do you think about the mixing of species?
BORDEU: Your question involves physics, morals, and poetics.
MLLE DE L'ESPINASSE: Poetics!
BORDEU: Without any doubt; the art of creating beings which do not exist, in imitation of those that do exist, is truly poetry. [372, 374]

The poetic experiment, here defined in materialist terms, is, as we have tried to show, deployed before our eyes and not commented upon directly. Like good little scientists, we observe the results of a whole series of concatenated transitive "poetic" effects. Diderot and d'Alembert talk to each other, which brings about in d'Alembert a dream state, a state at once mentally and physically productive of changes in his organization. Mlle de l'Espinasse and Doctor Bordeu read not only the recital of the dream, but even the "text" of his physical state (it is not insignificant that Mlle de l'Espinasse's interlocutor is a doctor who makes diagnoses). This causes mental reactions in the speakers during their conversation, and even provokes a physiological reaction—a state of mutual attraction or desire—in their attitude towards each other.

Can we then make an analogy between the kind of poetic experiment proper to a literary work and a recognizable scientific practice by positing that the literary equivalent of a single closed experimental system might be a single text thought of as a closed world? As a literary equivalent of a "black box"? As a matter of fact, we cannot. For in fact we read our own destiny as readers of this new kind of literature in the comportments of the readers who exist in the text. After all, just like Mlle de l'Espinasse, we are in the process of *reading d'Alembert's Dream*. We react, we read not only as logical beings, but as feeling creatures.

BORDEU: But what is a feeling being? A being abandoned to the mercy of his diaphragm. A touching phrase strikes the ear, a singular phenomenon strikes the eye, and all of a sudden an interior tumult breaks out, all the fibers in the network are agitated, shudders break out, we are seized with horror, tears run down our cheeks, we are suffocated with sighs. . . .
MLLE DE L'ESPINASSE: I recognize myself. [356]

We the readers recognize ourselves also; in the case of *The Nun*, for example, we are carried along with the marquis de Croismare, the supposed victim of a manipulation of his sensibility through the agency of a work of fiction. We do not read to *know*, we read to *feel*, even to rearrange our thoughts, to transform ourselves. Our author writes no more to *say* something explicitly than he does to manipulate, to act upon, to transform his reader into a different reader. Whence the fact that the novel is no longer organized around questions of logic or coherence, but around interest and suspense. Interest and suspense are themselves manifestations of this affinity that the reader is led to feel with the text. In this light it is also possible to understand the importance that Diderot, in his esthetic theories, especially those dealing with the theater, gave to the evocation of the involuntary physical states of the actors or characters. In the *Discussion on the "Natural Son,"* the *Paradox of the Actor*, or in the *Salons*, Diderot recommends that writers, actors, and even painters, provoke the desired physical—and therefore the analogous mental—states in the reader or spectator by the spectacle of analogous physical states in the actor, the subject of painting or the literary character.

In this same spirit, it would be interesting to account for the enormous difference between D'Alembert's "Preliminary Discourse" to the *Encyclopedia* and Diderot's article: "Encyclopedia." D'Alembert believes firmly in knowledge as a stable, coherent and easily packaged object . . . and for him education consists mainly of absorbing this content. For Diderot, however, there is no stable knowledge; moreover, the significance of reading resides not in its capacity to extract a content, but rather in the process itself—suggestive, inspired, even sometimes out and out mistaken—which proceeds through analogy and opposition as programmed by the cross-references. It is this process of reading that defines the nature of the "education" to be derived from the *Encyclopedia*, which attempted the incarnation of the complete knowledge of a century that defined itself precisely in terms of knowledge (this century is, after all, called the Enlightenment). But if we apply literally the epistemology just derived from *D'Alembert's Dream*, the *Encyclopedia* is less a collective scientific masterpiece than it is a literary work in which it is only the open and interminable process of the transformation of the readers that counts. Moreover, it is Diderot himself who says that:

> If the cross-references of confirmation and refutation have been prepared well in advance and with great address, they will give the Encyclopedia that characteristic which any good dictionary should have; this characteristic is to change the common way of thinking.[15]

15. "Encyclopédie" (1755), *Encyclopédie, ou Dictionnaire raisonné . . .* (Paris, 1751–80), 5, 640.

And why should this surprise us? After all, the Enlightenment was also the century that saw an enormous tradition of unfinished and interminable novels. From this point of view, Diderot succeeded with his *Encyclopedia* in writing the most enormous and most interminable Enlightenment novel which has ever been written. But it is *D'Alembert's Dream* that shows us how it is to be read.

*Experiments in Closure*

ROGER DRAGONETTI

# Joufroi, Count of Poitiers and Lord of Cocaigne

The so-called historical, or objective, reconstruction of a text, concerned primarily with setting down a univocal or polysemic semantic
structure derived from the signifieds of ordinary speech, is not to be
confused with the phenomenon of reading, which as a practice aims at
extracting the rhythmic affinities which literary language never ceases
to weave between the elements of sound (*son*) and meaning (*sens*). Far
from making itself out to be an activity which monitors the poetic text
via the norms of a representative model of everyday speech, the experience of reading transgresses this essentially reductive type of knowledge by integrating it into an auscultation of words in their plurality.
Such a move solicits and at the same time dissolves the many modes of
"scientific" linguistic representation precisely because this plural word
is *itself* language approached from the other side, unforeseeable, held in
reserve. To the reader, then, falls the task of gathering up the multiple
traces of the past's reverberations in the listening present.

   All this of course entails a wider conception of the enterprise
known as objectivization: accordingly, traditional guidelines must constantly be pushed back and rules reinvented, for the simple purpose of
making one's critical standards operative within new linguistic sectors.
More specifically, we must take care that the regulatory function of
objectivization (which is, it must be said, an activity of the *subject*) be
integrated into the practice of reading, this "art" predicated largely
upon chance occurrence—never entirely mastered by anyone—and
which for that very reason must take into account certain forces (within
the subject as well as within the text) arising from the coalescence of
three factors: calculation, chance and time. But however easy it is to
name these factors, it is not always possible *in practice* to separate them
into sharply delineated categories.

This article is adapted and translated from the author's *Le gai savoir dans la rhétori-
que courtoise* (Paris: Seuil, 1982).

If, in fact, a large number of medieval texts have come down to us in a lacunary state, due to the destructive ravages of time, this is not a sufficient reason to attribute to chance alone what is otherwise the impressive spectacle of a literature in shreds. After all, in the language of the lyric poet the "discovery" (*troveüre*) and the "hole" (*troueure*) resembled each other, down to the very letter. One can infer from this that the textual blanks might constitute the very dramatization of what courtly writing could neither say nor even sketch out. Although submerged in a theological culture governed by a belief in universal analogy, it is almost as if the medieval period were attempting to make manifest, through a remarkable sense of contrast, the true status of literary writing.

To be sure, the contrast is not so simple, and, viewed from another angle, the fragmentation of medieval literature becomes even more complex since the lines of demarcation between lacunae owing to chance and those which might have been the result of a calculated choice often remain uncertain. One must thus begin by risking conjectures in a reformulation of the problem—conjectures whose pertinence will reside in their capacity to extend our field of vision, within a formal analysis, to all the modes of liaison of poetic language. This initial extension will serve to loosen, to orient, and to reinforce what we might call the work of *proof* even if, as it is being reinforced, this "proof" always bears witness as well to its own impossibility in the field of literature.

It would be a mistake to make an overly sharp separation between the playful tone of certain medieval works and the graver, more dignified discourse of other works of the same period. It is certainly not a matter of erasing the differences but rather one of emphasizing that what is called *play (jeu)* is one of the fundamental dimensions of courtly literature. By this I mean that what animates the courtly text from the eleventh century at least until the thirteenth century is the spirit of *jonglerie* which turns poetic language into the magic instrument of countless mirrors reflecting their own fabulation.

Hence the vulgar tongue, whose flowering is perfected in the elements of rhythm and music, develops along with a sort of hilarity, a laughter ranging from trifling remarks to slapstick, to light sarcasm, and even to out-and-out mockery, without the linguistic component ever surrendering its rights to sovereignty over the play and the pleasure which it procures.

It is the concept of *gay saber*, characteristic of the poetry of the troubadours, which crystallizes the relation between literature and play. Carried along by the deep-rooted Dionysian *joy*, which the courtly poets celebrate in happiness and rapture, *gay saber* presupposes a dimension of craziness, facetiousness and pleasantry of which courtly poetry provides an abundance of examples. It seems to me necessary to insist upon these aspects of the *gaya sciensa* which governed for at least two centuries an entire rhetoric of lyric or narrative literature whose language is articulated essentially to the rhythm of the *contredit.* *

Certainly, the increasing prestige of the vulgar tongue, as the "barbaric" form of Latin in search of an autonomous form of expression, is one of the fundamental aspects of the modernity of medieval poetics, incorporating all that the idea of "modernity" implies with regard to difficulty and resistance to the reception of the novelty of a language destined to become "literary." However, the practices of the vulgar tongue did not simply mean a series of ruptures with the interdictions of a clerical Latin culture, but even a more difficult trailblazing through that forest of competing dialects spoken of by Dante in his linguistic survey of the Italian peninsula. Thus, "modern" usage, which consisted in the utilization of the mother tongue as a language of *poiesis*, rich in meaningful suggestions, also implied a sort of affirmation of power in competitions between partners of equal talent. The poets of the mother tongue were, in short, attempting to conquer a type of wisdom through their poetry, for, from the time of the troubadours' *gay saber*, it had become important to establish the new literary language as the locus of the most subtle inventions of thought at the level of the play of letters and words. I might add that the concept of "literary language," inscribed in the works themselves, was only rarely treated in the domain of theoretical reflection before the fourteenth century, and even then quite succinctly or elliptically.

If today we continue in speaking of "courtly poetry" after so many centuries and so many scholarly treatises on the subject, it is because the prodigious wealth of its inventions, occasionally masked under an appearance of realism, has never ceased to amaze us. But this realistic facade has a contrary effect, that of diverting the reader away from the hidden stakes of language as he blindly searches for historic truth (*his-*

---

*Dragonetti's idiosyncratic use of the term *contredit,* which will be maintained in the text, coalesces a hypothetical poetic genre (analogically based on the name of a real medieval genre known as the *dit*) with the term's etymological suggestion of contradiction. The result, as will become evident in the discussion which follows, is oxymoron, or paradox, elevated to the status of a poetic principle, in which the undoing of one's own poetic language suggests *not* its antithesis but rather some unpronounceable hermetic truth. [Editor's note.]

*toire)* and storytelling *(histoires)*. And yet even though the problem of
the historical referent all too often monopolizes the attention of the
learned critic, it would be an endless task to discuss in detail all that is
fragile in the criteria serving as a basis for the historical/biographical
arguments surrounding the medieval poet. The problem becomes even
more acute when the poet happens to bear certain resemblances to some
high-ranking official, in which case he assumes the right to cloak himself in the illustrious name as a means of affirming his own sovereignty.

The thirteenth-century Old French romance *Joufroi de Poitiers* provides an interesting illustration of the above discussion.[1] It confirms in
a striking way that courtly literature has never been other than the work
of the *gay saber* of language, the desire to grasp what is proper to it. As
the author of *Joufroi* puts it:

> Mais por savoir que en demeine
> Ai ma lengue, si faz ceste ovre,
> O ge en bien trover m'esprove.                    [ll. 4400–02]

But in order to know whether I possess my language, I produce this
work where I try my hand at being a good troubadour.

The transparency and fluidity of this romance have always led to its
acceptance, quite rightly I might add, as a model for the disconcerting
style of the *trobar leu.** Indeed, since Chabaneau[2] a number of com-
mentators have seen fit—quite justifiably—to draw the comparison
between the Geoffroi of this romance and the troubadour Guillaume IX,
who was also Count of Poitiers. What could be more in keeping with the
portrait of the first troubadour, whose *Vida* pictures him for posterity as
the *trichador de dompnas*, than the donjuanesque Geoffroi, who, in the
course of his adventures, becomes the lover of Agnès (wife of the Lord of
Tonnerre) and of Alis (the King of England's wife), and who furthermore
contracts two marriages: the first with Blancheflor, daughter of a bourgeois, and the second with Amaubergeon, daughter of his enemy, the
Count of Toulouse?

---

* According to the poetics of the troubadours, *trobar leu* or *plan* ("easy, clear composition") was considered the stylistic opposite of the *trobar clus* ("closed, obscure composition"). [Editor's note.]

1. All references to the romance will be taken from the critical edition prepared by
Percival B. Fay and John L. Grigsby, *Joufroi de Poitiers, Roman d'aventures du XIIIe siècle*
(Genève/Paris: Droz, 1972). Line numbers will be included in the text.

2. Camille Chabaneau, "Sur le roman français de Joufroi," *Revue des langues romanes*, 19 (1881), 88–91 and 22 (1882), 49.

The name Agnès, which also appears in the songs of Guillaume IX[3] and the name Amaubergeon, cited by the chroniclers of the troubadour[4] not to mention the presence in the romance of Marcabru, a contemporary of Guillaume of Aquitaine, help to justify a comparison between the two counts of Poitiers. Other characters, however, who are mentioned both in the *Vida* of Guillaume IX and in the anonymous romance, pose some problems for a chronological interpretation. We need not belabor the chronological hypotheses, since they are fully discussed by Fay/Grigsby in their introduction and followed by a review of the critical material which shows that even the most recent critics cannot get past the naive view of *Joufroi* as a realistic romance.[5] But we can still profit from the editors' remarks concerning the interventions of the strongly dramatized narrator, even though they themselves consider these interventions to be disruptive elements in the romance because of the awkwardness of the narrative transitions. In this essay my aim is, by way of the *gay saber* and its inventions in the field of the rhetoric of commonplaces, to show the link between courtly literature and the motif of *largesse*, one of the protagonist's dominant traits. In addition, I will attempt to understand the structure of the romance as a whole, taking into account the aforementioned storyteller's interventions.

Geoffroi initiates his exploits by distinguishing himself in a duel where, in order to defend the innocence of *Alis*, the Queen of England, he kills King Henry's seneschal. Seeking to become a knight, the youthful Geoffroi had obtained his father's consent to travel to King Henry's court. Word reaches him there of the death of his father, *Richier*, from whom he inherits not only "riches" but the title of Count of Poitiers as well. Determined to prove his knightly valor, Geoffroi then goes in search of tournaments and along the way encounters a minstrel named *Guy de Niele*, from whom he learns that a very beautiful damsel has been locked in a tower by her jealous husband, the lord of Tonnerre. Geoffroi promptly betakes himself to that town, where a tournament is being held, and throughout the festivities he camps beneath a pear tree which is growing opposite the tower. During this episode he passes himself off as the Lord of Cocaigne.

Some time later, Geoffroi, disguised as a hermit, and with a different Henri in attendance, returns to the town and obtains permission

3. Alfred Jeanroy, ed., *Chansons de Guillaume IX, duc d'Aquitaine*, CFMA 8 (Paris: Champion, 1972), l. 1, 24; ll. 5, 31, 55, 73.

4. Fay/Grigsby, 22. Cf. also Jean-Charles Payen, *Le Prince d'Aquitaine* (Paris: Champion, 1980), 159–68.

5. Op. cit., 9–26.

from the Lord of Tonnerre to build a hermitage on his lands. The spare exterior of this hermitage hides the fact that it is sumptuously decorated within, and from this place the hero's false profession of religion issues forth; strange testimony indeed, but one which will bear fruit, for Agnès of Tonnerre, freed from the tower, soon becomes the hero's lover. Geoffroi, however, decides to leave his beloved in order to go fight, not in Flanders but in England, against the enemies of King Henry. Even there he effectively escapes recognition by the king, for he once again conceals his identity, this time passing himself off as a mercenary, under the name of *Guiraut de Berri*. In the end the task of unmasking the alleged *Guiraut de Berri* and revealing to the English king the true identity of the Count of Poitiers falls to the troubadour Marcabru. This revelation, in turn, brings about the breaking off of the marriage which the false mercenary had contracted with Blanchefleur, for her social rank can no longer match that of the noble count.

I might add that Marcabru's original purpose in journeying from Poitiers to England was to pick up the trail of the vanished count, and to inform him of the destructive operations which Alphonse of Saint-Gilles, the Count of Toulouse, was carrying out on Geoffroi's lands. Geoffroi, before returning to Poitiers, goes once more to see the queen and becomes her lover. The final episode then recounts the defeat of the Count of Toulouse and the marriage between Geoffroi and his rival's daughter.

There are many traits which unite *Joufroi* and another anonymous, unfinished medieval romance, *Flamenca*.[6] But perhaps more significant are the differences. Besides Guillaume's fidelity to Flamenca, which contrasts so sharply with Geoffroi's promiscuity, one must note that there is no mention made of the hero of *Joufroi* having any literary expertise; only his chivalry and his largesse are instrumental in the story. However, in the Tonnerre adventure and in the episode in England we find a minstrel, *Gui de Niele*, sometimes called *Guion* (1. 923)—as if by a sort of grafting onto the etymology of *Guillaume*. And of course we find *Marcabru*,[7] the troubadour who leads the count back to his native land after his love for Agnès and Alis has carried him far from Poitiers. Let me emphasize, by this remark, the fact that each of these poets brings to light something which was meant to be kept hidden— that is, the beauty of the damsel locked in the tower and the identity of the Count of Poitiers.

6. Cf. Fay/Grigsby, 11–16.
7. The troubadour Marcabru is called "menestral traïtor" (treacherous minstrel) in line 3670.

Another difference in the two romances is that Geoffroi never acts alone; he always has a companion on his adventures (*Gui* and *Henri* in Tonnerre, *Robert* and *Marcabru* in England). The Poitou forms the link between these last two men, for both stand before the King of England and claim to come from that region: Robert for having lived there since his marriage, although he originally came from Anjou (ll.2901–03), and Marcabru for having been born there. The pertinence of these observations and the way in which one can discern a fabric of similarities and dissimilarities woven among the characters by the narrator will presently be demonstrated.

Finally, let it be added that Henri, the companion in Geoffroi's hermitage adventure, bears the same name as the King of England and that certain locutions surrounding this name (also written En-*ris* or Hen-*ris*) break down in a series of echoes which might be termed *ris*-ible and whose contagious effects are accentuated by the comic aspect of the adventure. One must then ask oneself whether this laughter which skims the surface of the text and figures in the division of the name *En-ris* does not justify the Old French epithet *rot* ("broken" or even "stripped,") by which the narrator, in line 1524, designates this servant who was forced, somewhat unwillingly, to "enter into religion." It is hard to say. What is certain is that besides the stifled laughter which one finds scattered through the romance (lines 2924 and 3537–39), the text is pervaded by a climate of suspicion which takes hold of the characters whenever something "true" is affirmed ("true" within the context of the adventure), and that this suspicion makes the fictional listener in the tale feel that he is being duped (*gabé*).

Such is the intuitive reaction of the lady of Tonnerre when her husband declares his love for her: "Avoi, sire, grant tort avez,/Si m'aï Deus, quant *me gabez!*" ["Come now, sire, you are very wrong, God help me, when you make fun of me!" (ll.1799–1800).] And she persists: "Se m'aït Deus, c'est vilanie/Quant vos penez *de moi gaber.*" [God help me! It's wicked of you to mock me so" (ll.1804–05).]

But Alis feels the same way when Geoffroi recognizes in the queen's chamberlain the mysterious messenger who had brought him a jewel box from a lady whose name he had kept secret but who now proves to be the queen herself (lines 3889–92 and 4163). And the situation is much the same for King Henry who feels *gabé* when Marcabru reveals the true identity of the Count of Poitiers (ll.3649–56). All of these manifestations of *gab*, which make up the story's games, are obviously thoroughly in keeping with Geoffroi's successive disguises, as when he stains his face with herbs (line 973), or changes his name or profession.

There may be a more hidden reason for the way in which the characters' language resists reality, a reason not unrelated to the nonsense of poetic speech. By a ricochet effect, the reader as well begins to mistrust this tale. Although the story itself is really quite banal, the words are arranged in a sort of vertiginous round (*rota*), as is demonstrated in the following passage where the *tours* ("turns" or "tricks") which Geoffroi prepares to play in the hermitage adventure with his companion, "un sarjant qu'Enris ot non" (line 1515), are reflected in the language used to express them:

> Le *rot* fait des blans dras vestir,
> Et haut reognier tot *entor*,
> Mult par firent bien lor *ator*.
> Et quant li cuens fu *atornez*,
> Une noit, ainz le jorn assez,
> S'enbla de Poitiers c'om nel sot
> For che sol li sarjant qu'il ot
> Fait *atorner* ensenble o lui;
> Si s'en vont a tapin andui
> Vers *Tornuere* la voie droite,
> O li cuers li conte covoite.                                    [ll.1524–34]

He had the "stripped one" (*rot*) dressed in white clothes, and "tonsured all around"; they took care over their "costume" and when the count was "ready," one night, well before sunrise, he left Poitiers without anyone knowing, except for the servant whom he had had "dressed" the same as himself; thus they went, in secret, both straight to "Tonnerre," where the heart guides the count (*le comte*) [or the story, *le conte*].

This is but one example, taken from the second episode of the adventure of *Tornuere*. The first episode recounts the fantastic "tournament" where the Count of Poitiers, under the name *Lord of Cocaigne*, emerges as the paragon of *largesse*.[8]

I have treated elsewhere this well-known motif of *largesse* for which Alexander commonly serves as a chivalrous model in medieval romances.[9] Therefore it should come as no surprise to find courtly language acting in obvious collusion with this imposing figure of munif-

---

8. For the medieval literary imagination, the land of Cocaigne was identified as a mythical "Land of Plenty."

9. Cf. My *La Vie de la lettre au moyen âge* (Paris: Seuil, 1980), 101ff.

icence, prodigality, delight (*jouissance*) in giving: all terms which may be summed up, in both registers, by the expression *répandre ses dons* (to spread or dispense one's gifts or talents). It is precisely this connection between *largesse* and poetic *inventio*, between wealth and falsehood, within the "Poitiers" metaphor, which we propose to demonstrate.

Geoffroi, already rich by inheritance, is constantly doling out everything people give him (either as gifts or in payment for services rendered); he even goes so far as to distribute all of the jewels which the mysterious lady has sent him by messenger. What could be more unsettling, in the eyes of all those who are showering gifts upon the Count of Poitiers, than this ruinous prodigality? Indeed, their concern is only matched by Geoffroi's serenity, as if for him the infinite renewal of wealth must arise from the very gesture of giving.

For example, when his father-in-law reproaches him for giving too much, Geoffroi replies:

> vos ne me donastes mie
> La largece, ne a ma vie
> Ne me la retoudrez vos pas.
> Beaus peres, bien sachiez san gas
> Qu'a ma vie toz jorn donrai,
> Et toz jorn riches reserai. [ll. 3573–78]

My *largesse* does not come from you and as long as I live you will not rob me of it. Father-in-law, know well and without jest that always in my life will I give and always will I become rich again.

Likewise, when Marcabru announces to Geoffroi that the Count of Toulouse is systematically ravaging the Poitou lands and has already burned all of the towns except Poitiers (line 3681), Geoffroi shows no anxiety, but instead replies:

> Nous referons les chasteaus buens,
> Qu'assez avons avoir et pierre,
> Et li areine rest legiere
> Mult a troveir en mon païs;
> Et si danz Anfos m'a sorpris
> D'ardoir ma terre par outrage,
> Encore i puet avoir damage. [ll. 3686–92]

We shall rebuild strong castles, for we have enough money and stones, and sand is easy to find in my country. And if lord Alphonse has attacked and insulted me, burning my lands, he can expect my revenge.

So great is Geoffroi's insouciance that he delays his departure in order to visit the queen. Thus, it is clear that the hero's *largesse* has paradigmatic value—it may even be said to constitute that which is primarily at stake in the romance.

It is especially in Geoffroi's relationship to Robert that this attribute of the Count of Poitiers can be interpreted as a congenital trait. Comparing himself with his lord, Robert, the brave knight, who, it will be recalled, did not come originally from the Poitou region, indicates his difference thus:

> Mais bien sachiez tot a estros
> Que ge ne vail pas meins de vos
> Por bien sofrir un grant estor;
> Mais plus avez assez richor,
> Et plus de moi poez doner.
> Ce vos fait vostre pris monter
> Et vostre malvestié covrir,
> Qu'avoir fait mainte foiz mentir.                    [ll. 2429–36]

But know well in truth that I am worth no less than you when it comes to withstanding a battle, but you possess and can distribute more riches than I. That raises your worth and hides your doubtful schemes, for wealth, time and again, gives the lie.

Wealth, then, disguises falsehood, but it is undoubtedly in order to push to its extreme this aspect of the difference remarked upon by Robert, that the Count of Poitiers, before leaving for England with his fellow trickster, decides to share with him his clothes and other possessions. In short, by putting him on an equal footing, Geoffroi expects to dispel any misunderstanding about a fundamental divergence. And although Robert enjoys, through his lord's generosity, half of the dowry which the latter will receive in marrying Blancheflor, he also experiences the horror of his treason when, through his own *malvestié,* and unbeknownst to Geoffroi, he shares the love of Queen Alis (lines 4180 ff.).

All this reveals to what extent Robert's *largesse* and shrewdness mirror Geoffroi's attributes, but always with that difference which keeps him dependent upon his lord. Robert only outdoes the Count of Poitiers, as Geoffroi himself notes the first time he portions out the wealth, by his courage in presenting himself at court stark naked (lines 2660–65), an action, one suspects, inconceivable for Geoffroi who loves embellishment and disguise in all their forms.

The question then presents itself in these terms: what is the source of the riches of the "comte" Geoffroi of Poitiers or of the "conte" *Joufroi de Poitiers*? And this brings us back to the question of whether the act of prodigality (*qui tient du prodige* [which is something of a miracle]) has any connection with the courtly language whose "aventure" appears to be dramatized by the romance.

If it is true that *Joufroi* does not in any way thematize the literary side, except by its transparency or indirectly, through the presence of the two minstrels, the words of the text should suffice to demonstrate in still another way the poet's subtle artistry which, in restoring commonplaces to their realm of play and pleasure (*jeu et joie*), never relinquishes the "facility" of the poetic *ornatus (ornatus facilis)* which turns the *trobar leu* writing of this unknown poet into a *jonglerie* apparently devoid of mystery.

Between Poitiers, land of origin, and Cocaigne, which replaces the native land when the hero ventures into Tonnerre, the text of the romance forms a link, such that, speaking in terms of language as fable, the two spaces (Poitiers and Cocaigne) become reciprocal metaphors for one another. This is but the first indication of a network of remarkably obscure relationships within the "clear" language of the text.

In this respect the Tonnerre adventure constitutes the rhythmic "heart" (to borrow a term used by the narrator in a homonymic play on the word *conte*) guiding the story: "Vers Tornuere la voie droite,/O li cuers li conte covoite" ["(They went) straight towards Tonnerre, where the heart guides the count (*le comte*) or the story (*le conte*)" (ll.1533–34).]

The preceding remark can be applied to the very name of that city, which, remarkable for its frequency in the text, is constantly changing its spelling: *Tornuerre, Torneuerre, Tornnerre, Torneure, Tornnere, Tornuere.* We have every reason to believe that the poet, breaking vowels down into diphthongs, doubling consonants and combining these two procedures, wants to make us aware of all the signifying possibilities of this place where Geoffroi displays his mastery at arms and his *largesse*, and where he uncovers the beauty of the unknown lady.

This dizzying quality attributable to the text's written notation contaminates the words themselves, drawing them into its sphere of mutating letters and revolving signification. Thus, the *Tornuerre* episode truly becomes a resonating space for the name itself, inasmuch as, in its first phase, at the foot of a tower (*tor*), the episode involves a tournament (*torneiment*), a battle (*estor*), and several comings and goings ("aller et *retor*") between the richly adorned (*atorné*) pear tree and the tournament (*torneis*) and, in its second sequence of events, the shrewd tricks (*tours*) of the two "tonsured" and well-adorned (*atornés*), hermits.

And if critics have asserted, perhaps somewhat too hastily, that this *realistic* story lacks elements of the fantastic, one need only stop to consider the "poirier," around which these two episodes turn, in order to be persuaded otherwise. Can there be any doubt that this "comte" and this "conte," abounding in adventures and words, make the "poirier" the magical center of the Count of Poitiers' munificence and of courtly language, whose abundance originates in the *land of Cocaigne*, land of the imaginary or of dreams if ever there was one, totally unknown and uncharted, as the people viewing these marvels emphasize?

> Mais mult ont de ce grant merveiles,
> Et sont esbaï come oeles,
> Qu'a sez serjant ont oï dire
> Que de Cocagne estoit lor sire,
> Si ne poent ome trover
> Que unques mais oïst parler
> De Cocagne en nul sanblant,
> Qu'enqui fu dit primierement.
> En la ville n'ot chevalier,
> Flamenc, Franceis ne Beruier,
> qui non alast veoir la nuit
> L'ostel lo conte et son desduit
> Por la merveille regarder.                                    [ll.1131–43]

But they are greatly astonished, and flabbergasted like sheep, for they heard from the [count's] servants that he was Lord of Cocaigne, and they can find no one who ever heard Cocaigne spoken of, in any way, before this moment. In the city there was no knight, whether Flemish, French or from the Berri, who did not go at night to see the count's encampment and his games (or to look upon this marvel).

Magical tree indeed, this *perier*, whose *ator* (adornment and lighting) was arranged for by the count:

> Et li periers geta clarté,
> Que maint gros cirge abrasé
> I ot don il fu toz jonchiez
> Plus espés qu'il n'estoit foilliez.                           [ll.1171–74]

And the pear tree radiated brightness, for it was dotted with many large, lighted candles, thicker than was the foliage.

This "mât de Cocaigne," in its fecundity, dispenses joys galore.[10] An exemplary symbol for all the games and fireworks of the highest *jonglerie,* for the prestidigitation and occult arts of courtly literature, inexhaustible dispenser of dreams in the realm of the *gay saber,* the "poirier" is also invested with the signs of the Count of Poitiers' *largesse:*

Ainz veïssiez toz avant traire
Ces jogleors et maint jou faire.
Li uns dançoit des esperons;
Bien s'en regarde les talons
Qu'il ne rechoit; li autre saut
Amont par mi un cerche aut;
L'autre tregetoit sus mantel;
Li uns regetoit li coutel,
Li autres des espees nues,
Et aus tranchant des poinz s'apue,
Et tunbe desus sanz dotance;
Li autre ovrent de *nigramance.*                    [ll.1147–58]

First one saw the jongleurs advance and put on many entertainments. One was dancing with spurs on, watching his heels carefully in order not to fall; another was jumping through a hoop held high; another did sleight of hand under his cloak; one threw a knife, another unsheathed swords, and fell fearlessly onto the cutting edge of the point; others performed necromancy [witchcraft].

And, not satisfied with this festival offered to the inhabitants of *Tornuerre,* the count, upon leaving the tower (*tor*), the adornments (*ator*), and the tournaments (*torneis*) in order to return ("faire *retor*") to his land, demonstrates his wild extravagance by turning this tree-of-plenty, this "poirier" of *Tornuerre,* into a genuine carousel mimicking the ever-turning words of the text. Imagine the sight: the nine horses won in the tournament and left as a gift for the lord of the city are attached to the tree's branches with reins of gold:

Toz les chevals athachier fit
Par les regnes des dorez freins
*Tot entor* le perier as rains.                    [ll.1306–08]

He had all the horses attached to the branches all around the pear tree by reins with gold bits.

10. The "mât de Cocaigne" (literally "mast of Cocaigne") corresponds to the "greased pole," a common object of diversion at village fairs. Prizes and candy are attached to the top of a pole which is "greased" in order to make it hard to climb.

As we follow the adventures of this "vagabond" count (*truant*, as he is often called), this amiable (*de bon "aire"*) count, this "errant" or "unbridled" count, who wanders far (*va grant "erre"*) in search of damsels and exploits, and concerning whom Agnès of *Tornuerre* did not know who he was (*qui il "ere"*),[11] we note that his meanderings and his tricks become less and less distinct from those of the anonymous narrator. The narrator intensifies and multiplies the marvels of his art, just as Geoffroi duplicates those of the radiant pear tree within the splendor of the hostel he has readied for himself upon arriving in England (lines 2803–22).

Beyond the written variations of *Torn-erre*, the persistent phonetic stress on the name ends up associating the "rolling" letter (the *r*) with the intoxication of the adventure. And this occurs to such an extent that, under the dizzying influence of the movement from decoy to decoy and from *erre* to *r*, a simple turn (or is it a trick [*tour*]?) of one of the letters in the word *periers* ("poirier") would suffice to change the Lord of Cocaigne, Count of *Poitiers*[12] (could it be an unintentional slip?) into the Count of the *Poirier*. For, to read the name *Tornerre* in yet another manner, the letter *t* of Poitiers appears as an embellishment ("un ornement") masking the *r*: T-orne-*r*, that is, *T* embellishes *r* (*atorne erre*).

This letter, represented as a head by the Phoenician hieroglyphic from which it derived, this letter which, according to thirteenth century definitions, *escorchoit la gorge*,[13] and *graigne*[14] like a dog gnawing on a bone, this letter *R* around which Villon constructed a ballad *Qui se termine tout par R* (line 935), rhyming with *erre* (path, route),[15] is also

11. For *truant*, cf. lines 3652, 3661, 3814, 3822. For *de bon aire* or *ayre:* lines 99 and 2737. It should be noted that the queen (*la reine*) and the lady of *Tonnerre* are also described in these terms (lines 246 and 1808) as is one of Geoffroi's valets (line 2563). For *erre* or *ere* from the verb *être:* line 1342. As for the verb *errer*, "to voyage," let us mention, among others, lines 926–27 and 1536–39 where a connection is established between "errer" and "Tornerre."

12. Variations in the dipthongs in the words *Poitiers* and *Poitou* are frequent: in *Joufroi* one finds *Poitiers* (line 92 and *passim*) and *Puitiers* (lines 1229 and 1395); in the song 11 of Guillaume IX: *Peitieus* (*Chansons*, 27). Likewise, for *Poitou*, one will find: *Peitaus, Poito*, and so forth. Furthermore, one notes that Geoffroi reveals his identify to Agnès with these words: *Dame, je sui cons de Poitiers* (line 1975) and: *Dame, ge sui cel a estros/ Qui herberga soz lo perier* (lines 1982–83). After this repetition within a single speech, Geoffroi responds to the lady who insists on knowing whether he is *really* Count of Poitiers (lines 2009–11): *Dame, je sui cuens voirement* (line 2013).

13. "Tore the throat." Cf. *Littré* under the letter *R*.

14. "Growls." Ibid.

15. Francois Villon, *Testament*, ed. Jean Rychner/Albert Henry (Geneva: Droz, 1974), line 938. Cf. also Thibaut de Champagne, *Chansons*, 57 (Chanson à la vierge).

the first letter of *Richier*, this "mauvais riche"[16] who is the *peire*, the father of Geoffroi. And this letter is inscribed at the heart of the *perier*, the tree which the new Count of Poitiers chose to *atorner*, making it the shining center of his munificence in *Tourn-erre* and thus attracting the attention of the beautiful prisoner.

When all is said and done, one senses a desire to hide the crudeness of the tree or of the letter behind a "hypocritical softness," as Villon says in the line beginning with that letter, in the *Ballade en R*, where his own name (François) is included as an acrostic:

> *F*aulse beaulté qui tant me couste chier,
> *R*ude en effect, ypocrite doulceur,
> *A*mour dure plus que fer a machier[17]

We are then surprised to note that this cover-up of the letter evokes the language of the narrator at the time of Geoffroi's first journey to England:

> . . . son *peire* a dit
> Que maintenant sanz nul respit
> Li face *son erre atorner*,
> Qu'i n'a plus soing de sejorner.
> Li cuens *son erre li atorne*.                     [ll.129–33]

His father says that now, without delay, he must "ready" his "luggage," for there is no longer any reason to put off the journey. The count "prepares his trunks" for him.

Is it in memory of the gesture of his *peire*, the Count *Richier*, that Geoffroi makes a lavish display of his *largesse* in order to *atorner* the *perier?* Surely, if one tries to exclude such letter play, the whole trickery (*trichier*) and wealth of the language vanishes, as does the relationship of the many *trichadors de dompnas* to their munificent models; for this reason, perhaps, the father's trickery (*[T]Richiers*) is reduced to the historical figure of a Count of Poitiers.

It is quite consistent with our approach that we should find words endeavoring to bring out, on the surface of their coded meaning, a second meaning which ascribes to the future heir of the Count (*comte*) of Poitiers an imaginary space, a country (*contrée*) which only exists within the story (*conte*) of the narrative. This is at least what we are given to understand by the account of the messenger who brings Geoffroi word

16. Cf. Paul Zumthor, *Langue, texte, énigme*, (Paris: Seuil, 1975), 45.
17. "False beauty which costs me so much, rough in reality, hypocritical softness, love harder than iron to the tooth," lines 942–44.

of his father's death: ". . . si lor conte/Qu'a Poitiers n'avoit point de conte" ["And he recounts to them that in Poitiers there was no count" (ll.641–42).]

Indeed, we know from elsewhere that it is the allegorical goddess *Tricherie* who rules as viscountess in Poitiers: "Que Tricherie est en Poitou/Justice, dame e viscontesse."[18] Thus, through these transliterations and shifts in meaning, the Poitou takes on its legendary existence as a land of imagination and poetic language, becoming, in short, that country which is the privileged space of beauty. And it is this very sense which one derives from the semantic ambiguity of the word *contee*, homonym of "comté" (feminine gender in Old French), when one hears the Lord of Cocagne declare to the Lady of Tornerre: "Vostre beauté me fu contee" ["Your beauty was recounted (*contée*) to me" or "Your beauty was my earldom (*comté*)" (1.1979).]

To speak of the *largesse* of courtly literature is to use "Poitevin," the double language of poetry—that language of contradiction poised at the edge of the unnameable, invisible fount—in order to express the inexhaustible wealth of invention which spurted from within the literature of that time and, as a torrent, poured forth unchecked across the whole of France, thanks to the succession of fabled "comtes de Poitiers" whose wealth is forever renewed, as Geoffroi declares of himself: "*toz jorn riches reserai*" ["I will always become rich again" (1.3578).]

The preceding helps to explain why, in *Joufroi*, the task of revealing the identity of the "comte de Poitiers" falls to the troubadour Marcabru. Only a troubadour was capable of recognizing a true count of the Poitou, especially one who claimed to come himself from that enchanted country. "Where are you from?" the king asks him, and Marcabru answers: "Sire, de Poito,/d'une terre don mult me lo" ["Sire, from Poitou, a land of which I am most proud" (ll.3619–20).] According to one messenger, the source of pride for Geoffroi, Lord of Cocaigne, is not Poitiers, but the *poirier*, which comes down to the same thing in the "Poitevin" language of the storyteller: "Al perier, dont il mult se loe" ["at the pear tree, of which he is most proud" (1.1325).]

Unmasked by Marcabru, who had recognized the essence of this Count of Poitiers (*son estre*, 1. 3666), what could Geoffroi do but insult the troubadour? Yet his insults are no different from those customarily directed at the *losangier*. From this point on, via the well-codified rela-

---

18. Raoul de Houdenc, *Le Songe d'Enfer*, lines 62–63, in A. Scheler, *Trouvères belges* (nouvelle série) (Louvain: Leferer, 1879), vol. 2, 179: "For in the Poitou Trickery acts as Justice, both lady and viscountess."

tionship between poet and *losangier*,[19] we see the accuser succumbing to the very same reproaches that he hurls at the accused, particularly since the denouncer is pretending to be someone else and "forever travels through the world seeking to fool women":[20]

Lors fu li cuens toz esperduz,
Quar bien sot qu'il fu coneüz,
Que Marchabruns el palais vit,
De cui sot que son estre ot dit.
Mult par [l']en a li cuens laidi
Por ce qu'il l'ot descovri.
Cent foiz l'apela lecheor
Et faus menestral traïtor;
Et Marchabruns li laisa dire,
Et en aprés li respont: "Sire,
Laissez or mes vostre tenchon,
Que je ne la pris un boton.                    [ll. 3663–74]

Then the count was all distraught, for he knew that he had been recognized as soon as he saw Marcabru in the palace; he knew well that he had revealed his whole being. The count covered him with insults because he had exposed him. One hundred times he called him scoundrel, false minstrel and traitor, and Marcabru let him speak and afterward answered him: "Lord, quit your debate (*tenson*) now, for I don't care a pin (literally, a button) for it."

While on the one hand Geoffroi had only to see Marcabru—and not hear his words—in order to feel exposed, Marcabru's disregard for the count's *tenchon* can remind us of the fictive nature of the *tenson*, a literary genre pitting poets against each other in what became frequently a sophistical debate. Indeed, in one *tenson*, Cercamon greets with disdain a certain Guillaume's questionable promise that an un-

19. The Northern French *trouvères* are forever accusing the *losangier* ("devious slanderer") of lies or even seduction, as if a mere accusation were enough to prove one's own authenticity as a poet. What is the most troubling, however, is the fact that both, poet and *losangier* use the same rules, the same commonplaces—in short, the same art of Love based on a rhetoric of absence. Expressed most simply, the *losangier* assumes a contrapuntal function in the courtly lyric. This figure of the poet's "other," his contradictory and diabolical double, serves to neutralize any substantial truth the discourse might contain and to relegate this "nothing," around which revolves the lyric's longing, to a totally exotic realm all its own. The particular form of the *contredit* invoked by the poet/*losangier* couple does not therefore involve the truth of the poetic discourse, but rather the art of producing an appearance of truth.

20. See the *Vida* of Guillaume IX (in Jeanroy, op. cit., 30); "anet lonc temps per lo mon per enganar las domnas."

named "count of Poitiers" will come to shower gifts on him: another curious crossover between the theme of *largesse,* the city of Poitiers, another Guillaume (or the same one?), and a debate developed along the lines of the *contredit.*[21]

This recurring connection between Poitiers and *largesse* explains why Geoffroi's companion, Robert, although having lived in the Poitou for a long time, would never be in a position to match the *largesse* of his Poitevin master: his origins are in the Anjou. This is also the reason why this same Robert, having to choose between love for Queen Alis and loyalty to his lord, will opt for the Count of Poitiers. We know that Robert is not allowed to be at the source of the marvels in this land of Cocaigne; it is rather his lot to receive and to share in their abundance thanks to Geoffroi, the lord who controls the secret of the fables' wonders (*prodiges*) and extravagance (*prodigalité*). Furthermore, what use would Queen Alis's friendship be to Robert, given that she has already sent the jewel box and the key to the Count of Poitiers? Having restated the Robert/Geoffroi relationship in terms of the opposition between Anjou and Poitou, one is reminded of a song of Marcabru which thematizes this opposition, suggesting as it does an antagonism and even a negative attitude toward the Anjou over and against the Poitou.[22]

A retrospective look at Geoffroi's adventures shows that the Count of Poitiers confronts his *own* enemies only at the end of the romance, for one certainly cannot consider enemies those adversaries whom he meets in the tournament jousts, which are manifestly for sport; the same applies to the seneschal, enemy of the queen, as well as to the enemies of the king whom Geoffroi fights as a mercenary. The only war which Geoffroi fights on his own behalf is the one he wages against Alphonse of Toulouse, and he does this not so much in order to defend the region of Poitou, for which he cares little, but rather to defend the city (*ville*) of Poitiers, the true seat of Geoffroi's—and the storyteller's—*quille.*[23] No matter whose *quille* is in question here, both are threatened by the *losangiers'* ruse, the *contrequille* of another *conte* and of another *comte,* figured in the romance by Alphonse de Saint-*Gille, Count* of Toulouse. The marriage of Geoffroi and Amau-

21. Cf. Alfred Jeanroy, ed. *Les Poésies de Cercamon* (Paris: Champion, 1922), strophe 6, line 54.

22. *Poésies complètes du troubadour Marcabru* ed. J.-M.-L. Dejeanne, Bibliothèque Méridionale, vol. 12 (Toulouse: Privat, 1909), Song 8, 32–36.

23. Note the *ville/quille* rhyme: given the transformation of *v* to *qu* they are virtually homonyms. Cf. my article, "Le Contredit de François Villon," *MLN,* 98, no. 4 (May 1983), 594–623.

bergeon, whose father, the Count of Toulouse, Geoffroi conquers and imprisons, brings the romance full circle, integrating into the Poitevin line the descendants of the ravager of the *comte* of Poitou, in somewhat the same way that the poet incorporated the *losangier*.

Having pointed out this crucial feature of *Joufroi*, let us now turn our attention to the narrator's interventions. Should one consider them a flaw of the romance, as so many critics have claimed? I think not. I would even go so far as to say that this other voice, which manages to interrupt the story so "awkwardly," functions as a variation on the same rhetorical strategy discussed above. This is what I now propose to demonstrate.

The source of this divergence between the storyteller's voice and the narrated material is present in the following passage from the prologue where the author stresses the constant value of love, always equal to itself (l. 44), always true, and thus capable of revealing the trickery which originates not in love itself, but in the knights and ladies and all who claim that love has degenerated:

> Ne unques ne fu plus veraie
> Qu[e] ele est or, qui bien l'asaie.
> Mais plus s'entendent en trichier
> Les dames et li chevalier
> Que il ne firent unques mes.                    [ll. 49–53]

> Never was love more true than it is now, for one who truly experiences
> it. But, more than ever, ladies and knights are becoming experts in
> trickery.

The narrator thus presents himself as one whose writing is faithful to a Love invariable in its very essence. And if the storyteller can in any way envisage the riches distributed by Love, it is in terms of a *largesse* which likens them to the jousts, the tournaments, the songs and the laughter of the narration, whose rhythms eventually coalesce in the adventure of the *perier:*

> Ne fait ele rire et chanter,
> Doner et joster et despeindre,
> Corz et torneiemenz enprendre?                    [ll. 38–40]

> Does not love make one laugh and sing, give and joust and spend and
> engage in festivals and tournaments?

From these two passages in the prologue one can infer that it is the trickery of the characters rather than the narrative fabric underlying their actions which is called into question. This questioning process does not, however, in any way alter Love. In other words, in the prologue, the author establishes a distance between the narrated adventure and Love's adventure, which is based on an entirely different law.

If one examines more closely the narrator's statements throughout the romance, one finds that his voice is different from those of the other storytellers, in that it only rarely intervenes to comment on the story. Instead, the narrator weaves his own adventures with those of his characters. And it is probably the gap between these two narrative voices which accounts for those abrupt transitions referred to as "awkward."

The distance between one story and the other is not always the same, however, tending to diminish as the story nears its conclusion. Indeed, while in the prologue the storyteller affirms his unconditional allegiance to Love's laws, in the final scene we find a narrator who is totally disillusioned. Between these two extremes a whole series of modulations provokes the upheaval whose most striking characteristics we shall now outline.

First of all, let us note that the narrator's first intervention takes place between the death of the reputedly invincible seneschal and the news of Geoffroi's father's death. After these events, Geoffroi may be said to have gained complete independence from his models of chivalry (the seneschal) and *largesse* (Richier), and, at the same time, from the narrator. For it is at the very moment when the son of Richier sets out to engage in his masquerades and trickery that the author reaffirms his decision never to oppose Love's law (ll. 593–94). Each successive intervention until the end of the Tonnerre episode goes in the direction of this counterpoint: the narrator resists trickery (l. 784), reaffirms his love for the faithful and beloved lady (l. 1220), and bears the suffering for a love which he is duty bound to keep secret (l. 1582).

But after Geoffroi's departure for England with Robert, there is a significant change in tone: while the Count of Poitiers stoops so low as to marry the daughter of a bourgeois, the narrator complains of having placed his love too high. He expresses scorn for the internal riches to be gained from the suffering undergone in such circumstances (ll. 2097–98); he envisages revealing his love, still a secret at that point, but by way of a discourse capable of deceiving even the *losangiers* (ll. 2942ff.). As it happens, along with the hope for a kiss (l. 2948), within the narrator there arises simultaneously an agitation which steadily invades him until he finds himself faced with a dilemma similar to that of Robert,[24]

24. Taking advantage of Geoffroi's absence, Robert has slipped into his lord's bed to

who is at pains to decide whether to be true to his lord or to the queen. At this point, the two stories nearly coincide. From this point on the storyteller will involve himself directly in the action of the romance, questioning the reader about Robert before offering his own opinion:

E vos, qu'en feïssoiz, seignor?
A toz vos pri par grant amor
Que chascuns son penser en die,
Qu'il en feïst a la fenie,
S'il fust en leu o cil estoit
Qui la reïne Alis tenoit.
Puis redira[i] ge mon corage
Aprés vos tuit, qui estes sage.                    [ll. 4211–18]

And you, what would you do, lords? I pray you all, out of great love, to tell me your opinion and what you would do if you found yourselves in Robert's situation, in love with Queen Alis. After all of you, who are so perspicacious, then will I tell you my thoughts [on the matter].

Unlike Robert, who decides to remain faithful to his lord, the narrator opts for the queen. The next intervention, the last of any importance, dramatizes a narrator completely distraught and "turned around" (*bestornez*) (l.4346), whose confusion pours forth in a lament, elaborately spun out in the style of the *contredit*. Here are some of its modulations:

Or pais! seignors, si m'escoutez,
S'orreiz con ge sui bestornez:
Ne sai si muer o si ge vi,
Ne sai que faz ne que ge di,
Ne sai quant chant ne quant ge plor, . . .

Ne sai quant ge ai o fain o seis,
O' si sui vilains o corteis,
Ne sai don sui ne de quel terre, . . .

Mi braz me resenblent dous maces,
Et li doi de mes mains limaces;
Mi pié me resenblent chasteus,
Et li ortels [i] sunt creneus. . . .

---

await the queen. Alis arrives and thinking she is kissing Geoffroi finds herself in Robert's arms. Robert falls in love with the queen, but would prefer not to wrong his master. Thus arises the internal debate which ends in the renunciation of Alis's love.

Si m'a bestorné lo corage
Une amor que ge ai servie;
Avoir cuidai leial amie
Et qui m'amasst de cuer verai,
Quant ge cest romanz comenchai.                    [ll. 4345–84]

Peace! Lords, listen to me that you may hear how distraught I am: I don't know whether I am dying or living, nor what I am doing, nor what I am saying, I don't know when I am singing nor when I am weeping. . . . I don't know when I am hungry or thirsty, I don't know if I am a scoundrel or a gentleman, nor in what land I was born. . . . My arms look like two clubs to me, my fingers like slugs, my feet resemble castles whose toes are the ramparts. . . . Thus has a love which I served turned my mind around; I thought I had a loyal ladyfriend who loved me with a true love, when I began this romance.

However much it might go counter to the narrator's heartfelt wishes, this lament ends with the resolve to terminate a romance which has exacted so much pain. Instantly the intervention is cut short and, in a turn to the banal, the narrative reverts to the hackneyed commonplaces of the genre: "Seignors, la guerre fu finee" ["Lords, the war was over" (l.4585).] And again, in the lines just before the romance breaks off:

Femne ot li cuens: oï l'avez,
Coment il se fu mariez.
Sa feme ame come sa dame,
Que molt par i ot bone fame
Et cortoise senz vilenie
* * * * * * (Interruption of romance) * * *
                                                   [ll. 4609–13]

The count took a wife: you have heard how he married. He loves his wife as his lady for in her he had found a decent woman, courteous without any meanness.

It is important to notice that this final intervention has every appearance of leading the tale towards a stereotyped ending, especially since the last of the three spellings of "femme" (*femne, feme* and *fame*), while surely dictated by its rhyme (*dame*), can nonetheless also be read as a homonym of "fame" (Latin *fama*), and can thus be said to give the final lines the appearance of a conclusion true to form: "For everywhere [the romance] had great reknown."

Whatever the case may be, one need only recall the end of the *Bel Inconnu* (applying the situation of Guinglain and his two ladyfriends to

Geoffroi and the narrator\* ), in order to see that even though the adventure of the Count of Poitiers ends in marriage, that of the storyteller and his true love is left hanging. And yet, after having traced the successive phases through which the narrative voice passes in following the metonymic movement of the story, it is the very rhythm of the *contredit*, so essential to courtly poetry, which comes to rest at the end of this contrapuntal romance. One can conclude from this that in spite of any enthusiasm or disillusionment with regard to Love, the narrator has remained faithful to that *Amors veraia* which cannot be expressed except through the *contredit*, that "true love" whose law he had claimed to respect. Much as in a *faux-bourdon*† which is sung note against note, the two voices in this story do not drown out the basic tune being carried by Love.

My previous claim, that the structure of *Joufroi* is based on the lacuna, is thus not without its reason. We need only consider the moments of suspension within the story produced by the narrator's interventions, even though these breaks are disguised and even cemented in on a massive scale by the storyteller's own account which feeds parasitically off the other in order to transport us to another world. At the very least, we must take care not to jump to the conclusion that this patchwork is due to artistic clumsiness, since the model for it is clearly inscribed at the beginning of the romance.

We might recall the duel between Geoffroi and the fearsome seneschal. This mortal combat is cut in half by a break in the action which at first looks like an ending, inasmuch as both rivals, having fainted at the same time, appear to be dead:

> Si che chevals et chevalier
> Cheient tuit enverselgravier
> Li uns lez l'autre estordiz.
> Ja fust des genz mult grant l'escriz,
> Quar cuidoient qu'il fussent mort.                     [ll. 469–73]

Horses and knights fall to the gravel, with both men next to each other, unconscious. Then the cries (*escriz*) of the spectators were very loud, for they all believed the two rivals were dead.

---

\* See the article by Alice Colby-Hall in the present volume for a discussion of the narrator in the *Bel Inconnu*. [Editor's Note.]

† In music, a late medieval technique of harmonization by which extra parts (voices) can be added to a plainchant using specific formulaic procedures of vocal transposition. The result is a more complex system of harmonies realized in the performance of a given work. [Editor's note.]

First of all, the homonym *escriz* combines the meaning of "cries" and of "writings," as if the author had wanted to make use of one single event to suggest the way in which the writing of such episodes tends to radiate outward. Similarly, the anonymous storyteller's inventiveness is bursting forth through a skillful transformation of this very commonplace into the nucleus of the formal laws destined to determine the entire romance. For it is at this very moment that the king steps in to impose silence and has the law of his reign proclaimed in a voice even more powerful than the cries of the spectators:

> Mais li reis fist crïer tan fort
> Son ban que cil qui parleroit
> Sanz nul respit penduz seroit;
> Por ce se tindrent quoi et mu.
> Quan li cuer furent revenu
> As dous vasaus qui jostré orent,
> En piez saillent plus tost qu'il porent.          [ll. 474–80]

The king had his proclamation to the effect that all those who spoke would be hanged immediately, declaimed so loudly that everyone remained still and silent. When the two vassals who had been jousting regained consciousness, they stood up as quickly as possible.

If we consider the implications of this episode, it is clear that the king's spiel functions as a model for the laws governing the narrative; in accordance with this model, the narrator's voice intervenes, interrupting the clamor of the adventure and silencing it so that a reprise can take place—but not without first reminding those "left hanging" by the adventure, and threatened with "hanging," of the very real presence of the rule of *fin'amor* governing the entire narrative. It is as though the narrative tale, regularly punctuated by a sequence of pauses, filled them up with the storyteller's voice; the latter, in this way comparable to that of the king's herald, proclaims the law of Love and its punishments during those intervals. Can we not say, in fact, that this royal authority and these *tailles* (taxes or cuts) are precisely what the poet desires in his first intervention following the seneschal's death when he announces the "sum" of his intentions?

> Mais se fusse de France sire,
> O de [tot] l'enpire de Rome,
> Si vos di bien de moi la some,
> Si ja Nostre Seignor me vaille,
> Que je feïsse en toz cels taille
> Que je soüsse jangleors
> De rien que fust encontre Amors.          [ll. 588–94]

But if I were King of France or of the whole Roman Empire, I tell you
well the sum of everything I would do. As long as Our Lord assisted me,
I would levy taxes (or, I would make cuts) on all those whom I knew to
be *jongleurs* (idle singers) of anything contrary to Love.

This clearly seems to be an allusion (actually rather obscure) to those
cuts (*taillades*) carried out by the author within the narrative material
in which he presents those unfaithful to Love's law. As far as Geoffroi's
adventure is concerned, this wish expressed by the author foreshadows
the "suspens(ion)" of the narrative which, in the fictional register, is
conflated with the punishment of hanging, as if it were a matter of
chastising by means of the breaks all those who, too subservient to the
realistic details of the story, may have forgotten its secret law.

In short, even if a formal treatment of the lacunae always risks
becoming a simple stereotyped maneuver once it has been discovered by
Love's followers, we should nonetheless trust the Poitevins' wealth of
invention: they know—but through what wisdom?—that commonplace speech holds within itself a vast reserve, a wealth of resources
which permit the reader to skirt the perilous terrain of platitudes.

Throughout this study we have given various examples of the rhetoric of incompletion and interruption; not only does this rhetorical
manipulation give every sign of being a part of the *trouvère*'s trade
secrets, but more specifically it seems to be a direct offshoot of the basic
premises of courtly poetry, which, in its assertion of literature as a
writing about the impossible, covers the ellipsis of meaning with masks
of varying dimensions. This is as much as to say that the game of the
*trobar* is always closed (*clus*) upon its secret and this above all where it is
most open (*leu*). Thus is postulated a practice of the language of Love in
which, as poets have always known, however much the possibility of
making a discovery is linked to the presence of an obstacle, the obstacle
must in turn create that *contredit* which ends up multiplying antithetical figures in an art of *gille*. *Losangiers*, treacherous knights, Counts of
Saint-*Gille*, even jealous husbands (*gilos*), such are the inverted figures
of the poet-lover grappling with his own words.

Ici prend fin le mien joyeux escrire
Dont on verra plusieurs gens assez rire

Here ends my joyous writing which, as you will see, will bring laughter
to many.[25]

Translated by Karen McPherson

25. Jean Lemaire de Belges, *Les Epistres de l'amant vers*, ed. Jean Frappier (Geneva: Droz, 1948), 37.

ALICE M. COLBY-HALL

# Frustration and Fulfillment: The Double Ending of the *Bel Inconnu**

In the biographical romances and *lais* of twelfth- and thirteenth-century France, the hero regularly marries or forms a permanent liaison with the woman he loves. It is easy, therefore, to understand the disappointment felt by many modern critics upon reaching the end of the *Bel Inconnu*, composed by Renaut de Beaujeu some time between the middle 1180s and 1230.[1] Peter Haidu has defended Renaut on the grounds that the latter experiments with lyric and narrative conventions in an intelligent, questioning, and deliberately tantalizing way.[2] Sophisticated experimentation of this type is certainly present, but I think it is possible to demonstrate that Renaut has provided us with answers as well as questions. In my view, there is strong evidence that Renaut understood extremely well the structural expectations of the medieval reader or listener and was able to hold his audience's attention by meeting these expectations in an amusing, subtle, and decidedly unconventional way. In order to make the uninitiated reader's dissatisfaction fully comprehensible, let me begin by offering a brief analysis of Renaut's plot.

---

*An earlier version of this paper was presented on December 29, 1976, at the meeting of the Modern Language Association of America in New York, under the title "Stylistic Ritual and Aesthetic Distance in the *Bel Inconnu* of Renaut de Beaujeu."

1. The *Bel Inconnu* was probably written between the middle 1180s and 1190, but may have been composed as late as 1230. See Renaut de Beaujeu, *Le Bel Inconnu*, ed. G. Perrie Williams, CFMA, 38 (Paris: Champion, 1929), vii–viii, and Alice M. Colby, "The Lips of the Serpent in the *Bel Inconnu*," in *Studia Gratula [to] ria: Homenaje a Robert A. Hall, Jr.*, ed. David Feldman (Madrid: Playor, 1977), 111.

All references to the *Bel Inconnu* will be to the Williams edition. Translations are my own.

2. "Realism, Convention, Fictionality and the Theory of Genres in *Le Bel Inconnu*," *L'Esprit Créateur*, 12 (1972), 37–60.

The main narrative, exclusive of the Prologue and Epilogue, can be divided into two parts. Part 1 (ll. 11–3914) ends with the rescue of Blonde Esmerée by the Bel Inconnu and the resulting revelation of his true identity. This climactic adventure releases the beautiful princess, Blonde Esmerée, from the physical effects of the spell placed upon her by the evil enchanter, Mabon. It is preceded by a number of challenging but somewhat less difficult encounters, from which the hero emerges victorious while traveling from Arthur's court to the princess' castle in the company of her fair messenger, Hélie. The most important of these is the defeat of Malgier le Gris, the tyrannical, irascible, and unloved suitor of the Pucelle aux Blanches Mains, who immediately offers to marry the hero and give him her lands (ll. 1991–2275). Fearing that she will prevent him from completing the rescue mission enjoined upon him by Hélie, he makes an uncourtly, surreptitious departure. Since Mabon is also a rejected suitor, it is not surprising that Blonde Esmerée likewise desires to marry the hero and give him charge over the domain she has inherited from her father, the King of Wales. Consequently, as Part 1 draws to a close, the Bel Inconnu, now called Guinglain, is faced with the dilemma of choosing between two offers of marriage, the second of which appears to be slightly more advantageous than the first from the material point of view. Both women are very much in love with the hero. He, for his part, is only mildly attracted to Blonde Esmerée and is clearly in love with the Pucelle, an extraordinary human being whose skill in the use of magic has transformed her into a veritable fay.[3]

Part 2 (ll. 3915–6246) concludes with a socially approved marriage of convenience to Blonde Esmerée. Prior to the wedding, Guinglain pays a second visit to the Ile d'Or, the white-walled, red-turreted castle of the Pucelle aux Blanches Mains, is pardoned for his previous breach of courtly etiquette, and enjoys the favors of his fairy mistress (ll. 3915–5054). In the course of his stay, he learns that it was her voice that proclaimed his identity and her subtle, clandestine support that made the entire rescue mission possible. However, he is to all appearances completely rejected by the fay once he decides to participate in the tournament announced by Arthur with the hope of luring him back to the court and to the arms of Blonde Esmerée, whom Arthur considers to be a suitable bride for Guinglain (ll. 5055–5429). After Guinglain has won the tournament (ll. 6088–90) and, to the best of his knowledge, lost

3. For a thorough analysis of the human characteristics of the Pucelle, see Sara Sturm, "The *Bel Inconnu's* Enchantress and the Intent of Renaut de Beaujeu," *The French Review*, 44 (1970/71), 862–69.

his beloved mistress, he quite understandably accepts Arthur's offer of a wife and a kingdom.

Guinglain's prowess has thus permitted him to enter into the kind of marriage that the average ambitious young nobleman would desire for practical reasons, but that is not the stuff of which romances are made. Such tales are not written to celebrate the marriage of convenience—to which they are hostile by definition—but the *mariage d'amour* or a permanent liaison characterized by mutual devotion. Fantasy and wish fulfillment are far more important here than the demands of everyday reality.[4]

Fully aware that the reader expects him to reunite Guinglain and the Pucelle, Renaut defends himself in the Epilogue, which deserves to be quoted in full:

> Ci faut li roumans et define.
> Bele, vers cui mes cuers s'acline,
> RENALS DE BIAUJU molt vos prie
> Por Diu que ne l'oblïés mie.                                6250
> De cuer vos veut tos jors amer,
> Ce ne li poés vos veer.
> Quant vos plaira, dira avant,
> U il se taira ore a tant.
> Mais por un biau sanblant mostrer                           6255
> Vos feroit Guinglain retrover
> S'amie, que il a perdue,
> Qu'entre ses bras le tenroit nue.
> Se de çou li faites delai,
> Si ert Guinglains en tel esmai                              6260
> Que ja mais n'avera s'amie.
> D'autre vengeance n'a il mie,
> Mais por la soie grant grevance
> Ert sor Guinglain ceste vengance,
> Que ja mais jor n'en parlerai                               6265
> Tant que le bel sanblant avrai.

Here the romance ceases and ends. Fair one, before whom my heart prostrates itself, Renaut de Beaujeu beseeches you not to forget him, for God's sake. He wishes to love you always from the depths of his heart; you cannot refuse him this privilege. If it pleases you, he will continue; or else he will be silent right now. But if you would but offer him a favorable glance, for your sake he would cause Guinglain to regain his

---

4. Françoise Boiron and J.-C. Payen, "Structure et sens du *Bel Inconnu* de Renaut de Beaujeu," *Le Moyen Age,* 76 (1970), 20, 25–26.

mistress, whom he has lost, in such a way that he would hold her naked in his arms. If you delay in doing this for him, Guinglain will be in such a sorry plight that he will never again have his mistress. Renaut has no other vengeance at his disposal, but this vengeance will be wreaked on Guinglain to his great misfortune, for I will never again speak of him until I have the favorable glance.

For the price of a *bel sanblant,* i.e., a favorable glance, the poet will compose a sequel in which the fay is restored to her lover's arms. Needless to say, this is a naughty ending; and it is not surprising that, in the twentieth century, some critics have accused Renaut of tasteless playfulness in a serious romance[5] or of a genuine inability to come to terms with the moral dilemma he has created.[6] Renaut's Epilogue does, without doubt, frustrate the desires of the reader; but is this frustration completely justified? What is, in reality, the narrative function of this tale of love and adventure? The Prologue (ll. 1–10) provides an early clue to Renaut's real purpose. Here we are told that the author has already written one or more *chansons* for his lady[7] and that he now wishes to offer her a romance. In a courtly *chanson,* the lover can only describe past joys and sorrows and the hope of future bliss; in a normal romance, the hero's successful pursuit of his beloved is assured. What better way to plead your own case than to imply that your tale is paradigmatic and that your lady should emulate its heroine? This is precisely the technique used by Aimon de Varennes in his *Florimont* and by the anonymous author of *Partonopeu de Blois.*

Suppose, however, that a writer desired to construct a story that was both a romance and a genuine narrative equivalent of a love lyric. This is the case with Renaut. Unlike the romancers just mentioned, he turns the autobiographical content of the typical *chanson* into a frame story portraying his own experiences and makes Guinglain's success in love entirely dependent upon his own. Three times during the course of the story, Renaut interrupts the narrative in order to comment on his relationship to his beloved. In the first passage (ll. 1263–71), our poet styles himself a victim of unrequited love: his lady is not his *amie* but

5. Boiron and Payen, "Structure et sens," 18.

6. Hans Robert Jauss, "Chanson de geste et roman courtois (analyse comparative du *Fierabras* et du *Bel Inconnu*)," in *Chanson de Geste und höfischer Roman,* Studia Romanica, 4 (Heidelberg: C. Winter, 1963), 76–77, and Madeleine Tyssens, "Les Sources de Renaut de Beaujeu," in *Mélanges Jean Frappier,* Publications Romanes et Françaises, 112 (Geneva: Droz, 1970), 1054.

7. In her edition of the *Bel Inconnu,* 195, Perrie Williams assumes that Renaut is referring to only one *chanson;* but "faire cançon" in line 3 is actually imprecise with regard to the number of songs involved.

only *la molt amee* ["the much loved one" (l. 1266)]. He sings for his lady while dying of love for her, and he would rather act foolishly than be unfaithful to her. Further on (ll. 4198–4209), he likens his own suffering to that of Guinglain, who has been temporarily rejected by the Pucelle as a result of his seemingly disloyal departure from her castle. Once Guinglain has achieved perfect bliss in the arms of the Pucelle, Renaut gives full expression to the hope that sustains him:

> En un jor me puet bien merir
> Plus que ne puis ja deservir.
> Molt doit on cele rien amer
> Qui si tost puet joie donner.                    [ll. 4831–34]

> In a single day, she can indeed give me greater recompense than I can ever deserve. One ought to love very much the person who is able to give joy so quickly.

These thinly disguised allusions to the object of his quest are followed by a paean of praise for ladies that closes with a revealing couplet: "Ha! Dius, arai ja mon plaissir / De celi que je ainme tant?" (ll. 4860–61). ["Ah! God, will I ever have my pleasure from the one whom I love so much?"]

It is only upon reading the Epilogue, however, that one can grasp the full structural import of the poet's remarks concerning his lady and also comprehend the true meaning of an enigmatic announcement that he makes immediately after the episode of the Fier Baiser:

> D'ore en avant vos vel traitier
> De Guinglain le bon chevalier
> L'istoire, qui mais ne faurra
> Tant con li siecles duerra.                    [ll. 3249–52]

> From now on, I wish to treat for you the story of Guinglain, the good knight, a story which will never end as long as the world endures.

In the Prologue, Renaut appears to equate the *istoire* he wishes to begin (l. 7) with the *roumant* that he desires to extract from a *conte d'aventure* (ll. 4–5), but it is the *roumant* alone that "ceases and ends" (l. 6247); and it does so with a significant reference to the future: "Puis fu rois de molt grant mimore, / Si con raconte li istore" (ll. 6245–46). ["Afterwards he was a king of very great renown, as the story recounts."] The story of this much renowned king will never be concluded unless the demise of the cosmos imposes an arbitrary termination upon it; whereas the romance will end, as biographical romances normally do, with the winning of a bride and a kingdom.[8] Renaut's *istoire* is not a romance in the usual sense of the word, but rather a narrativized *chanson*,[9] which, by definition, must not allow Guinglain's dream of love to be fulfilled in the here and now. An unclothed *amie* cannot lie in the hero's arms, or in those of the poet, within the confines of the two narrative structures indissolubly linked to each other by the Epilogue.

It is clear, I think, that the author wanted his reader to experience the frustration expressed in a typical *chanson*. Such a poem would not be complete, however, without a note of hope; and that note is indeed sounded. If Renaut's lady will deign to give him a favorable glance, Guinglain will regain the love of the fay. No sequel appears to have been written, nor could it have been, without destroying the lyric framework. Furthermore, as I shall attempt to demonstrate, the work needs no sequel since the reader can actually look forward to something more satisfying than the potential moment of happiness depicted in the Epilogue.

Though disappointed with the content of the ending, Hans Robert Jauss was impressed by Renaut's comments regarding the dependence of fiction upon external contingency; for, in the history of courtly romance, there is no earlier example of an author's awareness that his material is fictitious and can therefore be manipulated in such a way as to frustrate the reader.[10] Jauss is to be commended for having stressed the importance of the aesthetic detachment implied by the Epilogue. I, for my part, would go one step further and say that this attitude pervades the entire work and provides further justification for the much maligned conclusion. Renaut feels strong sympathy for his characters and is under the spell of Arthurian enchantment, yet his emotional commitment to the material is not so intense that he fails to notice the artificiality of the world he has created and the mechanical nature of the

8. For Renaut, *istoire* is a more general term than *roumant* and can therefore be applied to a narrative that does not fit into any well-known category. Consequently, this writer is even more precise in his use of these labels than Douglas Kelly supposes in "*Matiere* and *genera dicendi* in Medieval Romance," *Yale French Studies* 51 (1954), 147. Kelly rightly credits Renaut with offering us one of the first unequivocal examples of the generic use of the word *roumant* but treats the two terms under discussion as synonymous in Renaut's text.

9. The resemblance between Renaut's romance and a *chanson d'amour* has been noted by Paul Zumthor, *Essai de poétique médiévale* (Paris: Seuil, 1972), 343, and Jeanne Lods, "' Le Baiser de la reine' et 'le cri de la fée': étude structurale du *Bel Inconnu* de Renaut de Beaujeu," *Mélanges Pierre Jonin*, Senefiance, 7 (Aix-en-Provence, 1979), 418–19. They do not, however, show in detail how Renaut actualizes the narrative potential of the typical love lyric.

10. "Chanson de geste," 76–77.

literary conventions that govern both the lyric and the romance. Though he delights in genuine personal involvement with the subject matter, he lightheartedly refuses to take himself or his craft too seriously—whence the self-irony lauded by Fierz-Monnier.[11]

The reader is alternately captivated by the content of the narrative and pulled away from it by the reification of its component parts, which have become movable counters on the author's game board. It is as if Renaut were saying to his opponent: "Let me test your mettle. Do you think you are so familiar with literary conventions that you can anticipate my every move?" This is, in effect, the challenge offered the reader; and it is no less a source of diversion than the charmed life of an Arthurian knight under the protection of a fay.

The chief type of counter utilized by Renaut in his maneuvers is the long, stereotyped, laudatory and hyperbolic portrait, whose traditional function is to arouse admiration for the character in question and to imply that the personage is of noble birth and reasonably young, is essentially of good character, and will play a fairly significant rôle in the story. Not unexpectedly, the depiction of ideal feminine beauty—and it is always ideal in the true portrait—often serves the purpose of justifying the love of a knight for a lady.[12] A woman deemed worthy of formal portrayal is by definition important and, if she has a lover, either becomes his wife or establishes a permanent liaison with him, provided of course that the love is mutual. The same may be said, *mutatis mutandis*, of men who are granted portraits. Since the central figures in most romances are obliged to come to terms with love, it is not surprising that the pattern just described is illustrated by the majority of the thirty-two flattering portraits that had probably been composed by the time Renaut completed his poem.[13] Is it any wonder, then, that the experienced reader comes to regard the portrait as a mechanical clue to the outcome of the romance and, as a result, takes a certain perverse delight in trying to outguess the author? Can Renaut, therefore, be blamed for active participation in the very game his reader is playing with him?

Portrait 1, a lengthy description of Hélie (ll. 133–56), arouses the reader's curiosity since it may well indicate that Guinglain will win her hand, but this possibility is eliminated when it becomes clear that she is in the service of a noble maid whom Guinglain will attempt to rescue.

11. Antoinette Fierz-Monnier, *Initiation und Wandlung: Zur Geschichte des altfranzösischen Romans im zwölften Jahrhundert von Chrétien de Troyes zu Renaut de Beaujeu*, Studiorum Romanicorum Collectio Turicensis, 5 (Bern: A. Francke, 1951), 202.

12. Alice M. Colby, *The Portrait in Twelfth-Century French Literature: An Example of the Stylistic Originality of Chrétien de Troyes* (Geneva: Droz, 1965), 99–101.

13. For references, see Colby, *The Portrait*, 14–19.

The reader can assume that the hero will marry the damsel he has saved by undertaking an unusually dangerous mission, unless of course he has a prior commitment. Hélie's portrait simply shows that she is qualified to be her lady's messenger and deserves the attention she receives at Arthur's court.

The candidate proposed by Portrait 2 is Margerie, who is said to be extremely beautiful despite her violent display of grief (ll. 1525–54). This description is more laudatory and slightly longer than the one just analyzed, but the hero still does not become romantically involved. The girl's appearance is presented merely in order to explain Guinglain's sympathy and his offer to avenge her lover's death by doing battle with Giflet in the Joust of the Sparrowhawk (ll. 1629–44).

The reader begins to await a third, and perhaps decisive, portrait when he is given a brief introduction to the Pucelle aux Blanches Mains soon after Guinglain's successful joust with Giflet. Having learned that this young heiress is unusually attractive and also skilled in magic (ll. 1931–43), he suspects that a fairy mistress is waiting in the wings and is fully prepared for the detailed portrait which Renaut does not fail to provide (ll. 2217–58). As the townspeople lead Guinglain towards the Castle of the Ile d'Or after his victory over Malgier le Gris, the Pucelle's unwanted suitor, they joyously announce that he is now their lord and is about to see "the best lady that ever was" (ll. 2206–07), whom he will love and, if it pleases God, possess. As soon as the lady herself appears, and the portrait begins, the radiance of her beauty dispels the palace gloom and so astonishes Guinglain that he almost falls prostrate. Nature had moulded the maiden's features so artfully that, in the opinion of the author, no woman in the world had a more beautiful face or brow. Her eyes sparkled, her cheeks and lips were rosy, and her teeth were small and white. She had "a mouth well made for kissing and arms well made for embracing" (ll. 2239–40). She was "whiter than a flower" (l. 2231) and her blond hair was adorned with a gold thread and a chaplet of roses. In short, "no one had ever seen such a beautiful damsel" (l. 2258). Portrait 3 is longer, has greater rhetorical complexity, and bestows a higher degree of praise than either of the preceding ones. These factors, combined with the hero's initial reaction to the lady, are sufficient to convince the reader that he has finally identified the heroine, who will one day be the bride of Guinglain. This conviction is strengthened by the Pucelle's immediate love for the hero, her willingness to marry him without requiring any further test of his prowess, and the mutual passion that soon develops between them (ll. 2260–75, ll. 2441–71).

The initiated reader, smug and self-confident, begins to relax; but his patronizing smile disappears when he is confronted with Portrait 4 (ll. 3127–48), which does not correspond exactly to any of the thematic categories stored in his brain. Is Renaut's *wivre* meant to be a stereotypical fire-breathing dragon, an ideally ugly, serpentlike person, or an ideally beautiful human being imprisoned within the skin of a beast? It is hideous and large, its fiery red eyes gleam like carbuncles, and its flaming radiance fills the palace with a terrifying brightness. Yet, strangely enough, the poet declares: "Hom ne vit onques sa parelle, / Que la bouce ot tote vermelle" (ll. 3133–34). ["No one had ever seen one like it, for it had a bright red mouth."] Conventional serpents do not have appealing red mouths, and ideally ugly humans often resemble animals,[14] but a *bouce vermelle* can only belong to an ideally attractive man or woman.[15] Is it possible, then, that ideal beauty has been almost wholly metamorphosed into its opposite? The reader is mystified; and so is the hero, who seems to be having more difficulty dissecting the portrait than fending off the dragon. So fascinated he cannot move, he stares in wonder at its ruby lips which can no longer be prevented from planting a kiss upon his own, the long-awaited Fier Baiser. Guinglain falls into a deep sleep; and when he awakes, the serpent has become Blonde Esmerée, or, rather, Portrait 4 has been transmuted into Portrait 5 (ll. 3261–3300).[16] Renaut has moved another cardboard counter, and the reader's most logical hypothesis has proven to be correct. Just as Renaut's brief description announced the approach of Portrait 3, Portrait 4 has prepared the way for Portrait 5, but in a rather unusual manner.

The poet's description of Blonde Esmerée successfully forestalls any criticism of a knight who should fall in love with her or seek her hand in marriage. She is magnificently dressed, and her complexion is so fresh and rosy that no clerk could describe it. Nature has fashioned her body and limbs so well that there was never before such a beautiful woman in the world—except the Pucelle aux Blanches Mains, "for no maid is comparable to her," says the author (l. 3273). Renaut is not playing the game according to the rules. Traditional portraitists do not undercut their praise with unfavorable comparisons to others who are renowned for their beauty, not even when a lady is likened to Helen of Troy.[17] Portrait 5 is almost as long as Portrait 3 and, though less detailed as regards physical description, would be equally flattering, were it not

---

14. Colby, *The Portrait*, 72–88.

15. Ibid., 51–53.

16. For a detailed analysis of the hero's confrontation with the dragon, see Colby, "The Lips of the Serpent," 111–15.

17. Colby, *The Portrait*, 27–28.

for Renaut's deflating remark. Quite understandably, Guinglain gives Blonde Esmerée a *bel sanblant* when she offers him the opportunity to marry her and rule over her lands as king of Wales; but he avoids committing himself, saying that he cannot accept her proposal until he has talked with King Arthur and obtained his approval of the marriage (ll. 3384–3414, ll. 3595–3628). The princess loves Guinglain (l. 3672) and is clearly a desirable bride, but the Pucelle has already insinuated herself into his heart and even into the portrait of her rival.

The battle of the portraits continues in earnest when Guinglain returns to the Ile d'Or with the hope that his previous uncourtliness will be pardoned by the fay. As he approaches the city, he sees the Pucelle riding towards him in Portrait 6 (ll. 3936–94). She is just coming from the hunt with a sparrowhawk on her wrist and is followed by a sizable retinue. Renaut lavishes a total of fifty-nine lines on this elegant equestrienne and gives almost equal attention to her physical form, her costly gold-trimmed garments, and her dappled palfrey, whose harness rings sweetly with the music of a hundred little golden bells. The reader justifiably concludes that this aristocratic damsel is sufficiently beautiful, wealthy, and powerful to be a suitable bride for Guinglain and, moreover, is more than likely to be united permanently with the hero— after all, the portrait score is now two to one.

Renaut soon reinforces the reader's impression that these two are destined for each other by mobilizing a new type of counter, a stereotyped theme which I should like to call the compatibility topos. After Guinglain has been restored to the good graces of his lady, he is allowed to join her in a marvelous walled garden. As she comes forward to greet him, Renaut echoes and intensifies the praise meted out in Portraits 3 and 6 by means of an eleven-line series of comparisons proclaiming the superiority of her beauty to that of Helen, Isolt, Byblis, Lavinia, the fairy Morgan, and all other women (ll. 4344–54). This reminder of the maiden's charms is soon followed by a brief description of the wisdom, prowess, courtliness, and extraordinary handsomeness of Guinglain (ll. 4385–91). The import of these two descriptions is summarized as follows: "Que vos iroie je contant? / Molt furent biel et avenant" (ll. 4423–24). ["What would I tell you? They were very beautiful and attractive."] This seemingly trite observation is packed with meaning; for beauty is traditionally equated with nobility of character and high rank, whether determined by birth or by moral and spiritual excellence. In other words, given their similarity in beauty, there will be no misalliance if the hero and his fairy mistress are joined in wedlock.

A general indication of similarity or equality, exemplified by the line just analyzed, is the one essential constituent of the compatibility topos. This theme is often developed at some length with much stress on beauty, and the evaluation given may be the author's own or that of one or more characters. The topos may also include one or more references to the mutual love uniting the couple, as is the case here (ll. 4413–22). What can the reader predict from the presence of this topos? If mutual love is mentioned within the topos or elsewhere—and I have yet to find it missing in a twelfth-century text[18]—persons so described either marry or form a liaison that is terminated solely by death.[19] In this instance, the passion of the two lovers is said to be more intense than that of Tristan for Isolt (ll. 4421–22). Renaut seems to have a fairly precise kind of relationship in view.

Judging by the literary habits of his predecessors and contemporaries, a fairy tale ending will be forthcoming; but Renaut is about to make another move in the portrait game. While Guinglain is disporting himself with his mistress at the Ile d'Or, Blonde Esmerée arrives at Arthur's court and readily obtains permission to marry the hero (ll. 5281–95). This favorable response, though not unexpected, seems all the more defensible in light of the beauty of her body and the exotic richness of her clothing as depicted in Portrait 7 (ll. 5139–77). Quantitatively speaking, the score is now two to two; but Portrait 7, in which special attention is given to the maiden's garments, is somewhat shorter and less flattering than its counterpart, Portrait 6, and concludes with a general appraisal of her beauty that has already been outdone by the compatibility topos. No living woman had one-fourth the beauty of Blonde Esmerée (ll. 5176–77), whereas none of the noted beauties to

18. I have thus far discovered only one example of its absence, and that in the thirteenth-century romance of *Cristal et Clarie,* where a noble maiden, tormented by her passion for Cristal, begs him to give her his love on the grounds that they are of equal age and beauty (ed. Hermann Breuer, Gesellschaft für romanische Literatur, 36 [Dresden, 1915], ll. 1359–70). Her love is not returned because Cristal is bound by a prior commitment (ll. 1395–1402).

19. Excellent examples of this topos in texts that contain no full-blown portraits can be found in *Piramus et Tisbé,* ed. C. de Boer, CFMA, 26 (Paris: Champion, 1921), ll. 5–22, and in two romances of Gautier d'Arras, *Eracle,* ed. E. Löseth, Bibliothèque du Moyen Age, 6 (Paris, 1890), ll. 3614–43, and *Ille et Galeron,* ed. Frederick A. G. Cowper, SATF (Paris: Picard, 1956), ll. 568–74. The use of the topos to reinforce the narrative function of one or more portraits is well illustrated by the *Roman de Thèbes,* ed. Léopold Constans, SATF (Paris, 1890), ll. 3887–96; the *Lai de Narcisus,* ed. Alfons Hilka, in "Der altfranzösische Narcisuslai, eine antikisierende Dichtung des 12. Jahrhunderts," *Zeitschrift für romanische Philologie,* 49 (1929) 633–75, ll. 348–52; *Floire et Blancheflor,* ed. Felicitas Krüger, Romanische Studien, 45 (Berlin: E. Ebering, 1938), ll. 197–200; and by two romances of Chrétien de Troyes, *Erec et Enide,* ed. Mario Roques, CFMA, 80 (Paris: Champion, 1953), ll. 1462–96, and *Cligès,* ed. Alexandre Micha, CFMA, 84 (Paris: Champion, 1957), ll. 2706–20.

whom the Pucelle was compared were one-tenth as attractive as she (ll. 4344–50). As a result of Renaut's game-playing, the reader is fully conscious of the relative merits of the rivals. The Pucelle aux Blanches Mains should be declared the winner, but marriage to the runner-up would certainly be no misfortune.

After Guinglain wins Arthur's tournament, the king offers him the hand of Blonde Esmerée and demonstrates the desirability of the match in terms which constitute a one-sided version of the compatibility topos (ll. 6168–90). He praises her beauty, nobility, power, and wealth; he is even impractical enough to mention the princess' love for Guinglain; but there is never any reference to equality or mutuality. Arthur prefers to emphasize the fact that the hero will rise in status if he marries the future queen of Wales, even though it is obvious that his accomplishments have made him worthy of her. The frequently romanticized equality of the topos ill befits a *mariage de raison*.

Bound as he is by the structural laws of the *chanson*, Renaut can only offer Guinglain and the reader a sense of frustration as far as the present is concerned. But no such constraints apply to the future, and that future can be encoded in the text by a skilful writer who has mastered the grammar of expectations with which the experienced reader approaches a romance. Renaut is in no sense a novice, as some critics have supposed;[20] and there is every indication that his intended audience consists of persons familiar with a large number of *chansons*, romances, and *lais*. He does not underestimate the intelligence of the initiated reader; instead, he gives him the pleasure of deciding what ending would fulfill the promises of the truncated plot. Renaut's counters are all aligned on the game board, and it is the reader's turn to play.

What sort of fulfillment will Guinglain attain in the reader's imagination? It is clear that whether they marry or not, the hero and the fay will be permanently united by a bond of love. Marriage is certainly not out of the question, since Blonde Esmerée could step aside by taking the veil,[21] as does the first wife of Eliduc in Marie de France's *lai* of that

20. Gaston Paris, "Etudes sur les romans de la Table Ronde: *Guinglain ou le Bel Inconnu*," *Romania*, 15 (1886), 12; William Henry Schofield, *Studies on the Libeaus Desconus*, Harvard Studies in Philology and Literature, 4 (Boston: Ginn and Company, 1895), 108; Urban T. Holmes, "Renaut de Beaujeu," *Romanic Review*, 18 (1927), 334–36, and *A History of Old French Literature from the Origins to 1300*, 2nd ed. (New York: Russell and Russell, 1962), 178; and John L. Grigsby, "The Narrator in *Partonopeu de Blois*, *Le Bel Inconnu*, and *Joufroi de Poitiers*," *Romance Philology*, 21 (1967/68), 538.

21. Anthime Fourrier (*Le Courant réaliste dans le roman courtois en France au moyen âge*, vol. 1 : *Les Débuts [XIIᵉ siècle]* [Paris, 1960], 299–300) has demonstrated that this Merovingian practice was still tolerated by some churchmen in the twelfth century despite the fact that it was strictly forbidden by canon law.

name. An enduring illicit relationship is, however, more in harmony with the structural patterns of the poem. The results of the portrait contest indicate that Blonde Esmerée is an eminently worthy partner for Guinglain, so worthy, in fact, that one has difficulty imagining her complete disappearance from the hero's life. Renaut tells us nothing except that Guinglain became a king of very great renown (l. 6245) and that, in the proposed sequel, he will once more hold the fay in his arms (ll. 6256–58). What justification is there for devising a conclusion that is markedly different from the one sketched by the author himself? Let us not forget that the poet has already favored Guinglain and the Pucelle in an explicit comparison with Tristan and Isolt. Moreover, in the *Tristan* of Thomas, the hero does ultimately marry a certain Isolt of the White Hands, thus creating a second triangle involving two women rather than two men. Renaut is perhaps subtly avenging the second Isolt by giving the attractive rôle to his own Maid of the White Hands.

Many modern readers have expressed disapproval of the present dénouement, but without reaching any consensus regarding an appropriate bride or mistress for Guinglain. Some of them would prefer that the fay play a more limited rôle and that the hero love and marry the woman he set out to rescue at the beginning of the romance, since this sequence of events is more in harmony with the plot structure chosen by the later medieval German, English, and Italian writers who devoted romances to the same theme and who may have imitated Renaut himself and/or utilized his source.[22] Moreover, as Gaston Paris points out, marriage to Blonde Esmerée would be in keeping with the biographical romance tradition.[23] The majority of critics, however, would opt for some form of loving union between Guinglain and the Pucelle aux Blanches Mains, either because the true Celtic fay would not relinquish her hold on the mortal she loved[24] or simply because this ending is more satisfying, given the emphasis already placed on the fay and the need for a consistent presentation of the poet's idealized fictional world.[25]

22. Paris, "Etudes," 6, 12–14, 20–22; Max Kaluza, ed., *Libeaus Desconus,* Altenglische Bibliothek, 5 (Leipzig: O. R. Reisland, 1890), cxxxxii; Schofield, *Studies,* 40–42, 56–59, 106–10, 154–64, 197–99, 208–38; and Tyssens, "Les Sources," 1053–55. Schofield dissects the *Bel Inconnu* objectively without commenting on its literary value, but one has the distinct impression that Renaut's departures from the "purer" forms of the story are not looked upon with favor.

23. "Etudes," 6.

24. Emmanuel Philipot, review of Schofield's *Studies, Romania,* 26 (1897), 302–03, and Lucy Allen Paton, *Studies in the Fairy Mythology of Arthurian Romance,* Radcliffe College Monographs, 13 (Boston: Ginn and Company, 1903), 173–76. Paton criticizes by implication in the same manner as Schofield (see n. 22).

25. Holmes, *A History,* 178; Jauss, "Chanson de geste," 76–77; and Boiron and

This disagreement is highly illuminating, for it strongly suggests that both solutions are correct and that the reader can justifiably devise an ending that allows them to coexist. It is safe to assume, I think, that in the lyric poet's dream world of wish fulfillment, Guinglain possesses both a wife and a fairy mistress. He enjoys the challenge of earthly kingship and the honors it bestows on him without losing the opportunity to escape at times into a paradise of love where all responsibility is forgotten.

The lyric portion of Renaut's double ending can be viewed as a subtle criticism of the happiness portrayed in the typical romance or *lai*.[26] Most commonly, the hero enters into a *mariage d'amour* which does not deny him the material advantages of a *mariage de raison*. He assuredly derives far more joy from life than did the average nobleman; but marriage increases his moral, social, and political duties; and his wife, however much beloved, is not the wish-maiden of his dreams. Would a permanent, nonadulterous union with a fay solve this problem? For a time, perhaps; but, as a rule, young warriors grow weary of perpetual bliss and break away from a prison of love, no matter how idyllic it may be, in order to enjoy the challenge of adventure and combat. What was it, after all, that wrested Guinglain from his lady's arms if not the lure of tournaments? The third solution proposed by courtly narratives is an intense adulterous liaison. Since, however, the torments of such a relationship are at least equal to its spiritual glories, Renaut rejects this possibility in favor of his own *Tristan without Tragedy*.

At the close of the romance, Guinglain acquires a kingdom and a wife whom he finds attractive but does not love. In a lyric extension to the romance, he embraces his fairy mistress once more; and the reader, relying on the structure of the preceding narrative and the expressed

---

Payen, "Structure et sens," 25–26. Renaut's innovative conclusion "is unusual in the tradition of the *roman* in that it is unsatisfactory to poet and hero alike," according to Sara Sturm, "The Love-Interest in *Le Bel Inconnu*: Innovation in the *Roman Courtois*," *Forum for Modern Language Studies*, 7 (1971) 241–48.

26. Peter Haidu ("Realism," 56) maintains that Renaut is playing with the literary conventions of two discrete narrative genres, since a fairy mistress from the Celtic Other World is "the normal reward of the hero in a *lai*." Haidu's statement concerning the *lai* appears to be based on a misreading of Boiron and Payen, "Structure et sens," 21, and Jean Frappier, "Remarques sur la structure du lai: essai de définition et de classement," in *La Littérature narrative d'imagination* (Paris: 1961) 23–37. In reality, very few *lais* are of the fairy-mistress type; whereas a close look at the courtly tales of the late twelfth and early thirteenth centuries shows that fays and faylike women may bring happiness to the hero of either a *lai* or a romance. As for the *chanson*, Haidu limits its use to what I call the frame story.

hopes of the author, imagines that the hero will eventually obtain the best of this world and of the Other World, that he will, in fact, succeed in possessing both a wish-maiden and a wife. Like the lover on Keats' Grecian urn, Guinglain is "winning near the goal"; and the pleasure of imagined fulfillment awaits everyone who reads Renaut's text.[27]

27. The following study did not appear in time to be discussed in the body of this article: Alain Guerreau, "Renaud de Bâgè: *Le Bel Inconnu,* structure symbolique et signification sociale," *Romania,* 103 (1982), 28–82. Unlike Boiron and Payen (see n. 4), Guerreau is so pleased with the socio-political rightness of Guinglain's marriage and its effectiveness as an antidote to the temptations of knight errantry that he does not analyze the literary effect of the usual ending. He does, however, present convincing evidence (29–33) that the author of the romance was actually Renaud Bâgé, seigneur de Saint-Trivier (c. 1165–1230). *Biauju* (l. 6249) is probably a scribal error for *Baujieu* (alternate spelling: *Baugieu*), which can be posited as a plausible Franco-Provençal form of the place-name Bâgé around the year 1200.

JOSUÉ HARARI

# The Pleasures of Science and The Pains of Philosophy: Balzac's *Quest for the Absolute*

> Celui-là qui lève ce voile de plomb dont une puissance jalouse
> enveloppa le sanctuaire des causes premières, celui-là dompte la terre;
> il est le lion pour la force, le cerf pour la vitesse, la mine d'or elle-
> même pour la richesse, le maître des rois dont il dédaigne les
> sceptres, et marche égal au destin. Que n'est-il immortel, il serait
> Dieu.
>
> —Falthurne

*La Recherche de l'Absolu* belongs to the group of narratives Balzac published under the heading *Etudes Philosophiques*. But the reference to "philosophy" provides only an extremely vague criterion to link texts such as *La Recherche de l'Absolu*, *Le Chef-d'oeuvre inconnu*, *Gambara*, *Massimila Doni*, *Louis Lambert*, etc. For while common denominators among these texts can be recognized, the connections seem, at first glance, unrelated to a "philosophical" context or content. Unless, of course, one argues that any study entirely governed by the operation of an Idea should be labeled as philosophic—and then what novel of Balzac would not fall under this heading? Short of that, what are the common denominators which establish the particularity of the *Etudes Philosophiques*?

The most visible common denominator is that all the main characters of the *Etudes* are "mad" creators whose works are never completed, but left in ruins by death or "madness." A second characteristic that differentiates the *Etudes* from the main body of the *Comédie Humaine* is the nature of the ambition at stake. As throughout the *Comédie*, ambition obsesses each hero and is relentlessly pursued, but its means and goals change radically. As Marthe Robert puts it:

> Indeed, there the ambitious man is no longer the calculating man, the disillusioned and informed realist, the careerist initiated into the mysteries of the social workings, who knows how to hone his weapons while awaiting his hour of success; he is rather the seeker of an abso-

135

lute, the contemplative solitary whose spirit demands the possession of a non-divisible truth encompassing the One and All.[1]

Robert hastens to add that one must distinguish between authentic seekers of the Absolute such as Louis Lambert ("The only one who merits such an imposing title") and the fakes, such as Balthazar Claës:

> The novel entitled *The Quest for the Absolute* proves how little import it is necessary to accord to Balzac's rubrics as principles of classification, for in spite of the archaic oddness of his speculations, Balthazar Claes remains a Bastard true to the type: his Absolute is nothing but a collection of alembics and retorts with nothing more spiritual about it than the ordinary affairs of the other parvenus.[2]

This is an important point to which I will return.

Another parallel links the seekers of the Absolute in the *Etudes:* each moves in a sphere beyond that of the common man, the sphere of thought, and in that realm thought overflows the technical means available to these creators and in the end ruins their works. This is the well-known Balzacian theme of thought that kills. Thus thought—"The great solvent of the human species"[3]—kills the thinker in *Louis Lambert,* art kills painting in *Le Chef-d'Oeuvre inconnu,* the idea of science kills science in *La Recherche.* Claës, Frenhofer, and Gambara burst out of science, art, and music, respectively, just as Raphaël in *La Peau de chagrin,* in the words of Ramon Fernandez, "bursts out of life."

A final common denominator among the seekers of the Absolute is that they do not "return." The *Comédie Humaine* was born the day Balzac came up with the idea of systematically applying the principle of the reappearance of characters:

> A great step has recently been made. When they saw some of the already-created characters reappear in the *Père Goriot,* the public un-

1. *Roman des origines et origines du roman* (Paris: Grasset, 1972), 277. Except where otherwise noted, all translations are my own.
2. *Ibid.*
3. The thesis concerning the destructive nature of thought was neither new nor rare at Balzac's time. As early as the second half of the eighteenth century on, Tissot had demonstrated in *De la Santé des gens de lettres* the dangers that sanity runs by risking outlandish expenditures of cerebral energy. With the work of Brunaud (*De l'hygiène des gens de lettres,* 1819), Georget (*De la physiologie du système nerveux et spécialement du cerveau,* 1821), Broussais (*Traité de physiologie appliquée à la pathologie,* 1821) and Réveillé-Parise (*Physiologie et Hygiène des hommes livrés aux travaux de l'esprit,* 1834), the idea that overly intense intellectual activity has dire effects had become commonplace in nineteenth-century pathology. On this subject, see Moïse Le Yaouanc, *Nosographie de l'humanité balzacienne* (Paris: Librairie Maloin, 1959), 27–61.

derstood one of the most daring of the author's intentions, which was that of giving life and movement to an entire fictional world within which characters will subsist. . .[4]

Thus Rastignac reappears twenty-five times, Bianchon twenty-eight, Frederic Nucingen thirty-one, Vautrin six, etc.[5] The reader of the *Comédie Humaine* is always on familiar ground because he continually meets characters he has already met elsewhere. But the same reader will not recognize Claës, Gambara, Frenhofer, or the other creators of the *Etudes Philosophiques* because not one of them makes the comeback list. If the "return" is Balzac's stroke of genius, the genius himself, ironically, is excluded from the characteristic mode of existence of Balzacian society.

One could argue that this is because Balzac in his analyses of great creators in the *Etudes* is taking up the romantic theme of the incompatibility between the spiritual nature of the genius and ordinary society.[6] But the emphasis Balzac puts on warning us about both the excess of genius and the madness of the creator (because for Balzac madness is always a tendency to push thought beyond itself, a sort of excess of genius which overwhelms genius itself) nonetheless requires explanation. Ramon Fernandez was the first to point out how peculiar it is that Balzac "reserved for his *Etudes Philosophiques* the clinical analyses of genius which make up its pathology"[7]—all the more so since Balzac also produced a number of successful geniuses (Bianchon, Savarus, etc.) in the *Comédie Humaine*. In that case, why do the *Etudes* only present failed geniuses, geniuses who seem to constitute the pathological anatomy of the *Comédie Humaine*, "mad" creators who are systematically characterized by "an abnormal dilation of the mind"?

Establishing a phenomenology of the genius or madman in Balzac would no doubt clarify how he conceives the nature of the faculties of intellectual consciousness. From it one could draw a sort of topology or economy of the human brain. But it would not enlighten us as to the

---

4. Félix Davin, *Introduction aux "Etudes de Moeurs au XIXᵉ siècle"* in Balzac, *Oeuvres complètes* (Paris: Pléiade, édition Castex), 1, 1160. Published in 1835, this text—signed F. Davin—was inspired and later revised by Balzac himself.

5. Fernand Lotte counts 573 characters who reappear in *La Comédie Humaine*, of whom at least 211 are in four novels and 58 in ten novels. See his "Le Retour des personnages dans *La Comédie Humaine*" in *L'Année balzacienne*, (1961), 233.

6. "Indeed, men seem to have more respect for vice than for genius, for they refuse to believe in the latter. It would seem that the beneficial results of the secret toil of the scholar are so distant that society is afraid to reckon with him in his lifetime. . ." *The Quest of the Absolute* (Philadelphia: George Barrie and Son, 1899), 29. All further references to *La Recherche* will be to this translation and will appear in the body of the text.

7. *Balzac ou l'envers de la création romanesque* (Paris: Grasset, 1980), 89.

*reasons* for which the dynamics of genius are of a fundamentally excessive and abnormal nature in the *Etudes*. I believe the above questions must be redirected not towards the mad creators but towards the object they are seeking. In other words, what kind of knowledge does Balthazar seek when he pushes the principle of chemistry to the extreme? Or Frenhofer the artistic principle? Or Gambara the musical principle? Or Louis Lambert the philosophic? What kind of knowledge does creative thought seek that causes it always to end up as abnormal thought? Or, to ask the question in a more controversial way, why in Balzac does research that is "philosophical" (in the broad sense of the word) always denote an unsatisfactory state of mental health? *La Recherche de l'Absolu* yields at least the beginnings of an answer to these questions.

## I. GENESIS

On a first level, *La Recherche* offers an image of the scientist seen throughout the literature of the nineteenth century. But once the novel has been read, the reader realizes that it is less a question of science in the text than of problems concerning the family relations of the Claës among themselves and with the world. For every page on which science is a subject of discussion, we read twenty pages about inheritances and judicial comings-of-age, wasted fortunes and their financial ramifications, notarized acts and contracts between father and children, and so forth. In short, *La Recherche*, which explicitly presents itself as the story of knowledge and science—we will discuss subsequently the genuine scientific component of the novel—in fact proposes an exhaustive analysis of the social and familial relations of the Claës, and thus turns out to be yet another study of manners. Why then does Balzac attempt to give the impression that something else is at stake?

One explanation comes immediately to mind. In the beginning, the novel *Les Jeunes Gens*, the first sketch of *La Recherche*, was intended precisely as a *Scène de la vie privée* that would analyze the family disturbances caused by a father who is a great creator entirely caught up in his search for the Absolute. The original edition of *La Recherche* repeats fairly clearly the outline of *Les Jeunes Gens*.[8] The central themes—death of the mother, inadequacies of the father, struggle between daughter and father—remain sufficiently intact to allow the conclusion that although the title of the novel changes, the family drama

8. See on this topic the discussion in the Pléiade documentation to *La Recherche de l'Absolu* (Paris: Pléiade, édition Castex) 10, 1566–69.

proceeds as before. Beyond this fact, and unlike the other novels of the *Comédie Humaine*, little is known about the conception of *La Recherche de l'Absolu*. In her monumental thesis on *La Recherche*, Madeleine Fargeaud shows that in its genesis there are no false starts, no rewritings, no intermissions in the process of writing. The title *La Recherche de l'Absolu* appears for the first time on July 1, 1834, and the manuscript is complete eight weeks later.[9] The mystery surrounding the birth of *La Recherche* deepens when one adds that it is a freestanding work where no other characters from the *Comédie* enter, that it is the only work of the *Comédie* with a scientist as the central character, and the only one set in Flanders. As Fargeaud summarizes, *"La Recherche de l'Absolu*, a Flemish and scientific accident in the *Comédie Humaine* is, at the same time, not the most Balzacian of the author's creations."[10] However, the combination of chemistry and Flanders is not as accidental as Fargeaud implies; in fact, this conjunction will help us to reconstitute the project of Balthazar Claës.

Curiously, as far as the narrative is concerned, Balthazar's research is much less visible than are the disastrous results it provokes. Balthazar Claës does make a number of important discoveries, but all of them are left behind, brushed aside so that he may go beyond them. The text leaves no room for doubt about the reality of these discoveries:

> In August, 1813, about a year after this narrative begins, although Claes had made some fine experiments, upon which, unfortunately, he looked with contempt, his efforts had been unsuccessful so far as the principal object of his investigations was concerned. [131]

Whereas Balthazar pays no attention to his experiments and thus nullifies his scientific work through disinterest, by contrast his destruction of a number of other things is quite real and active. At the simplest level he squanders several fortunes; six, according to the townfolk (298). He destroys money—"his mania had devoured about seven million without results" (295), specifies Pierquin the notary—and diamonds, gold, and silver plate, all of which his research turns into smoke (69). He also "destroys" the work of other creators, paintings by Rubens, van Dyck, Rembrandt, Titian, Murillo, "all authentic and of the first importance," whose collection for the Claës gallery was the fruit of "three centuries of patient research" (48). And finally even the pride of the Claës house-

9. Madeleine Fargeaud, *Balzac et "La Recherche de l'Absolu"* (Paris: Hachette, 1968), 21. Fargeaud's documentation regarding *La Recherche* is outstanding; much of our own work would not have been possible without her source work.

10. Ibid., 22.

hold, the unique wood panels "considered Van Huysium's greatest work" (18), are sold.

But Balthazar does not just destroy material goods; on a second level he destroys the social network in which his family is inscribed. Conjugal love undergoes the ravages of the Absolute. His wife Pépita recalls to him on her deathbed that she is the victim of his quest:

> You men of science drain the soil around you as great trees do! I, a poor, feeble plant, could not rise high enough, I expire half-way up your life. . . . Spare, spare our children! May these words echo in your heart! [169]

But her warning plea is effective only for a brief instant, as Balthazar will quickly forget his paternal obligations in the face of the fury for the Absolute, at the family's peril and expense.

Balthazar's scientific work thus destroys a whole set of riches and social relations, but these disastrous results do not account for the research itself. The nature and object of Balthazar's "Quest" have yet to be specified.

## II. THE SECRET

A first set of characteristics: the man seeking the Absolute buys an immense quantity of chemical products. Balthazar has test tubes, retorts, siphons, batteries, and many specialized instruments, all used for his research. He takes advantage of the reports sent to him by the Parisian chemical supply house, Protez and Chiffreville, who "frequently communicated the results obtained by chemists in Paris, in order to save him unnecessary expense" (64). But the contents of these reports, which might clear up part of the mystery of Balthazar's work, are not discussed or communicated to the reader. Never does Balthazar explain of what his experiments consist; not in terms of chemical reactions, nor of experimental conditions, nor of his understanding of scientific instrumentation, never, in sum, in terms of technical givens or scientific theories on the basis of which we might understand the failure or success of his research. There is no equivalent of the kind of theoretical discussion, for example, Frenhofer holds on the subjects of perspective, light, unity of composition, when presenting his conception of painting in *Le Chef d'Oeuvre inconnu.* In fact, for a man of science and a would-be chemist, Balthazar speaks about chemistry very little in the novel—three times, to be precise.

The first time he speaks of chemistry, Balthazar only recounts to his wife what the Polish gentleman Adam de Wierzchownia taught him about chemistry, a passage to which we will return in a different context. The second time, when he tries to explain to his daughter his latest experiment in order to obtain money from her, Balthazar is almost immediately interrupted by Marguerite and the discussion is aborted when she accuses him of irresponsibility ("I shall have the strength to combat your madness" [215]); and he, furious, hurls insults at her. The third time, Balthazar, more in need of money than ever, speaks to Marguerite to explain to her the latest, and last, experiment he has thought up, after which, says he, "nothing more will be possible. If I do not find it this time, I must abandon the search for the Absolute" (224). But the narrative is cut off when he realizes he cannot establish any kind of scientific communication with his daughter: " 'If you knew all that is at stake, you would not use such words with me. Listen, I will explain the problem to you . . . but you would not understand me!' he cried in despair" (231). Since Balthazar's interlocutor, whether wife, daughter, or valet, is always on a lower level in the hierarchy of scientific knowledge, no transmission of information can take place.[11] Structurally speaking, Balthazar is thus never granted the opportunity to articulate the details of his research.

A second characteristic of the secret surrounding this research concerns the laboratory. Given how meticulous Balzac's descriptions usually are, the absence of any description of the laboratory is astonishing. The parlor especially, but the other rooms in the Claës house as well, are minutely described in La Recherche, but the laboratory, the focal room for the narrative, is hardly described at all. What is more, although it is the room in which nearly all the scientific research takes place, it is surprising to see how seldom the protagonists of the drama, and the reader as well, ever enter it. Aside from Balthazar and Le Mulquinier, no one really enters the laboratory. Pépita decides only once to try her luck at penetrating the secrets of her rival, science, so well protected by the laboratory: "She was determined to insinuate herself secretly into that mysterious workshop of seduction, and to acquire the right to remain there always. . . . She had hardly opened the door, when he [Balthazar] rushed at her, seized her, and pushed her roughly back into the hall, where she nearly fell from top to bottom of the stairs" (59–70). The scene concludes with Balthazar's apologies and his firm reminder to his

11. Cf. on this point Madeleine Ambrière, "Balzac Homme de Science(s)" in Balzac. L'Invention du roman (Paris: Belfond, 1982), 52.

wife of his strict orders forbidding her from interrupting his work in the laboratory.

Marguerite, in turn, will visit the scientific sanctuary, but Balzac's description of this scene focuses less on the laboratory than on one machine, and above all, on the fantastic effect that the vision of Balthazar, engulfed in gases and fumes, has on Marguerite:

> As she entered, she saw her father in the center of an enormous room, brightly lighted, filled with machines and dusty implements. . . . That aggregation of retorts, crucibles, metals, fantastically colored crystals, specimens hanging on the walls or tossed upon the furnaces, was dominated by the figure of Balthazar Claes. . . . His eyes were fastened in a ghastly stare upon a pneumatic machine. The receiver of the machine was capped by a lens formed by double convex glasses, the space between them being filled with alcohol; and in that lens were concentrated the rays of the sun which entered the room through one portion of the rose-window of the garret. The receiver, the disc of which was insulated, was connected with the wires of an immense Voltaic battery. . . .
>
> The sight of her father, who, as he almost knelt by his machine, received the sun's rays full upon his face, and whose sparse locks resembled silver threads . . . contributed to make a deep impression on Marguerite, who said to herself in dire dismay: "My father is mad!" [212–13]

Near the end of the novel, Balzac again describes the pneumatic machine, from a little closer up. We do not really see the laboratory, but Balthazar makes a few gestures indicating the subject of the experiment he is working on and expressing in a fragmentary way his thoughts about the crystallization of carbon before he recalls his promise to Marguerite to abandon chemistry and leaves the laboratory for his exile in Brittany:

> Here is a combination of carbon and sulphur . . . in which the carbon plays the part of electro-positive element; crystallization must begin at the negative pole; and in case of decomposition, the carbon would tend thither in a crystallized form. . . . Rest and time are conditions essential to crystallization! . . . We must look out for that . . . it is possible. . . . But what am I thinking about? We have nothing more to do with chemistry, my good fellow, we are going to collect taxes in Brittany. [254–55]

Without a doubt this is the only occasion in *La Recherche* when we are given a chance to guess what Balthazar's research is, at least on the experimental level. We know that at the time Balzac was writing his novel, a number of chemists had been working for several years on the problem of liquefying carbonic acid gas (carbon dioxide). These chemists hoped pure liquid carbonic acid might dissolve carbon, thus yielding, under the right conditions, crystallized carbon—diamonds. Whatever the further implications might be, it seems clear that it is this sort of experiment with diamonds that Balzac attributes to Balthazar Claës.

Third characteristic of Balthazar's secret: unlike most of the other tales in the *Etudes Philosophiques*, *La Recherche* contains no scene of a decisive test, no final confrontation where the work of the hero is judged. Frenhofer reveals the secret of his painting to Poussin, and Gambara plays his celestial music to a packed house, but this moment never happens for Balthazar. And this despite the fact that the text tells us clearly, and more than once, that the scientist's research lies at the heart, or rather the head, of the chemical discoveries of the time: "Science had progressed. Claës found that progress in chemistry had tended, unknown to the chemists themselves, in the direction of the object of his investigations. Men who had devoted themselves to the higher problems of science believed as he did that light, heat, electricity, galvanism, and magnetism were different effects of one and the same cause" (194). One might expect that the connection with Protez and Chiffreville, or simply Balthazar's reputation as a scientist (or even as a mad scientist), would lead a Parisian or European scientist to try to meet Balthazar to discuss the present state of his research, his past experiments, the results he obtained, and so forth. However, no chemist ever shows up to disturb or evaluate the science of Claës from the outside. Only at the very end of the novel is there a scene where the beginning of a confrontation that could become a decisive test happens. Very excited, Balthazar wants to say something—his eyes, the text tells us, project his thoughts —but his paralysis prevents him from speaking. His son-in-law, Emmanuel de Solis, tries to calm him in what has become the usual manner, by reading him the morning newspaper:

> As he unfolded the paper Emmanuel saw the words: *Discovery of the Absolute*, which startled him, and he read to Marguerite an article concerning a lawsuit relative to the sale of the Absolute, by a celebrated Polish mathematician. Though Emmanuel read the heading in a low voice to Marguerite, who requested him to omit the article, Balthazar overheard him.
>
> Suddenly the dying man raised himself on his hands, cast upon his terrified children a glance that blinded them like a flash of lightning . . . he raised one hand, clenched in fury, and cried in a voice of thunder the famous word of Archimedes: EUREKA!—I have found!—

He fell back upon his bed with the dull thud of a lifeless body; he died uttering a ghastly groan. . . [305–06]

Thus Balthazar takes his secret with him to the grave, without ever giving us the chance to find out if this secret was in the end a real discovery—the discovery of the Absolute—or just the manifestation of the scientist's madness.

The problem to be solved is then the following: why is this research, so enigmatic and so devastating, never explained in the novel? It is hidden so thoroughly that by the end of the novel we almost wonder if Balthazar Claës is not simply a first-class fraud and *La Recherche* really a joke on Balzac's part. For after all, what the Absolute represents, what it means, what it is, what Balthazar's research is—all these points, seemingly essential for understanding the novel, are never explained. After the first fortune has disappeared, Mme Claës wonders, "But what was he seeking?" (65). And after the death of her mother, when three more fortunes have been swallowed up, Marguerite asks herself the same question: "Great Heaven! What is he seeking?" (222). A few months later she has gotten no further in discovering the object of this research that, for lack of better terms, she speaks of as "the unknown (X)" (237). But the most unsettling thing for us, the readers of the novel, is that our only chance to understand the nature of this Absolute which destroys everything but is never really defined in the narrative, resides in our duplication of the deciphering process attempted by Marguerite and Pépita.[12] Fortunately, and in spite of the narrative's insistent silence, three different hypotheses about the nature of the Absolute can be advanced.

## III. HOW MANY ABSOLUTES?

*The Alchemical Absolute*
Despite Sainte-Beuve's suggestion, in an article on *La Recherche*,[13] that Balzac had drawn his entire idea from a tale published three years earlier under the title *Hermès dévoilé*, which featured an alchemist named Cyliani, Balthazar cannot be considered an alchemist in the traditional sense of the word. Even allowing for Balzac's well-known habit of creat-

---

12. Balzac's use of "point of view" permits and reinforces the secrecy surrounding Balthazar's project. Although Balthazar is the central character in the plot, in the *narration* he is not; the reader's view thus remains restricted first to that of Pépita, and then to Marguerite's point of view.

13. *Revue des Deux Mondes*, 15 November 1834.

ing stories out of ideas and events he came across by accident, the superficial narrative similarities between Cyliani's story and that of Balthazar are not sufficient in themselves to qualify the latter's quest as an alchemical one. Nor is Gaston Bachelard's equation of unconscious scientific imagination with frustrated erotic desire any more convincing when it is used to associate Balthazar's quest with the alchemist's search for the philosopher's stone.[14]

Where Sainte-Beuve's thematic approach led him to make a vulgar equivalence between two narratives with the same subject, Bachelard's psychoanalysis poses the stakes correctly (the relation of science and sexuality) but, as is typical of all "wild" psychoanalysis, he gives a doubly false interpretation. Firstly, Balthazar is as little an alchemist as Pépita is sexually unattractive, disgraced or unapproachable. One has to read only a few pages of La Recherche to realize the seductive powers of Pépita—"The Spanish blood did its perfect work in the granddaughter of the Casa-Reals, and made the science of varying pleasure ad infinitum instinctive in her. . . . Her Spanish eyes were bewitchingly beautiful when she saw that he considered her lovely in négligée attire" (38, 42). Balthazar, it might be added, seems to do very well under his wife's "care." Secondly, the phenomena of displacement and sublimation from the wife to science that Bachelard diagnoses are not particular to Balthazar; it is a trait that he shares with all of the Balzacian monomaniacs. Moreover, what Bachelard does not say is that these phenomena are totally unrelated to a Balzacian psychology of the scientific unconscious. They are the direct expression of Balzac's conception of the organism as composed of a fixed sum of energy whose concentration into one unique point brings about a disruption of the equilibrium of the human machine. This conception of the organism, in which body and thought are one, takes the form of a psycho-physiological determinism that affects all Balzacian characters.[15] Whence the fact that if thought absorbs the whole of the vital energy available, it affects and ultimately

14. See the chapter entitled "Libido et connaissance objective" in Bachelard's La Formation de l'esprit scientifique (Paris: Vrin, 1967), especially 185–187: "One cannot ponder a mystery, an enigma or a chimeric enterprise for long without sexualizing, in a more or less veiled manner, its principle and vicissitudes. . . . As we see, it is the complaint of the unhappily married man. He is easy to imagine in the guise of the scientist who abandons his hearth for his laboratory and who goes seeking in the 'beauties of science' ecstasies his disgraced wife prohibits him. One finds here a valid explanation for Balzac's Quest for the Absolute."

15. As Lucienne Frappier-Mazur puts it: "Monomania . . . shows up as a transfer of energy . . . which gives intellectual sublimation priority over conjugal love" in L'Expression métaphorique dans "La Comédie Humaine" (Paris: Klincksieck, 1976), 238–39.

annuls the functioning of all other organs. This would explain, for example, why in *La Recherche* Balthazar's head reaches gigantic proportions while his other organ(s) shrivel away—"the lower portions of his body were slender" (26).

As for Balthazar's explicitly alchemical side, to be sure he does speak of making diamonds and enriching his family, and continually reminds Pépita and Marguerite, when they complain, that he is working "for the glory and fortune of his family" (64). But in fact all his promises "of wealth and jewels" (225) are nothing more than a way to excuse himself to his family. When Pépita announces the first of their numerous bankruptcies, Balthazar smiles fondly at her and declares, "But, my angel, tomorrow it may be that our fortune will be without bounds," and goes on with a formulation that deserves emphasis: "Yesterday, while in search of *much more important secrets*, I believe that I discovered a means of crystallizing carbon, which is the substance of the diamond" (76). That is to say that alchemy, making diamonds (one of the clues we had traced earlier), is of secondary importance to Balthazar. What he seeks is something entirely different. Misinformed neighbors and the town gossips share Bachelard's misreading and think Balthazar seeks the philosopher's stone. But they are the exception, and the majority of intelligent people, those who know something of chemistry, such as Emmanuel, do not hesitate to recognize the genuinely scientific nature of the scientist's research: "Unfortunately, my dear Marguerite, although, as the head of a family, he is doing wrong, from a scientific standpoint he is doing right, and a score of men in Europe will admire him while everybody else calls him mad" (222). This remark of Emmanuel switches our focus on Balthazar's research from alchemy to the scientific assumptions and experiments of his time.[16]

*The Scientific Absolute*

Balthazar Claës is a traditional chemist of his period, the beginning of the nineteenth century. In his youth he frequented the circle of scientists around Lavoisier becoming "his most enthusiastic disciple" (33). Note that at that time, despite Lavoisier's praise for Balthazar's work, chemistry had no sinister effect on the young man, who indeed neglected it in favor of the beautiful women of Paris. However, Balthazar

16. If one is to understand the implication of Emmanuel's remark, Balthazar is in fact at the crossroad between alchemy and chemistry. In so placing him Balzac inserts a magical tradition into a positive discipline: Balthazar's brand of transcendent chemistry thus represents an attempt to explain *scientifically* the problems that were raised earlier by the practitioners of the occult sciences. Bachelard missed this aspect altogether.

always maintained an interest in chemistry, since he kept a library which contained, among other scientific books, those which Pépita Claës reads in her attempt to understand her husband's work: "I have read Fourcroy, Lavoisier, Chaptal, Nollet, Rouelle, Berthollet, Gay-Lussac, Spallanzani, Leuwenhoëk, Galvani, Volta, in a word, all the books relating to the science you adore" (77).[17] And as we noted, Balthazar does make important chemical discoveries, even if he ignores them in seeking something else: he has combined chlorine and nitrogen, decomposed certain metals, and when his wife begins to cry, the only thing he can think of to comfort her is to tell her of his successful decomposition of tears. How, then, should one translate Balthazar's involvement with chemistry?

As regards this science, Balthazar duplicates quite exactly the experiments of the chemists of his time. The combination of chlorine and nitrogen was an experiment successfully performed by Pierre-Louis Dulong in 1812, while the analysis of tears refers to the famous experiment of Fourcroy and Vauquelin in 1790. By the same token, the only two experiments actually described in *La Recherche de l'Absolu*—the one with the pneumatic machine Balthazar hopes to use to reduce metals, and the one that brings about the combustion of a diamond—repeat earlier work by Lavoisier and Guyton de Morveau in France and Humphry Davy in England. Even the pneumatic machine described in the laboratory had just been invented by the chemist Adrien Thilorier, who received the Academy of Science prize in mechanics in 1832 for his machine to liquefy gases. Thus Balthazar carries out true classical chemical experiments and Balzac is probably not exaggerating when he writes to Mme Hanska, "Two members of the Académie des Sciences taught me chemistry in order to keep the book scientifically true. They made me alter proofs ten to twelve times."[18] Moreover, when Balthazar tells Pépita how he was introduced to the problem of his research, he situates it in the way that Adam de Wierzchownia left it to him, and this problem is indeed the classical problem of the chemistry of his time:

Chemistry divides creation into two distinct portions: organic and in-

17. Nollet and Rouelle belong to the phlogistonist camp; Lavoisier, Fourcroy and Chaptal to the New French Chemistry (anti-phlogistonist); Berthollet and Gay-Lussac to the current constituted by Reaction-Chemistry. Spallanzani and Leuwenhoëk, however, were biologists who studied protozoa and blood globules. Both Galvani and Volta who discovered respectively electric current and the Voltaic pile also worked on the physiology of muscles. This list of the great names of chemistry poses a problem to which we will return when we discuss the experiment of the watercress seed.

18. *Lettres à Madame Hanska* (18 Octobre 1834), quoted in the "Introduction" to *La Recherche*, op. cit., 10, 628.

organic nature. . . . Now, analysis has reduced all the products of organic nature to four elementary substances: three gases, nitrogen, hydrogen, and oxygen; and another non-metallic solid substance, carbon. Inorganic nature, on the contrary, which varies so little . . . includes fifty-three elementary substances, whose different combinations form all its products. Is it probable that the elements are more numerous where fewer results are produced? [101]

The argument of M. de Wierzchownia-Balthazar can readily be followed. It consists in reasoning that if living things, so complex and varied, can be reduced to four elements, then inanimate substances, much less complex, ought to be reducible to a number of elements as small if not smaller:

My former master's opinion, therefore, was that those fifty-three substances have a common basic principle, originally modified by the action of a power which has ceased to exist today, but which human genius should be able to re-establish. [102]

Wierzchownia is formulating here the hypothesis of a "unitary chemistry" which was an important force for the philosopher-chemists at the beginning of the century.[19]

But Balthazar also seeks to resolve a number of other scientific questions that the text only suggests. He tells us that his Polish "initiator," convinced of his ability to explain "the supreme secret of all the effects produced by nature" (104), had told him of the following experiment:

Plant the seeds of some organic substance, water-cress, for instance, in some inorganic substance, say sulphur. Water the seeds with distilled water, in order that no substance of which we know nothing may find its way into the product of the germination. The seeds sprout and grow in a soil of which we know the composition, feeding only upon substances known to us by analysis. Cut the stalks of the plants several times, in order to procure a sufficiently large quantity to produce several drachms of ashes when burned, so that you will have an appreciable bulk to operate upon: well, upon analyzing the ashes, you will find silicic acid, aluminum, calcium, phosphate, and carbonate, magnesium carbonate, sulphate and carbonate of potash and oxide of iron. . . .

19. Humphry Davy in his *Elements of Chemical Philosophy* (translated into French in 1813) and, a few years later, William Prout, had both suggested that hydrogen might be the common base of all the elements. This conception of simple substances as formed by the condensation of a single element, such as hydrogen, is picked up by Balthazar when he explains to Pépita the process of decomposing metals by gasification (133).

Now, these substances do not exist in the sulphur, an elementary substance, which served as soil for the plant, nor in the water used to water it, the composition of which is perfectly well known; but, as they do not exist in the seeds either, we cannot explain their presence in the plant except by supposing an element common to the substances contained in the water-cress and to those in which it has grown. [103]

This experiment poses the following problem: how can a simple substance such as sulfur be transformed into a substance composed of several elements? How can the life present in a watercress seed cause pure sulfur to be diversified into substances as varied as those contained in the watercress plant, as shown in analyzing its ashes? But the problem of how an organic, living substance can arise from a homogeneous and unique simple substance, and produce elements of a different nature, is a problem of a *different order*. Lamarck had proclaimed in 1802 that the things that animals and plants have in common should constitute the domain of a new science to be called biology. Soon thereafter, biology had already come to mean that science which concerned itself with the totality of vital phenomena including botany, zoology and physiology. In this context, posing the problem of the unity of nature and its capacity for diversification—in other words, wondering whether at the origin of all living things there is a single unique substance that diversifies itself, through time and history, to produce plants, animals, and sentient beings—is no longer a problem of chemistry, but one that rightfully belongs in the realm of biology. One might almost have thought that the names of the biologists Leuwenhoëk and Spallanzani had slipped inadvertently into the chemistry reading list that Mme Claës consulted to learn her husband's science. But now we see that the "error" is willful, as is confirmed by the fact that the question pertaining to the biological unity of nature is at the heart of the chemical experiments of *La Recherche de l'Absolu*. And M. de Wierzchownia is perfectly aware of this (as is Balthazar), because he continues his discussion of the watercress seed to draw identical conclusions about the silkworm and even, he says, "of man himself, who often has legitimate children entirely unlike their mother and himself" (105).

The real history of the watercress experiment is especially enlightening regarding the displacement of the problematic of Balthazar's research from chemistry to biology. Balzac copied the text of this experiment virtually word for word out of the second volume of Berzélius's *Traité de Chimie*. But the conclusions he draws from it come from his reading of the three volumes of *La Physiologie Végétale ou exposition des forces et des fonctions vitales des végétaux* (1832) of the Genevan botanist Pyrame de Candolle. Discussing nutrition, reproduction, and the influence of external agents on plants, Candolle had put forth a theory of a single principle capable of producing the great variety of plants in vegetable physiology. The same idea of a single principle and the interrelation of natural beings appears in his earlier work *Théorie élémentaire de la botanique* (1813), where he affirms that all individuals born of the same seeds are not absolutely alike among themselves.[20] Balzac passes over the conclusions of Berzélius about the watercress seed experiment when he borrows his account of it, because Berzélius for his part was quite careful not to postulate a "common principle" for all the effects of nature. On the contrary, Berzélius had stated some scientific reservations about the experiment, recalling that a hypothesis is not a demonstrated truth, and at the most he had timidly hypothesized "common elements" in the various substances found in the ashes.[21] But Balzac chooses to graft the unitary conclusions of the naturalist philosopher Candolle onto Berzélius's experiments, for they then permit M. de Wierzchownia to conclude that creation is a function of a biological absolute: "From that infallible experiment, I deduced the existence of the *Absolute!* A substance common to all created things, modified by a single force, such is the precise and clear statement of the problem presented by the Absolute, a problem which seemed to me *capable of solution*" (103–04).[22] Recalling here that the biological argument of the unity versus the diversity of nature was conceptualized and debated by early nineteenth-century scientists less as a scientific and more as a philosophic problem leads us to our third hypothesis about the Absolute.

*The Philosophical Absolute*
What does Balthazar gain from his multiple speculations about unitary chemistry and his dream of the biological unity of matter? He aims to

20. Quoted by Fargeaud, op. cit., 190; see also the Pléiade documentation, op. cit., 10, 1636.

21. "I believe that one could be led to conjecture here that the different bodies found in the ashes, that is potassium, calx, magnesium, aluminum, ferric oxide, silicic acid, sulfuric acid, and phosphoric acid, *are composed of elements that are common to all of them*" Traité de Chimie, 2, 269, quoted in Fargeaud, op. cit., 308.

22. This statement calls to mind the important reflection in the "Avant propos de la *Comédie Humaine*," in which Balzac declares that "the Creator used a single pattern for all organized beings," *Oeuvres Complètes*, op. cit., Pléiade, 1, 8. Thus Balzac, also, is haunted by his character's dream. Where Balthazar attempts to define scientifically the substance of everything, Balzac's own enterprise is a kind of quest for the Absolute in which every aspect of life must be reduced in the *Comédie Humaine* to a single principle that can explain all of the *Comédie's* fictional humanity.

resolve *scientifically* all the questions he asks of chemistry and of biology, but nonetheless the deeper meaning of these questions still always seems to lie elsewhere. It is the *leitmotif* we find in Balthazar's regular formulation, "In searching for *much more important secrets,* I made such and such a scientific discovery," and in the single question on the lips of all the other protagonists, "What is he seeking?" If Claës neglects the scientific import of his discoveries, seeking to go beyond them, and subordinates his research to a hypothesis that is never openly spelled out, we can only conclude that this hypothesis—the Absolute, or the system of the Absolute—even if it is, or tries to be, based on experimental discoveries, is not fundamentally a scientific hypothesis, but a hypothesis of a different order. That is, the scientific hypothesis of the unity of matter and its diversification is subordinated to the philosophical hypothesis concerning the relationship between man and the act of creation. In Balzac's series of "Questions intéressantes pour les connaissances humaines," this aspect of the problem confronting Balzac is raised:

> What would be the way to substitute for the words of Metaphysics a language of conventional and simple signs which might, *as in the exact sciences,* prevent errors from slipping in and which, by making it proceed from demonstrated propositions to propositions still to be resolved, from truth to truth, would give it the possibility of reaching the most unknown things and of tearing aside the last veil of nature?[23]

This "scientific" knowledge which will deliver up nature's secret is, to be sure, knowledge relative to the act of creation: that is Balthazar's objective. His language is that of experimentation but his quest is entirely in the philosophic realm. What he truly seeks is a way to place himself at the point where, on the one hand, all the diversity of nature is reduced to a single substance and, on the other hand, from which he might reproduce living organisms in all their abounding variety. In scientific terms, this is the point at which all of chemistry could be reduced to the analysis of a single substance and all of biology could be deduced from this same substance. In philosophical terms, it is the point where all that is multiple finds its unity and where unity manifests itself as the point from which all diversity is created. In other words, this is precisely the focal point where God is situated.

If we return for a moment to the earlier scene where Marguerite is in the laboratory and we refocus on Balthazar's description in light of

---

23. Collection Lovenjoul, Manuscript 157, folio 83.

the above remarks, the figure of Balthazar takes on new meaning. When first describing the Claës house, the reader will recall that Balzac points out the resemblance of the attic window to "the rose-window over the grand portal of a cathedral" (15). Now, he has Balthazar kneeling in front of a machine that is described as a monstrance: at the top it has two convex pieces of glass—"the receiver of the machine was capped by a lens formed by double convex glasses . . . [which] concentrated the rays of the sun which entered the room through one portion of the rose-window of the garret" (213)—but with no host in between them. Instead Balthazar, "as he almost knelt by his machine, received the sun's rays full upon his face, with his sparse locks resembling silver threads" (213), is praying to the divine illumination coming down through the window. The symbolism of the scene is graphic enough to dispense with any commentary other than Balthazar's words to Marguerite: "In a moment, you see, the most powerful force which a chemist can command will manifest itself, and I alone . . ." (214).

This same theme is treated explicitly this time when Balthazar explains to his wife that matter is the absolute principle of all phenomena:

> Man is a retort. For instance, according to my theory, the idiot is the man whose brain contains the smallest amount of phosphorus, or any other product of electro-magnetism; the madman, he whose brain contains too much of it; the ordinary man, he whose brain has a moderate supply; the man of genius, he whose brain is saturated with it to a suitable degree. . . . Just think if I should be the first to find it—the first to find it—the first to find it!"
>
> "Accursed Science, Accursed demon! You forget, Claes, that you are committing the sin of pride, of which Satan was guilty. You encroach upon God's prerogative."
>
> "Oho! God!" [108–09]

Mme Claës interrupts Balthazar again to point out to him that chemistry has the power to decompose substances but that it is not given to it to recompose inorganic elements after the fashion of living nature: "Analyze flowers, fruits, Malaga wine; to be sure, you will discover their elements . . . but can you, by putting them together, produce those flowers, those fruits, that Malaga wine? Will you control the incomprehensible effects of the sunlight? Will you obtain the atmosphere of Spain? To decompose is not to create" (109–10). To this, Balthazar replies crisply, "If I discover the coercive force, I shall be able to create" (110). Balthazar seeks, then, and *he believes he can find,* the secret of creation.

## IV.  EUREKA

At this point, we must perhaps again ask whether Balzac is not teasing us when in *La Recherche* he claims to resolve scientifically the philosophical problem of creation. The magnificence and misery of philosophy seem to come precisely from the possibility of posing the question of the Absolute, and from the impossibility of answering it. In any case, to ask an insoluble question such as that of the Absolute, to ask it in its properly philosophic form, one needs a great brain—or a lot of phosphorus, in Balthazar's terms. No doubt this need for a giant brain for philosophical thinking is the reason for which all the philosopher-creators in the *Etudes Philosophiques* suffer from an "abnormal dilation of the mind." But then Balzac is kidding us with his story about the Absolute![24]

In fact, the suggestion that the Absolute might be a sham is made in *La Recherche* from another angle, but the implications to be drawn from Balzac's seeming playfulness are serious indeed. For example, the last chapter of *Les Jeunes Gens*, "Vente de l'Absolu," corroborates the last page of *La Recherche*, when, the reader will recall, Emmanuel reads an article "concerning a lawsuit relative to the sale of the Absolute, by a celebrated Polish mathematician" (306). But if the Absolute was sold, then it must have been found. And in fact, a check of the documentation gathered by Madeleine Fargeaud on *La Recherche* shows that Balthazar is probably modeled on a Polish mathematician, "Hoëné Wronski . . . encyclopedic brain, often obscure, complex, mystical, and a mathematician of brilliant illumination. . ."[25] In his *La Réforme du savoir humain*, Wronski claimed to have discovered the law of creation and to have invented a philosophy whose principal object was to unveil the absolute goal of humanity. Wronski, to whom the Absolute appeared on August 15, 1803, wanted to initiate his contemporaries into this supreme good. But the Germans were not interested in this revelation and

24.  Indeed, if one looks back to the original version of *La Recherche (Les Jeunes Gens)*, the next to last chapter certainly suggests that the question of the Absolute is a trick question. It asks, "Does an absolute of some sort exist?" Yes, it turns out, but not at all the kind we expect. Fargeauld's documentation shows, for instance, that in 1832 there was a "merchant of Absolute" who sold cloth in the Passage Colbert. Even closer to home, Théophile Gautier remarks that on the wall of the garden in the rue Cassini where Balzac lived one could read the following sign: "Labsolu, brick merchant." But this Labsolu (or l'Absolu) may not really have been Balzac's neighbor because, according to other reports, on the inside wall of Balzac's courtyard huge black letters spelled out "Factory of the Absolute!" Cf. the chapter "Les Sources vivantes" in Fargeaud, op. cit., 53–86.

25.  Ibid., 72.

Wronski, in need of money, decided to sell the Absolute to a gentleman from Nice in quest of learning, M. Arson. But Arson eventually decided that the Absolute was getting too costly. Having already spent 300,000 francs on the Absolute and its inventor, he sued Wronski, which brought about a famous trial known as the trial of the "Yes or No."[26]

It is this episode of the "German" Absolute that Emmanuel reads from the newspaper. At a symbolic level, the existence of Wronski's Absolute put together with Balthazar's *Eureka* suggests the possibility of the discovery of a "French" Absolute. But unfortunately for French philosophy, Balthazar never gives us the key to this Absolute, for he dies at the very moment of its discovery. This conjunction, like the one discussed earlier regarding the lack of information about Balthazar's work, brings the following question to mind: does Balzac's novel attempt to demonstrate that the Absolute is a reality which is not of the order of language? This hypothesis would at least explain why the Absolute cannot be named, cannot be articulated, in the text of *La Recherche.*

What then does this hypothesis imply? If Balthazar Claës does find himself at the focal point he seeks—the unique point where all of nature converges and is born again—then it necessarily follows that nature, in order to produce what it has produced, needs nothing but itself. Everything can be produced out of the one, the same, the identical. There is no need for the other, for alterity, for sexuality, nor even for any notion of relation at all. To find what Balthazar Claës seeks is to place oneself at the focal point of nature, the originary and primal point of creation where otherness is not needed. The Absolute is thus a reality sufficient unto itself, a reality not derived from anything but from which all other realities derive. It is the creative principle reduced to the unique, and it is a paradoxical sexuality lacking the binary: desire without relation to the other.[27] This is precisely the point towards which Balthazar is aiming, the point that denies the fundamental character of any relation to the other.

Let us look at this hypothesis a little more closely. First of all, the argument that the first and fundamental point in nature excludes sexuality is a common contemporary theme, to be found at the heart of the philosophy of nature at the beginning of the nineteenth century and which is developed in the weightiest scientific texts. It is a well-documented fact that the eighteenth-century naturalists had discovered the

26. Pléiade documentation, op. cit., 10, 1567.
27. I am borrowing here from remarks made by Michel Foucault during a seminar on the nature of the relationship between desire and knowledge from Sade to Nietzsche.

concepts of fertilization, regeneration and above all of asexual reproduction. This "prebiological" coming-to-consciousness had naturally led scientists like Geoffroy Saint-Hilaire, Cuvier, Blainville, Dumézil and Latreille to debate the question of the unity versus the multiplicity of living species in the domains of botany and zoology.[28] Balzac is teaching us nothing particularly new on this subject. Contrary to Bachelard's reading, the force of his novel does not come from having posed the problem of repressed or paradoxical sexuality in-between the lines of *La Recherche de l'Absolu*, but from the attempt to represent a character in a position that denies the relation to the other. Balthazar Claës is in fact, quite precisely the man of desire without relation. We meet here one of the most venerable themes in Western thought: that knowledge cannot acquire or have access to the truth except on the condition of liberating itself from desire and especially from sexual desire. But if knowledge must free itself from desire, paradoxically it still cannot be freed from the desire for knowledge. However, this desire will then constitute itself as a pure desire for knowledge, that is, a desire without relation. As a result, the libido of the man of knowledge, the scientist, is a libido which cannot support a relation to anyone else. "Science is your life," Pépita tells Balthazar, and adds, "a great man can have neither wife nor children. Walk *alone* in your paths of misery! Your virtues are not those of common men, . . . you cannot belong to a wife or a family" (169). Thus the quest for the Absolute—for absolute knowledge—has meaning and can be anchored in the novel only because Balthazar's desire is a desire without relation: sexual, familial, or linguistic.

A number of additional elements in *La Recherche* support this hypothesis about the special role or place of the scientist. The reader quickly recognizes, first of all, that knowledge exists only at the exclusion of the sexual relation. The text indicates quite clearly that Balthazar can only do research if sexual relations are suspended, and inversely, that each time the sexual relation is revived, knowledge disappears. For this reason, each time Balthazar takes up his experiments again, he leaves the parlor, the space of exchange, of the family, of love, in other words the site of reciprocity with the other, and goes upstairs, where he locks himself up in the laboratory: "Science absorbed Balthazar so completely that . . . he was neither husband nor father nor citizen; he was a chemist" (152). We must also recall here the first reconciliation between the spouses. Pépita asks Balthazar for explana-

---

28. For an enlightening discussion of this topic see Jean-Paul Aron, "Science et Histoire: le temps de la biologie au début du XIXᵉ siècle en France" in *L'Endurance de la Pensée* (Paris: Plon, 1968).

tions he refuses to give; she faints, and at that moment he becomes aware that something serious is going on. As the scene continues, it becomes apparent that it is indeed in the mode of sexuality that the reconciliation takes place. In effect, Pépita seduces her husband and it is at this moment that she drags out of him a promise to abandon chemistry:

> "I want to destroy your laboratory and chain up your science," she said, her eyes flashing fire.
>
> "Very well, to the devil with chemistry!" . . .
>
> "Let us say no more about all this," she said with a smile and glance overflowing with coquetry. "Tonight, my Claes, let us not be only half happy." (114–15)

The reconciliation with Pépita/renunciation of chemistry is sealed by total happiness, and what is total happiness when one is married if not renewing sexual relations with the other half? Unfortunately for Pépita, the pendulum will later swing back towards science with the result we have now come to expect: "A complete separation between the husband and the wife was the result of that year. Claës slept apart, rose early, and shut himself up in his laboratory . . . he became weaned from her" (159).

The second example of this problematic which links science and the familial relation is given at the time of the triple marriage of the Claës children. It is a glorious evening, and the parlor scintillates with prestigious guests richly dressed and with splendid wedding gifts. The reading of the marriage contracts begins, following the Claës ritual according to which the parents are singled out as the focal point of the ceremony. Balzac's text spells out clearly the triumph of paternity over science: "This hommage rendered by that whole assemblage to the paternal authority which, at that moment, shone resplendent with regal majesty, gave to that scene a flavor of antiquity. *It was the only moment in sixteen years when Balthazar forgot the search for the Absolute*" (284–85, my emphasis). But all of a sudden, Le Mulquinier appears in the middle of the group, like a madman, holding in his hand a diamond that he gives to Balthazar, telling him, "I went to the laboratory . . ." (286). Balthazar, visibly shaken, begins ranting about science and his research. Silence falls over the room and Balthazar, taken aback, glances over the crowd and, dismissing Le Mulquinier with a gesture, gives the diamond to Marguerite at the same time that he tells the officiating notary: " 'Let us proceed.' That remark sent such a thrill through the assemblage as Talma used to send through the spell-bound audience in certain roles. Balthazar had resumed his seat, saying to himself in an undertone: 'I must be the father today, and nothing else' " (287). Thus, science gives way before the sexual and familial relation sanctioned by the rights of marriage and paternity.[29]

The last episode that helps clarify this problematic of the Absolute occurs at the end of the book, when Balthazar believes he has attained the Absolute and suddenly dies. The scientist attains the Absolute only on the threshold of death, in other words at the very moment when there is a total rupture of all possible relations with others, and *a fortiori* of the linguistic relation. Now one understands better why the Absolute Balthazar seeks can never be transmitted through the sexual relation, nor through the social relation, nor through the linguistic relation; the essence of this Absolute is that it cannot be pronounced inside a relation to anyone. Absolute Knowledge is that which is sufficient to itself, it is that which is expressed and attained outside of the other. It is for this reason that the knowledge—the quest for the Absolute—that is the subject of the novel paradoxically cannot at any time be disclosed, since it will be achieved only outside of any relation, at death's door: "[He] cried in a voice of thunder the famous word of Archimedes: EUREKA!— *I have found*—He fell back upon his bed with the dull thud of a lifeless body; he died uttering a ghastly groan. . . ." (306).

The original manuscript of *La Recherche* ends with the above sentence. On the page proofs, Balzac made one last important touch-up: ". . . and his distorted eyes expressed, up to the moment that the physician closed them, his regret that he had not been able to bequeath to science this solution of an enigma from which the veil was torn away too late by the fleshless fingers of death." This final addition, the last sentence of the novel, objectifies the discovery of the Absolute, confirming that Balthazar Claës is the metaphor of the scientist whose desire for Absolute Knowledge cannot be realized anywhere but in solitude, in any way but in silence, and at any time but at the moment of death.[30]

29. The reverse is also true. When Pépita early on in the novel tells Balthazar that he is spending too much of the family's money, and asks him how his daughters will be able to marry, Balthazar replies: "I will make you rich when I choose. . . . You can well afford to wait when I am consuming myself in superhuman efforts" (215). The remark that they will marry when, and after, he makes them rich means, in reality, that as long as science reigns unchecked in the household, sexuality and marriage will have to wait.

30. It is important to note that we are not given in *La Recherche*, as most of Balzac's critics tend to say, a reflection on the open-ended nature of desire. Those who see in *La Recherche* a variation on *La Peau de chagrin* argue that the possession of the desired object

## V. THE FABLE IN RETROSPECT

From the preceding analysis it is clear that Balzac has encoded the secret of the Absolute on at least three levels. We have thus far analyzed the first two: a *thematic* level which describes Balthazar's quest as the other protagonists (and thus the reader) see it, and a *symbolic* level whereby the text suggests certain things that it cannot articulate openly given the nature of the Absolute. In analyzing the third level—the *structural* level which, in this case, is blurred by the operation of the other two— we shall attempt to demonstrate that the key to the *Recherche's* own philosophical "secret" resides in the fact that it manages to encode a formulation of the Absolute upon the very configuration of the central characters, otherwise presumed to be merely contingent or anecdotal. We have already seen that Balthazar's life is patterned according to the structure of his chemical Absolute (multiplicity of substances reduced to one), since the ultimate statement of such total unity is the paradoxical silence and inexpressibility—the solitude—of death. But in a second, even more clever ironic turn, a replication of the *biological* Absolute (diversity produced from the one) is found in the otherwise inexplicable narrative shift toward Marguerite in the second half of the novel. We will attempt to provide support for the above claims by piecing together the fragmented clues concerning Balthazar's Flemish ancestry and Marguerite's ambiguous sexuality.

What role does Flanders play in *La Recherche?* First, we learn from its history, according to Balzac, that it had been subjected successively to the invasions of the Burgundians, the Spaniards, the French, the Germans and the Dutch. From these enforced "associations" Flanders was compelled to absorb the manners, customs and products of its neighbors. Two long pages of *La Recherche* are devoted to the nature of Flemish trade which caused the products of Italy, Spain, England, Austria, and even India, Japan and China to *converge* in Flanders (8–9). As a result of its effort to retain whatever it acquired from elsewhere, Flan-

---

suppresses desire as such and hence the desiring being. Gaeton Picon gives an eloquent formulation of this view: "The limit that the Balzacian hero runs against and whose death is only a symbol, is not an accessible totality but an already realized totality" (*Balzac par lui-même* [Paris: Seuil, 1956], 161). This scenario, which sees in Raphaël Valentin a "totalized" desire that reduces him to complete passivity—a kind of metaphoric death anticipating his real death—cannot be applied to Balthazar. For him, the cause and effect relationship between death and the realization of desire are inverted. We cannot say that Balthazar must die as soon as he has discovered the secret of the Absolute, but rather that it is precisely by virtue of his being on the threshold of death that he can possess the secret. Death is the necessary condition for the fulfillment of Balthazar's desire and not its consequence.

ders came to represent early on in its history the land of cosmopolitanism and diversity—"Flanders could hardly be looked upon except as the general warehouse of Europe" (9). This was true down to the period when the Flemish people learned to amalgamate these multiple cosmopolitan currents and to forge for themselves a unity that belonged properly to them: "The discovery of tobacco welded together the scattered national features with smoke. Since then, notwithstanding the clipping of its territory, the Flemish people has existed through the pipe and beer" (9). So much for the point of convergence—and nullification of diversity—that comes to define the unity of Flanders.

But Flanders is also characterized as the land of concentration—concentration of "the treasures and the ideas of its masters and its neighbors" (9). Predictably, the Claës family embodies Flemish concentration at all possible levels: economic concentration—"the vast fortune amassed by his ancestors" (12); geographic concentration—the Claës family marries into the Spanish family de Molina and assimilates its territories (12); social concentration—"They [the Claës] formed alliances only with families of the purest burgher blood" (13); political concentration—"a woman had to be able to point to a certain number of sheriffs or burgomasters among her kindred to be admitted into their family" (13); finally, this concentration is redoubled when Balthazar Claës-Molina, Comte de Nourrho, marries Mlle Josephine de Temninck (Pépita), granddaughter of the Duc of Casa Réal—"its [the Claës family's] treasures were increased by Mademoiselle de Temninck, who contributed several fine pictures by Murillo and Velasquez, her mother's diamonds, and the superb presents sent her by her brother" (40). By 1805, the time when the story of La Recherche begins, the long-established Claës instinct for concentration had transformed Balthazar's mansion into a museum replete with the most diverse legacies that had accumulated for six generations: valuable art objects, Dutch, French and Italian paintings, Japanese and Chinese porcelain, furniture, silver, and even "one of the finest collections of tulips ever known" (48).

Structurally, Balthazar is defined as this ultimate concentration point:[31] he is the end point of a gigantic legacy, the point of convergence and arrival not only of Flemish diversity but also of all the Claës successions and riches. As he belongs to a family of weavers, one could say that symbolically he is the finished product—the simple and homogeneous product—woven out of the strands of all the previous generations. Thus

31. See on this topic the brilliant article of Pierre Laszlo, "Concentration et faillite," in Nouveau Journal de Chimie, 3:1 (1979).

one recognizes from the unique position Balthazar occupies, and the symbolic meaning associated with it, the very precise characteristics of the chemical Absolute he pursues.

The first half of *La Recherche* closes with the death of Pépita, at which time Marguerite takes over, according to her mother's wishes, the management of the household. But shortly thereafter, Marguerite realizes that the set of social and economic relations between the Claës and the world can only be reconstituted on the condition that the man who resists all relations be excluded. She thus confronts her father in these terms: "I come, father, in the name of all the Claës, to order you to cease your experiments. . . . I have on my side your ancestors and honor, which speak louder than chemistry. Families take precedence over science" (216). Within pages of this warning, Marguerite goes into action: she replaces Balthazar first as head of the family by taking onto herself "the majestic rights of paternity" (245), and then literally expels him from his own house and sends him away to Brittany for seven years.

Let us now examine how Marguerite—as the central character of the second half of the narrative—embodies the biological Absolute her father desired. First, on a metaphorical level, as soon as she displaces Balthazar, she becomes a substitute mother for the children (as Pépita had admonished her), but she also plays the role of their father since she invests their money and assesses their revenues. In relation to her father, she also plays a maternal role— "Angel whom the heavenly spirits should applaud . . . how many times have you given life again to your father?" (288)—and even that of the father after Balthazar relinquishes to her the rights of paternity— "his oldest daughter awed him . . . from the day when he renounced his already compromised paternal authority" (275). Marguerite is thus both the mother and father of the Claës family. She is the point of origin from which all the family ties that science had destroyed are resumed and renewed, the single and unique principle from which all the Claës world is born again.

But all the while the family is being "revived" there is a brief scene during which Emmanuel declares his love for Marguerite and offers her his newly inherited fortune:

> —"This moment, my best beloved," she answered, "wipes out many sorrows, and brings a happy future nearer! Yes, I accept your fortune," she continued, while an angelic smile played about her lips, "I know a way to make it mine." *She glanced at the portrait of the ancestor Van Claes, as if to invoke a witness.* . . . "Alas! my poor love, are we not doing something that we ought not to do?" she said, deeply moved; "for we shall have to wait a long while."

—"My uncle used to say that adoration was the daily bread of patience, speaking of the Christian who loves God; I may love you so, for I have long confounded you with the Lord in all my thoughts; I am yours, as I am His." [261–63, my emphasis]

In this characteristic description, Balzac condenses a number of qualities that typify the nature of Marguerite's and Emmanuel's relationship: innocence, asexuality, Christian devotion. Clues to this relationship were already apparent during their first encounter in the novel. In this earlier scene, Balzac had systematically focused on Emmanuel's feminine characteristics: he is "maiden," with a "keen sensitiveness" and "a charm peculiar to young girls," and his "feminine movements" are harmonized with "his melodious voice" (142–43). Moreover, Marguerite and Emmanuel exchange their first glances when they catch each other looking at "a picture by Guido representing an angel" (146).[32] This first meeting under the sign of the Spirit symbolizes the pure and disincarnate nature of their love, which leads the two "sister" souls—compared respectively to the purity of a diamond (199) and the virginity of a pearl (225)—to ultimately join in the mystical oneness we have witnessed in the scene quoted above.

If we pursue further the argument of Balthazar's biological Absolute, which states that sameness must manifest itself as the point from which diversity is created, we see that the "lovers'" relationship—articulated along clearly homogeneous lines, asexual as well as unisexual, since both are angelic and feminine figures—is going to be the principle of (re)production of the social and economic empire Balthazar had destroyed. Marguerite, with the help of Emmanuel, first arranges the weddings of her brother and sister with their Flemish cousins, thus reconstituting the Claës wealth from its Flemish side; then, she marries Emmanuel and in so doing she "recovers" the wealth of his uncle who had acquired, at some point in the novel, the county of Nourrho from the Claës. The Hispano-Flemish dispersion that had occurred throughout Balthazar Claës's lifetime is entirely reconstituted in less than five pages! And it is built on this homogeneous relation, in which the generating principle is a paradoxical sexuality, a symbolic oneness.

One other symbolic episode in La Recherche ought to be mentioned here as it supports our hypothesis about Marguerite. This Absolute that

32. This is the only painting in the Claës gallery which is even partially described in La Recherche. A note in the documentation (Pléiade, 10, 1655) identifies the painting as Guido Reni's La Salutation angélique which represents the Virgin, Saint Joseph and two angels.

Balthazar is looking for, he does manage to find after all, and not only at the moment of his death. We recall that just before leaving for exile, Balthazar was involved in an experiment he had to abandon before its completion. Seven years later, upon his return for the wedding of the children, he does not go up to the laboratory, but Le Mulquinier does, and finds a diamond that he brings to Balthazar. It isn't the Absolute yet, but it is one step on the way to the Absolute. And Balthazar says: "Chance, in seven years, has produced, *without me*, a discovery I have been trying to make for sixteen years" (286, my emphasis). What does this remark mean, and what does the diamond mean? First, it is clear that the diamond could only be formed in the absence of Balthazar. If it is true that what the scientist desires is to arrive at the point at which nature creates from the identical without a need for the other, it follows that nature can accomplish the miracle of the diamond only in the absence of Balthazar. But secondly, read from another perspective, if Balthazar were not present during the constitution of the diamond, Marguerite was—and she was reconstituting the family wealth at the time. In effect, it is then not Balthazar but Marguerite who, symbolically or by osmosis, makes the diamond: they both represent the point out of which nature creates from the identical. This is why, in a highly symbolic gesture, Balthazar turns to Marguerite—" 'All nature will belong to us, we shall be above everything—and through you, my Marguerite—Margarita!' he continued, with a smile, 'your name is a prophecy. Margarita means a pearl' " (225)—and gives her the diamond, thus inscribing her life story within his biological Absolute.

This openly symbolic reading of Marguerite's role with relation to Balthazar's biological Absolute is confirmed on the scientific level. In arguing on behalf of this Absolute, M. de Wierzchownia, we recall, had given as one example of its existence the fact that "man himself, often has legitimate children entirely unlike their mother and himself" (105). Not only does Balthazar adopt this view but his own daughter embodies it: "Strangely enough, and physiologists have never been able to explain the phenomenon, [Marguerite] had not one of her father's or her mother's features" (120). If we pursue the biological record, we discover that Marguerite's "difference" produces, paradoxically, a return to the good Claës heredity. For if she does not resemble her parents, nevertheless, "she was the living image of her maternal grandmother" (120). The point of this backward jump from the eighth generation (Marguerite's) to the sixth (the grandmother's) is to bracket Balthazar's generation— the dissipating generation. This genealogical bracketing supports the point made earlier: namely, that the familial, social and economic world of the Claës can be reconstituted only if Balthazar, the man of the nonrelation, is excluded from it. And Marguerite implements the exclusion not once but three times. Firstly, the biological exclusion is inscribed in her genes; secondly, she enforces the physical exclusion in the narrative; and thirdly, she excludes Balthazar on a symbolic level during the scene of mystical love, since her symbolic union with Emmanuel is *witnessed* not by her father but by the ancestor: "[Marguerite] glanced at the portrait of the ancestor Van Claës, as if to invoke a witness" (262).

This brings us back full circle to one of our original questions regarding the protagonists of the *Etudes Philosophiques*. Like Balthazar, none of the other seekers of the Absolute—Frenhofer, Gambara, Louis Lambert, etc.—has a place in society. They must be excluded from Balzacian humanity, for their search is precisely that which is only meaningful outside of any and all possible relations with the other. The search for the Absolute is fundamentally and profoundly antisocial. That is why every "creator" of the *Etudes*, unlike the other characters of the *Comédie Humaine*, must not return, so that the writing of the *Comédie* can proceed.[33]

33. I wish to thank Richard Lockwood for his valuable suggestions that are incorporated throughout this essay, and Wilda Anderson for her generous help with regard to the scientific background of *La Recherche*.

## D. A. MILLER

# Balzac's Illusions Lost and Found

For F. M.

It has become easy to show how the closural decorums set up by a text are exceeded by the disseminal operations of language, narrative, or desire—so easy in fact that the demonstration now proceeds as predictably as any other ritual. Whenever a text makes confident claims to cognition, these will soon be rendered undecidable, and whatever ideological projects it advances will in the course of their elaboration be disrupted, "internally distanciated." Full, focused psychological subjects will be emptied out and decentered as invariably as desire will resurface at the very site of its apparent containment. Altogether it would seem as though the possibility of a fixed, settled closure were recovered in the fixed, settled character of the arguments against it.

Yet the point of remarking the orthodoxy of recent thinking about closure is not to dismiss the considerable productivity of such thinking, and far less to deny the textual phenomenon to which it so profitably calls attention. Rather, to the extent that the "failure of closure" has been transformed into a compelling, even compulsive critical success, it may well be a text's most powerful and seductive effect. In recent criticism, for instance, sometimes despite the most rigorous intentions to the contrary, the effect has operated to preserve for literature—as the very category of the literary—an almost or even frankly ontological difference from the worldly discourses in which it would otherwise be implicated. Whether the failure of closure is greeted with philosophical melancholy (over the fact that meaning can never be pinned down), political relief (that a work's suspect ideological messages don't finally cohere), or erotic celebration (of a desire that erupts when and where it is least wanted), it always gives evidence of a process which is, on one hand, inherent in textuality and, on the other, radically outside and subversive of all that a given text mundanely "wants to say." Capable of demystifying the official projects to which it is inevitably committed, literature would thereby transcend them and constitute itself as a distinct and separate category with its own peculiar privilege. What this privilege allows is suggested if we consider the quasi-political values that implicitly invest its affirmation. As the contest is usually staged,

164

closure enfolds the modalities of a massive, right-thinking repression, while its various "others" carry the more delicate, but also lighter burden of subtle, unconventional subversion. Due allowance made for the newly bleak and "disturbing" values to which it now plays host, literature thus tends to remain what it has been since the category first came into its own in the nineteenth century: a sanctuary for values seeking refuge from an inhospitable world.

Suppose, then, we understand the failure of closure as a textual ruse designed to produce, among others, this very effect: the "literature-effect." Suppose we take that coming-to-fail not as a negative phenomenon, but as a positive strategy, not disruptive but constitutive of a text's social implication and usefulness. Suppose we assume, in other words, that a text has "always already" put to use that which appears to bring the order of its discourse into question. Our attention would shift accordingly from the "problem" of closure to the various textual-cultural interests involved in producing and maintaining the problem. And once the dimension of power were thus introduced into the discussion of closure, then the enterprise of the traditional novel, for instance, which may be situated precisely at the threshold of the modern problematics of closure, would also have to be redefined. It would no longer (or not just) be the doomed attempt to produce a stable, centered subject in a stable, centered social order, but rather (or in addition) the more successful task of forming a subject habituated to displacement and psychic mobility, in a social order whose power is secured through a series of "more or less cunning decompositions."[1] The phrase comes

---

1. Honoré de Balzac, *La Peau de chagrin*, ed. M. Allem (Paris: Garnier Frères, 1967), 59: "A l'origine des nations, la force fut en quelque sorte matérielle, une, grossière; puis, avec l'accroissement des agrégations, les gouvernements ont procédé par des décompositions plus ou moins habiles du pouvoir primitif. Ainsi, dans la haute antiquité la force était dans la théocratie; le prêtre tenait le glaive et l'encensoir. Plus tard, il y eut deux sacerdoces: le pontife et le roi. Aujourd'hui, notre société, dernier terme de la civilisation, a distribué la puissance suivant le nombre des combinaisons, et nous sommes arrivés aux forces nommées industrie, pensée, argent, parole. Le pouvoir, n'ayant plus d'unité, marche sans cesse vers une dissolution sociale qui n'a plus d'autre barrière que l'intérêt." *The Fatal Skin*, [FS], trans. Cedar Paul (New York: Pantheon Books, 1949), 59 ["At their birth nations depend to a certain degree on concentrated, brute material force. Then, as settled communities grow, governments proceed more or less skilfully to parcel out primitive power. For instance, in remote epochs, national strength lay in theocracy, the priest held both the sword and the censer. Later, two men functioned as ecclesiastics: the sovereign pontiff and the king. In these our own times, society, which is the last word in civilisation, has distributed power among a number of groups and so we have the forces called business, thought, money and oratory. This disintegration of authority is leading to a social dissolution against which the only barrier is interest."] Yet if the strategies of modern power are thus perceived as at once scattered and scattering, this exemplary recognition is ultimately surrendered when power's "cunning decompositions" come to be interpreted as "social

from Balzac, whose work (specifically, the so-called Vautrin trilogy: *Père Goriot, Illusions perdues,* and *Splendeurs et misères des courtisanes*) will be used to broach such a redefinition in what follows.[2]
We begin with an ending:

> Rastignac, resté seul, fit quelques pas vers le haut du cimetière et vit Paris tortueusement couché le long des deux rives de la Seine où commençaient à briller les lumières. Ses yeux s'attachèrent presque avidement entre la colonne de la place Vendôme et le dôme des Invalides, là où vivait ce beau monde dans lequel il avait voulu pénétrer. Il lança sur cette ruche bourdonnant un regard qui semblait par avance en pomper le miel, et dit ces mots grandioses: "A nous deux maintenant!"
>
> Et pour premier acte du défi qu'il portait à la Société, Rastignac alla dîner chez madame de Nucingen. [*PG* 309]

> Thus left alone, Rastignac walked a few steps to the highest part of the cemetery, and saw Paris spread out below on both banks of the winding Seine. Lights were beginning to twinkle here and there. His gaze fixed almost avidly upon the space that lay between the column of the Place Vendôme and the dome of the Invalides; there lay the splendid world that he had wished to gain. He eyed that humming hive with a look that foretold its despoliation, as if he already felt on his lips the sweetness of its honey, and said with superb defiance,
>
> "It's war between us now!"
>
> And by way of throwing down the gauntlet to Society, Rastignac went to dine with Madame de Nucingen. [*OG* 304]

Earlier in *Père Goriot* Balzac told us that "l'étudiant n'était pas encore

---

dissolution," and when, as a result, the molar unity that power has resourcefully foregone is once again put forward as an implied political aim. It is as though the passage ambiguously grounded both operations I have ascribed to the traditional novel above: the desperate centering inspired by the prospect of social disintegration, and the subtle decentering enjoined by—the other face of such disintegration—the diffuse structuration of modern power. At greater length, it could be shown how the first operation is only a provisional maneuver in the service of the second.

2. References will be made parenthetically in the text to the following editions: *Père Goriot [PG]*, ed. P.-G. Castex (Paris: Garnier Fréres, 1963); *Illusions perdues [IP]*, ed. A. Adam (Paris: Garnier Frères, 1961); *Splendeurs et misères des courtisanes [S & M]*, ed. A. Adam (Paris: Garnier Frères, 1964). When unaccompanied by the abbreviations given in brackets above, page numbers will refer to the last work so specified. The English translations are taken from the following editions: *Old Goriot [OG]*, trans. M. A. Crawford (Harmondsworth, Middlesex: Penguin Books Ltd, 1959); *Lost Illusions [LI]*, trans. Kathleen Raine (New York: The Modern Library, 1967); *A Harlot High and Low [HHL]*, trans. Rayner Heppenstall (Harmondsworth, Middlesex: Penguin Books Ltd, 1975).

arrivé au point d'où l'homme peut contempler le cours de la vie et la juger" (245) ["the student had not yet reached that stage in his development when he could stand aside from the current of life, and consider it with detachment" (242)], but now, as Rastignac stands on the heights of Père Lachaise above the *beau monde* of Paris that submits obligingly to his gaze, he appears to have attained that promised position of raised consciousness and total vision. As Peter Brooks comments, "society and city have been seized in their totality and essence, in a gathering together of essential structures, relations, meanings made legible."[3] The scene thus stages a moment of truth, in which, having relinquished his illusions about the world, Rastignac comes into possession of the knowledge that will unlock for him the mysteries of Paris. Furthermore, just as the bewildering confusion that society initially presented to Rastignac had its subjective counterpart in his abundantly complicated psychology, so the moment at which Rastignac recognizes the essential orderliness of the social order coincides with a psychological simplification, in which his character, purged of the blurring sentimentality that he sheds as "sa dernière larme de jeune homme," ["the last tear of his youth"] is confirmed in its strength and decisiveness. The completion of education thus involves, in addition to the acquisition of knowledge, a depletion of the subject who comes to know. And on the basis of such cognitive and psychological clarifications, the novel grounds the persuasiveness of its ending: not as an arbitrary end point, but as an appropriate closure. For though the novel closes by conspicuously opening a new narrative sequence—*aller dîner*, as Roland Barthes might have encoded it—such blatant open-endedness only testifies to a career whose direction and final felicitous destiny are so assured that it can go without telling. Confirmation is provided in the rest of *La Comédie humaine*, where this career is alluded to in its various stages, but Rastignac never again appears as its full-fledged protagonist.

All of this would be conventional enough—the traditional novel typically secures its conclusion as a moment of truth whose dominant mode is psychological resolution—if the ending did not simultaneously negate all that it claims for itself as such. For with Paris "tortueusement couché" ["spread out below"] under the gaze that Rastignac "throws" (*lança*) upon it, as though the city were a beehive whose honey he had already begun appropriating, the moment of truth is at the same time a scene of erotic fascination, a dramatic relapsing into an acute state of

---

3. Peter Brooks, *The Melodramatic Imagination: Balzac, Henry James, Melodrama, and the Mode of Excess* (New Haven: Yale University Press, 1976), 140.

desire. And if, as Balzac insists throughout the *Comédie,* the possession of knowledge coincides with the renunciation of desire,[4] then Rastignac's vision, though no longer lachrymose, may be none the less blinded. The eroticism of his gaze dictates quite naturally his return visit to Madame de Nucingen, and also makes for the irony of the grandiose challenge that licenses that visit. "A nous deux" can indicate an alliance as well as an opposition,[5] and Rastignac's "bad faith" is rooted in the fact that he can find no better way of beating Society than by wanting to join with it. Much as the truth about the world is revealed to be only the truth of one's desire for the world, the apparently bellicose gesture merely facilitates submission to the world as it is socially given. Similarly, psychological fulfilment—implicitly, the chief goal of desire—will demand for its realization the evacuation of psychology in a subject whose inwardness has been strictly reduced to the internalization of social codes, norms, and practices. In none of Rastignac's subsequent appearances in the *Comédie* is he equipped with a psychology remotely comparable in extent or depth to the one he is given in *Père Goriot.* The ample "point of view" that he has provided in this novel will henceforward be limited to the objectively registered behavior of a role: here the dandy, there the *intriguant,* finally—summing up and rewarding the entire process of "self-discipline"—the Minister of the Interior. It is as though his richly resistant subjectivity had become a function of his own desire for success, a desire which in the course of being realized eliminated the very possibility of its being "his own." Never will Balzac show Rastignac in a moment of gratification, in contented, triumphant possession of the humming Parisian hive he avidly covets here. He may be a brilliant success, but so far as we know, he never *has* a brilliant success, for that success has been permitted by the replacement of a psychological subject by its social functioning. In this light, the apparently superficial open-endedness of the novel's last recorded action becomes more substantial. Unlike, say, in Jane Austen or Trollope, where a character's final identification with the social order issues in a nonnarratable state of affairs, here that identification commits Rastignac to further action in the world, to ongoing narrative.

---

4. The best known example occurs in *La Peau de chagrin,* when the antiquary tells Raphael: "*Vouloir* nous brûle, et *pouvoir* nous détruit; mais savoir laisse notre faible organisation dans un perpetuel état de calme" (37). ["To Will scorches us; To Act destroys us; but To Know steeps our frail organism in perpetual calm." (*FS* 36)]

5. As in a toast, or as in this usage from Balzac's trilogy: "A nous deux, nous donnerons du courage à Léontine" (*S&M* 413) ["Between us, we'll give Léontine heart" (*HHL* 347).]

Whether or not the subsequent stories are actually told matters less than the fact that they are necessarily entailed.

The scene thus situates for us a number of paradoxes. The lucid moment of truth is also a blinding moment of erotic fascination. The assumption of a critical distance from Society promotes a thorough-going integration into it. The self comes into its own at the same time as it is voided of its own inwardness. And finally, the moment of closure only signals the displacement of narrative and the necessity of its further production. I shall suggest that what holds these paradoxes together, determining their social value, is the structure of Balzacian "disillusionment." Though Brooks is certainly right to posit Rastignac's "disillusioned consciousness" behind "the gesture of possession" it entitles him to make,[6] this is perhaps a stranger phenomenon than he quite shows. How is it that the disillusioned consciousness—generally thought (and sometimes with Balzac's own novels for examples) to be an unhappy one whose insights doom it to passivity and withdrawal—turns a profit? We need to focus on the pure potentiality of the disillusioned moment here: bounded on one side by Rastignac's release (from the specific commitments and investments he has just foregone) and on the other by his subjection (to the commitments and investments he must now proceed to make). His "gesture of possession" is thus better named his fantasy of possession, of the possibility of all things being possessed: a possibility that must vanish as soon as one thing actually *is* possessed, when the restrictions that this moment derives its euphoria from suspending must be resumed, and when, as a result, the ambiguity of that possession (of it or by it) will come to impose itself. "A nous deux maintenant!" arrests Rastignac, so to speak, on the threshold of exchange: where, having liquidated one set of goods and not yet having fully bargained for another, he seems exuberantly capable of appropriating all qualities insofar as he might appropriate any. This exhilarating moment, therefore, is a projection, an abstract form demanding its content, an empty exchange awaiting its articles. Precisely as such, however, it requires for its completion a sequel—the concrete specification of Rastignac's vision—which must of necessity abolish it and mark the return to the committed, constrained state of affairs preceding it. And already, we note, this return is anticipated in the disproportion that ironizes Rastignac's passage from his grand and universal challenge to the petty and particular "premier acte" that it inspires.

In *Illusions perdues*, disillusionment is worked through beyond the

6. Brooks, 139 and 140.

moment of pure potentiality to its necessary aftermath, and at every point where the well-advertised operation of the title is shown to occur, whatever pathos is associated with losing illusions might be more appropriately assigned to the inevitability of finding them again. Since disillusionment is often considered the quintessential nineteenth-century experience, it becomes particularly interesting to observe that, in the very novel that is often considered the supreme representation of this experience, no disillusionment really occurs. Certainly, Lucien de Rubempré repeatedly undergoes what might be called a phenomenology of disillusionment, though the fact of repetition would alone be sufficient to cast doubt on its authenticity. Consistently, moreover, the moment of ostensible disillusionment is exposed as a mere phase: a psychological adjustment which permits the transition from one "illusion" to another, structurally identical to it. An exemplary instance of this takes place during Lucien's visit to the Paris Opera. "Doublement éclairé" ["Doubly enlightened"] by the Parisian *monde* and by madame d'Espard, Lucien "vit enfin dans la pauvre Anaïs de Nègrepelisse la femme réelle," ["saw at length poor Anaïs de Nègrepelisse as she really was"] and the real woman proves to be "grande, sèche, couperosée, fanée, plus que rousse, anguleuse, guindée, précieuse, prétentieuse, provinciale dans son parler, mal arrangée surtout!" (*IP* 181) ["a tall, thin withered woman with a blotched complexion, red hair, angular, stiff and affected in her manner, precious in her tastes, provincial in her speech, and, above all, badly dressed!" (*LI* 179)] But this enlightened perception is only an effect of Lucien's dazzled submission to the mediation of Parisian society. On one hand, his evidently disabused vision sees more than is there, for Louise, the text has just reminded us, "était restée la même" ["was still the same."] On the other, it doesn't see enough: "Lucien ne devinait pas le changement que feraient dans la personne de Louise une écharpe roulée autour du cou, une jolie robe, une élégante coiffure et les conseils de madame d'Espard" (182) ["Lucien could not foresee the change that was soon to be wrought in Louise's appearance by a scarf to soften the line of her neck, a well-cut dress, a different hairstyle, and Mme d'Espard's advice" (180).] The functioning of his ostensible disillusionment *within* an economy of illusion, tenaciously conserving the energy of its cathexes, becomes explicit when we find that "en perdant ses illusions sur madame de Bargeton . . . . il fut fasciné par madame d'Espard; et il s'amouracha d'elle aussitôt. . . . [C]ette reine apparaissait au poète comme madame de Bargeton lui était apparue à Angoulême" (190–91) ["as his illusions about Mme de Bargeton faded . . . under the spell of Mme d'Espard, he fell in love with her

on the spot. . . . (T)his queen seemed to the poet all that Mme de Bargeton had seemed to him in Angoulême" (*LI* 189).] The same pattern in
which a disillusionment-effect serves the displacement of illusion, thus
preserving it, can be seen throughout the novel. During the supper at
Florine's, thanks to Lousteau's cynical revelations about the world of
journalism, Lucien "avait . . . vu les choses comme elles sont" (360)
["had seen things as they are."] But the consequence of this insight is
that "il jouissait avec ivresse de cette société spirituelle" ["he was
intoxicated with the pleasure of being in such intellectually brilliant
society." (329).] Far from discouraging a career in journalism, Lousteau's
dismal *tableau* actually seduces Lucien into one, and the illusion about
literature is simply exchanged—via the delusion of disillusionment—
for an analogous illusion about journalism. Not dissimilarly, at the end
of the novel, having taken Carlos Herrera's illuminating "cours" on
history and ethics, Lucien is simultaneously taken by "le charme de
cette conversation cynique" (713) ["the charm of this cynical discourse" (658)], with the result that he is once again willing to undertake
the social itinerary he was preparing to abandon forever. An evidently
profound disillusionment thus "ends" the novel, as in *Père Goriot*, by
laying claim to a new beginning. In the place of an ending, the novel
simply declares its intention, along with its protagonist, to *trade places*:
"Quant à Lucien, son retour à Paris est du domaine des *Scènes de la vie
parisienne*" (752) ["As for Lucien, his return to Paris belongs to the
*Scènes de la vie Parisienne*" (695).] What is tendered in exchange for
closure is the very fact of exchange itself.

It is hardly a question of denying the social "alienation" as which
disillusionment is demonstrably rehearsed. To the extent that he has
been committed to the archaic desire for particular objects or persons in
a world requiring their perpetual exchange, the Balzacian *ambitieux*
regularly encounters a stinging dispossession: of his writing, his success, his lover, etc.[7] But unlike many of its readers, Balzac's fiction

---

7. The logic underlying such characteristic peripeties of Balzacian ambition has
been well described by Richard Terdiman, in his discussion of the initiation process in
Balzac: this process "has as its referent, and tests the possibility of domination over, a
concrete structure of interests and power-relations. . . . But the would-be subject, once
initiated, finds himself immersed in the structure of relations over which he sought
control, discovers that he is involuntarily speaking the referent *as its own object*. The
social system the initiatory process sought to determine in fact thus determines the
process even in its seeking; the power over which control was sought turns out to be *power
over those who seek power*" ("Structures of Initiation: On Semiotic Education and its
Contradictions in Balzac," *Yale French Studies* 63, 1982, 216).

never hypostatizes this aspect of disillusionment (as the evidence of a critical consciousness), but places it within a more inclusive process which quickly reappropriates it. Like Rastignac's, Lucien's disillusionment is the psychological effect and condition of an exchange. In a society rigorously structured on the principle of exchange, therefore, disillusionment cannot be, as Theodor W. Adorno has claimed, "the experience by which men are split off from their social function," but rather the experience in which they are identified with this function most completely.[8] Nor is it even the case that the alienation Adorno finds here serves merely to mask a deep-seated adaptation, since, in a precise sense, the alienation *is* the adaptation. For as much as desire is checked in this experience, it is commensurately freed, unbound from its investment in a particular person or object and rendered once more available for investments to come. Disillusionment "mobilizes" desire in both senses of the word: on one hand, it frees desire into circulation and thereby, on the other hand, in a society whose functioning demands just such circulation (of money, women, roles, stories), it *constrains desire to active duty.* Accordingly, insofar as desire is momentarily decathected in disillusionment, it promotes in the long run an overall libidinal investment in the social processes themselves, dominated by categories of exchange and transfer. It betokens grief, then, only as does Freudian "mourning": in the work of surmounting grief. Hence, though ambition regularly issues in disillusionment, disillusionment regularly issues in renewed ambition, often reshaped as well into a less vulnerable, more adequate form.

It follows that the structure of disillusionment must be misunderstood when approached from the point of view of a character's psychology, which is chiefly determined by its relationship to this structure. It is no more naive to take Lucien's disillusionment at face value than it is, peering into his character, to reduce the social conformism that emerges from his disillusionment to categories of moral psychology such as self-deception, hypocrisy, and the like. The automatic quality of the process by which one illusion is "lost" and almost simultaneously replaced by another suggests that the structural mechanism at work far transcends the grasp of either the psychology of a character or the psychologism of a reader. One notices that Lousteau preaches against journalism from within the practice of it, and by now it should not be hard to see that the preaching is exactly what enables the prac-

---

8. Theodor W. Adorno, "Balzac-Lektüre," in *Noten zur Literatur* (Frankfurt: Suhrkamp, 1974), 140 (my translation here and in n. 11).

tice. As, par excellence, the "stock-exchange of the spirit," journalism requires its practitioners to persevere in disillusionment to the point where the "moment" of disillusionment becomes the enduring state of cynicism. Such cynicism, considered as the impoverished, all but depleted psychology of the mechanism of exchange, is the indispensable condition of success in Balzac. If Rastignac succeeds where Lucien fails, it is not on account of the usual differences of character brought forward when this question is raised. Rastignac's manly decisiveness and Lucien's effeminate abulia are traits which merely reverse, by way of authorial value judgment, the relationship of each to the mechanism in operation. It is rather the determined Rastignac than the flighty Lucien who is the more truly mobile protagonist, willingly identifying himself, not with particular objects on either side of exchange, as Lucien tends to do, but with the sheer process of exchanging them. At all events, the disillusionment of neither ever mounts the slightest resistance to the social order whose good things the one goes on to "possess" only because, unlike the other, he knows when and how to relinquish them. And as we will see in a moment, social conformism motivates even the most disabused and antisocial of Balzac's characters, Carlos Herrera-Vautrin himself. Ultimately, *Illusions perdues* demonstrates that no authentic disillusionment ever occurs in the social world to suggest that no such disillusionment ever *can* occur there. This, I think, is finally how we ought to gloss the novel's curiously tautological title. For if, as Lucien says in a letter to Louise, illusion is the name we give to belief "plus tard" (201), after, that is, it has been given up, then an illusion is always already lost, and a nonredundant rendering of the title would be either *Croyances perdues* or simply *Illusions*. Unless, of course, as I have been suggesting, what is lost is precisely the practicability of losing illusions, in a world which has radically eliminated the possibility of negation.

*Splendeurs et misères des courtisanes* presents the most extreme version of the loss-of-lost-illusions, which, in the last incarnation of Vautrin, it reenacts as an identification of criminality with the police. But the transformation of the escaped convict into the chief of the Parisian Sûreté does not simply unmask the apparent resistances of criminality, which proves ultimately bound to the very power that is set against it; it redefines the police as well, whose elaborate activities can no longer be plausibly reduced to the repressive task of enforcing the interdicts of the law. The shock of Vautrin's cop-out is mitigated by the fact that what the narrative here realizes has been thematically anticipated from the beginning: "On ne peut devenir que ce qu'on est" (*S & M* 80) ["You can't become what you aren't" (*HHL* 75).] On one hand, the arch-criminal works exactly like the police. Vautrin has no trouble securing for Esther the police document that will confer on the prostitute her official rehabilitation—or even in getting the resume in an agent's dossier from the Prefect of Police himself. At one point, Vautrin's dress and manner can strike passers-by as that of a "gendarme déguisé" (72) ["a constable in disguise" (68)]; at another, he actually does disguise himself as a police magistrate sent by the Prefect to interrogate Peyrade. When the London police rid themselves of a troublesome murderess by sending her to Paris, she simply enters Vautrin's own service, which the text doesn't hesitate to call a "contre-police" (268) ["counter-police"]. On the other hand, the police work exactly like criminals. Whereas passers-by might take Vautrin for a *gendarme déguisé*, "un homme d'esprit" would intuit the potential thief in Cotenson (127); and whereas Vautrin disguises himself as a policial emissary, Peyrade camouflages himself as a bohemian who loudly proclaims his "horreur de la police" (136) ["contempt for the Judicial Police" (113)]. And their criminality sometimes goes beyond mere appearance, as when Peyrade breaks the rules of the force by hiring himself out as a private detective to Nucingen, or when, on a larger, world-historical stage, he organizes with Corentin and Cotenson a "Contre-Police" for Louis XVIII (143). Continually analogized to one another—Carlos Herrera is the Spanish Corentin, Paccard is Vautrin's Peyrade, etc.—police and criminals are quasi-instinctively brought together "sans le savoir" (179) ["without knowing it" (153)] in the duel that only the name of legitimacy prevents from being a perfect play of mirrors.

The affinity, even the interchangeability of criminals and police is, of course, a commonplace of nineteenth-century fiction, where it typically functions to consolidate the field of delinquency as distinct from the realm of middle-class civil society. The latter can then be qualified as both uncontaminated by crime and unencumbered by the visible and explicit constraints of the police. Preoccupied in chasing one another, cops and robbers thereby seem to leave *us* alone.[9] But Balzac releases the cops and robbers from the quarantine in which they are usually confined by explicitly connecting police practices—technically the same as criminal ones—to the practices of the social world at large. "A Paris, comme en province, tout se sait. La police de la rue de Jérusalem n'est pas si bien faite que celle du monde, où chacun s'espionne sans le savoir" (259). ["In Paris, as in the provinces, everything gets around. The

---

9. The pattern summarized here is elaborated in D. A. Miller, "The Novel and the Police," *Glyph* 8 (Baltimore: The Johns Hopkins University Press, 1981), 128–37.

police in the rue de Jérusalem is not so well organized as that of society, where everyone spies on everybody without knowing that he is doing it." (217)] Indeed, the characteristic excitements produced by Balzac's representation of the social world come precisely at those moments when social banality suddenly appears charged with the designs of a vigorous micropolitics: when the Camusots' dull "chambre à coucher" [bed chamber], for example, becomes a lively "chambre de délibération [council-chamber]." The social *milieu* thus ceases to be a "middle" separating two extremes from one another and from itself. And it loses this protective integrity in other ways as well. The theme of prostitution, for instance, scandalously migrates across class barriers from Esther to the society women like Madame de Sérizy and the Duchesse de Maufrigneuse who embody a similar sexual license; and beyond gender divisions from "ce qu'il y avait de plus femme dans la femme" ["what is most female in the female"] to what is most female in the male as well, when, like Lucien, he is kept by his own kept woman.[10] Similarly, Vautrin's Platonized homosexuality provides the context for a heterosexuality in which sexual relations with women are subordinated to the far more cathected transactions of power between men, or to the narcissistic process of self-affirmation within men. Rather in the way that Freudian psychopathology ends up problematizing "normality," Balzac's representation of Society takes seemingly marginal and relatively external phenomena to epitomize what is central and inherent to it.

One might note that police and criminals express their affinity to one another, just as the social milieu expresses its affinity with both, "sans le savoir." One might suggest, in other words, that the various social continuities between center and circumference, norm and deviation, can only be manifested "unconsciously," cloaked in ignorance or denial. Yet if ignorance evidently makes for the smooth functioning of the social order, so and no less, paradoxically, does knowledge. Despite the many declarations of its supposed rarity, and though it is frequently divulged *in confidence*, as knowledge whose efficacy depends on keeping it secret, cynicism enjoys an extremely wide distribution in Balzac. It surfaces at least sporadically in nearly all his characters, who nonetheless remain incapable of producing or even contemplating any "escape" from the social order that is instead, as we say, cynically main-

10. In the manuscript of *Splendeurs et misères*, the Duchesse keeps Lucien's letters "à cause des éloges données à ce qu'il y a de plus femme dans la femme" (*S & M* 734) ["because of the praise of what is most female in the female"]; in the published version, these eulogies are given "à ce qu'elle avait de moins duchesse en elle" (588) ["upon what was least duchesslike about her" (*HHL* 492).]

tained. One thinks how, in a novelist like Dickens, cynicism is arrested both by the vague hope of social reorganization and—in the meanwhile, as it were—by the concrete project of reencoding social differences in less arbitrary, more stable moral terms. Or one thinks how, in Dostoevsky, cynicism is transcended in the divine, where such differences, superficial or substantial, no longer matter. If cynicism unfolds in Balzac to a fullness unparalleled in nineteenth-century fiction, this is because the possible subversive social consequences of cynicism—feared and contained in the humanism of Dickens or the religion of Dostoevsky—are never in any danger of occurring. The best defense against the dreaded consequences of cynicism, Balzac shows, is cynicism itself: an eroticized knowledge constituted in too near a proximity to its object not to be another one of the latter's seductions. Cynicism finds its truth in conformism for the same reason that it finds its mode in paradox. Intimately bound alongside a *doxa* which provides the entire content of its reflections, it is always prevented from doing anything but pay hommage to the received opinions that, in its paradoxical turn, it too receives and passes on.

If Vautrin's practices do not differ from the police's, or even from those of the worldly on whose behalf the police do their work, why then does he fail to realize his schemes? After all, though these schemes are attributed to his antisocial desire for "vengeance," once Lucien becomes the vehicle of such vengeance, they conform perfectly to the most ordinary world aspirations. The failure to achieve them would be the more striking in proportion to the horrified admiration with which the text insists on Vautrin's social, policial expertise: the penetrating surveillance of his gaze, his unmatched mastery of cultural codes, his protean ability in disguise and plotting, the absolute autonomy of his will. If with all these advantages, Vautrin fails, it is finally because—supremely disillusioned as he imagines himself—he is not disillusioned enough. No less than his "creature," Vautrin is motivated by specular dreams of presence. The desire to be, to have Lucien, fatally attaches him to a specific object rather than to social processes themselves. Until his "conversion," Vautrin is an anachronism: an individualist not only in the obvious sense that his counterpolice must be a small, all-too-private enterprise in comparison to the vaster corporate-bureaucratic organization of the official force, but also because what inspires him are fantasies of individual possession, possession of individual objects by individual subjects. This comes out most clearly in his sexual infatuations, his victimization by types. For though Vautrin is able to see and manipulate "the arbitrariness of the sign" at most other levels, when confronted by a Rastignac or Lucien, he is entirely willing

to grant the appearance all the erotic authority of the reality. A semiotician, as such, can never fall in love, for that experience is based on an
assumption that the "outside" intrinsically corresponds to the "inside." (In this light, "tricking" would be the semiotician's chosen mode
of sexual expression.) To the extent that Vautrin is enamoured, he abdi-
cates his semiotic competence, not because he misreads the signs, but
because in this domain he fails to understand them as signs at all. More
broadly, Vautrin's untimely possessiveness comes out in his fantasies of
power  as something to have and to hold. One recalls from *Père Goriot*
his dream of becoming a plantation owner in the American South,
"avoir des esclaves, gagner quelques bons petits millions à vendre mes
boeufs, mon tabac, mes bois, en vivant comme un souverain, en faisant
mes volontés" (*PG* 126) ["to have slaves, earn a few nice little millions
selling my cattle, my tobacco, my timber, living like a monarch, doing
as I like" (*OG* 131).] Perhaps unsurprisingly, it is the arch-criminal in
Balzac who entertains the most reactionary ancien-régime conception
of power as a monolithic concentration in a single person. In a world,
therefore, where he must encounter the elusively dispersed nature of
modern power, diffused in techniques and norms, Vautrin is bound to
disappointmemt. His creatures slip from his grasp, like Rastignac and
Lucien, or play him false, like Europe and Paccard. Only with the loss of
Lucien—not just the loss of the specific object of his ambition, but the
loss of *ambition for a specific object*—do Vautrin's machinations at last
bear fruit. He successfully replays the failed scenario of saving Lucien
with Théodore Calvi, an ex-boyfriend from prison, with whom, sug-
gestively, he has been only sexually, not romantically, involved.[11] In

11. Adorno writes about Balzac's treatment of homosexuality: "Faced with the
irresistible imposition of the principle of exchange, he perhaps imagined in this pro-
scribed love, a priori desperate, something like love's unmutilated image: he ascribes it
to the false cleric, who as the head of a criminal gang has renounced the exchange of
equivalences (*Äquivalententausch*)" ("Balzac-Lektüre," 142). Yet we do better to understand Vautrin's homosexuality as the advance guard of sexual modernism than as this
archaic sentimental refuge. The moment when, on Calvi's reappearance, Vautrin recognizes his homosexuality in its desublimated form is also the moment when his character
is most attuned to social exigencies and most expert at the operations they require. It is
as though the recognition completes the process of modernizing him as a subject of
exchange, by casting his unmanageable love into the more negotiable form of sexual
commerce. In the end, Vautrin's homosexuality is not opposed to "the exchange of
equivalents," which on the contrary aptly defines it. It thus announces the development
that, a hundred and fifty years later, will allow sociology to observe: "Parmi toutes les
sexualités, l'homosexualité masculine est sans doute celle dont le fonctionnement rap-
pelle le plus l'image d'un marché" ["Of all forms of sexual behavior, male homosexuality
is undoubtedly the one whose functioning most recalls the image of the market place"]
(Michael Pollak, "L'homosexualité masculine, ou: le bonheur dans le ghetto?," *Communications* 35 [1982], 40).

several senses, Vautrin ends by becoming Rastignac. Between the cynical detachment he assumes from society and that already built into and required by the proper functioning of that society, there is no longer any distance. Like Rastignac, moreover, Vautrin obstinately maintains an oppositional stance when the very possibility of one is about to collapse. If he now displaces his desire for revenge within the police force itself, proclaiming his intention to get even with Corentin, the emptiness of that desire is revealed in the last sentence of the novel: "Après avoir exercé ses fonctions pendant quinze ans, Jacques Collin s'est retiré vers 1845" (*S & M* 657) ["After having exercised his functions for some fifteen years, Jacques Collin retired in 1845 or thereabouts" (*HHL* 554).] The whole career of Vautrin as head of the Sûreté has been elided, as the sovereign power he fantasized and tried to possess has been attenuated in the exercise of "functions." Once again, the moment of true insight into the world leads to a psychological evacuation as well as a commitment to further narration, both here explicitly coinciding with the activity of policing. And the last incarnation of Vautrin is only the most obvious figure for a functionalism whose triumph, in the name of the police, affects the entire representation. In the same way that Vautrin is now transformed from character into functionary, so the densely woven novelistic texture of *Père Goriot* has been gradually voided to become the feuilletonesque narrative functions of *Splendeurs et misères*, and these functions are implied to be even barer in the elided adventures of Vautrin's police career. Clearing the ground not just for the routinized exercise of policing functions, but also for their routinized representation, Balzac's novel of disillusionment is appropriately concluded at the end of the Vautrin trilogy, but only because it there asks to be completed in a quite different genre which will nonetheless precisely honor its request: the *roman policier*.

It is perhaps already clear why we must extend our thematic discussion of disillusionment to the larger question of the operation of novelistic form. For the theme of disillusionment recurs in the Balzacian novel's own relationship to what it represents. To see the inadequacy of Lucien's perception of his own disenchantment, for instance, is at the same time to be installed within the disenchanted perception of the narration. When this narration disillusions us about disillusionment, it thereby reclaims the validity of the experience for itself. The Balzacian novel discredits the experience of disillusionment within the representation only by this means to rehabilitate it as the basis on which the narration is entitled to speak. No doubt we can say—positioned by the narration as its readers, we cannot but say—that the narration's perception is truly superior to Lucien's, which it deconstructs. But there are several reasons for suspecting that Balzac's narration belongs to the pattern of coincidences that it seems to be betraying and that the representation of the mechanism of disillusionment is in fact its repetition. For one thing, the treatment of disillusionment is the prime thematic means by which the Balzacian novel wins the adherence of its readers. The cognitive clarity of the narration, produced as an effect of its contrast with the mystified perception of the characters, asks to be consumed as part of a libidinal investment. If in order to be read, the novel must be enjoyed, then the narration must continually practice a charm which is perfectly analogous to that of Lousteau's diatribe or Vautrin's pedagogy. Its insights need to seduce us, and insofar as we are seduced, in entranced "possession" of the truth, the novel has succeeded in escaping our critical scrutiny. Cultivating an affective detachment from the world and thus—what is supposed to be the same thing in Balzac— coming truly to know it, we simultaneously cathect that affect onto the novel, desiring it, and thus—what would also be the same thing in Balzac—never quite understanding it.

How is the reader "operated" in Balzac? What processes must this reader necessarily engage? It only stands our seduction by the text's own disillusionment-effect on its head to argue resentfully—as even some of Balzac's most interesting recent critics have done—that Balzacian narration realizes a fantasy of sovereign semiotic power and total narrative control. Clearly, the evidence for such a fantasy can easily be found: in the biographical resumes that are as full as the dossiers of the police; in the ready-to-hand explanations for whatever occurs; in the continual exhibitionistic display of the narration's superior vision, in which we get, and are always reminded of getting, the supreme panoptic privilege of watching the watchers themselves. But if in these ways the Balzacian novel submits to the hold of the same ancien-régime conception of power that motivated Vautrin, it also more profoundly modernizes such a conception: in its espousal of a logic of displacement and dispersion, its willingness to abandon its positions in exchange for new ones, its ultimate obedience to the category of the *functional*. What Fredric Jameson has called, for instance, "a rotation of character centers" in Balzac precludes imaginary identification with characters in favor of an identification with the process of shifting itself.[12] To read a novel like *Splen-*

---

12. Fredric Jameson, *The Political Unconscious* (Ithaca: Cornell University Press, 1981), 161: "This rotation is evidently a small-scale model of the decentered organization of the *Comédie humaine* itself." In the light of Balzacian disillusionment, however, we cannot accept his suggestion that this decentered organization *antedates* the emergence of a centered subject. Rather, we should say, this decentered organization has always-already engendered the correlative fantasy of a centered subject, who is therefore

*deurs et misères* is successively to occupy a whole, but not complete, set of social positions, absolutely attached to none. Similarly, there are no grounds for speaking of a narrator in Balzac, if by narrator we understand a simulacrum of a *person*, for this kind of individual focalization is precisely what the narration, by multiplying, works to by-pass. One identifies not with a narrator, but with a narration—or better, no *one* identifies at all, since when the notion of the person is removed from one side of the equation, it is also gone from the other. The same principle that detaches us from identifying with persons makes the Balzacian description, apparently overflowing with detail, ultimately so abstract and even skimmable. The point of such description is only that it always has a point; the specific details are thereby evacuated in a meaning which could be derived from a different, and hence interchangeable, set of details. The suffocating local particularity of the Balzacian novel is only its point of departure, the point which the dynamism of the narrative consists in *leaving behind*, as "one" is assimilated to techniques, procedures, functions.[13] Along the same lines, as Gérard Genette has best demonstrated, the apparently compulsive need to make sense in Balzac produces considerable incoherence if the various explanations are taken together as parts of a unified understanding.[14] What matters in Genette's demonstration, however, is not its somewhat malicious observation, made as it were behind Balzac's back, that the novelist is being inconsistent—a complaint that finally emerges from a rationalist sensibility as Balzacian as the Balzac it finds to snipe at. Rather, what the discrepancies reveal is the ultimate dependency of the Balzacian text on a conception of narrative functionality. Thus, if the same qualities are adduced in different places as causes for opposite effects, this is only to say that for the reader of Balzac, sense has no absolute basis, but changes with the narrative need and the social context. Like

on the verge of being emarginated from the outset, and able to defend his "integrity" only through his willingness to be dispersed.

13. "The exclusion of money from circulation would constitute precisely the opposite of its valarization as capital, and the accumulation of commodities in the sense of hoarding them would be sheer foolishness. (Thus for instance Balzac, who so thoroughly studied every shade of avarice, represents the old userer Gobseck as being in his second childhood when he begins to create a hoard by piling up commodities)" (Karl Marx, *Capital*, vol. 1, tr. Ben Fowkes [New York: Vintage Books, 1977] 735). If Balzacian narrative confirms Marx's thesis, it is not so much by illustrating it along the lines suggested in this passage, as by continually enacting it as the principle of its formal construction. See Adorno "Balzac-Lektüre," 148–49; and Fredric Jameson, *Marxism and Form* (Princeton: Princeton University Press, 1971), 10.

14. Gérard Genette, "Vraisemblance et motivation," in *Figures II* (Paris: Seuil, 1969), 81–86.

everything else in Balzac, meaning too must adjust to the demands of its functional station.

This is finally why the Balzacian novel, committed to processes of circulation and exchange, is incapable of coming to an end, why it must mark its endings by the promise and necessity of further narration. There simply is no principle of arrest, as there would be if a decisive sense could be established, or even a settled personal identification. The lack of such a principle shows up thematically in Balzac's unorthodox representation of the police, who in *Splendeurs et misères* seem less interested in preventing crime and arresting criminals than in merely supervising a wealth of intrigues, as though the efficacy of policing were now carried not in and by means of an ending, but in the smooth facilitation of narrative processes themselves. This is also why it is mistaken to think that the failed closure opens up, as anything more than a masking effect, transcendent possibilities (such as "freedom") which could be used to justify and characterize "liberal society" or, for that matter, "liberal arts" like literature. What social integration means in Balzac, we have seen, is not arrest and settlement (which would either establish our freedom by putting limits on it, or extend its domain by failing to secure them), but an eminently narratable "exercise of functions." There is no reason not to reverse this proposition and say that what the narration's own exercise of functions drills us in are precisely the basic structuring principles of nineteenth-century social order. This is not an order which values or even requires a fixed self, or the sense of an ending, but aspires—as the disillusioned Balzac is the first to admit—to the condition of money: to its lack of particularity, to the mobility of its exchange, to its infinitely removed finality. In its subscription to such principles, the Balzacian novel finds its redeemable social value.

GERALD PRINCE

# La Nausée and the Question of Closure

La Nausée is the story of a thirty year old man who, after years of travels and adventures, has settled in Bouville to complete a history thesis on M. de Rollebon. At the beginning of the novel, Antoine Roquentin feels that "something has happened":[1] he is given to fits of nausea that he cannot explain and the world around him—tobacco packs, door handles, stones, walls, suspenders, tramway seats—appears to be just as sick. He decides to "keep a diary in order to see clearly" (5). At the end of the novel, after having understood the meaning of nausea ("it is Existence revealing itself and it is not pretty to see, Existence")[2] and after having rejected many ways of acting like a jerk and trying not to face the contingency of being—adventure (it is found only in books); his work on M. de Rollebon ("a dead man can never justify a living one")[3]; power and money (the bourgeois of Bouville are bastards); knowledge (the Self-Taught Man is an imbecile); the consolations of reminiscence (the past is dead), psychology (Roquentin is "neither a virgin nor a priest" [15]), or nature (it is disgusting); debauchery (he has tried it and it did not work); action (but do what and for what?); love (Roquentin and Anny have nothing to tell each other); friendship (Roquentin and the Self-Taught Man have nothing to tell each other); humanism (!); and even suicide (it is not much of a solution; besides, it is frightening)—at the end of the novel, the protagonist decides to leave Bouville and to go vegetate in Paris. For the last time, he sits at the "Railwaymen's Rendezvous"

1. Jean-Paul Sartre, La Nausée in Oeuvres romanesques, ed. Michel Contat & Michel Rybalka (Paris: Gallimard, Bibliothèque de la Pléiade, 1981), 8. All references are to this edition. The translations are mine, with a strong assist from Lloyd Alexander's translation (New York: New Directions, 1964).
2. See Sartre's prière d'insérer in the edition of his Oeuvres romanesques, 1695.
3. Ibid., 1695.

where, for the last time, he hears *Some of These Days*, a song which represents for him an antinausea. He then understands that he has always wanted to *be* and that he could save himself by creating a being as opposed to an existent, a work of art. "Tomorrow it will rain on Bouville" (210).

According to this account of *La Nausée*—which is fairly adequate, I think, and certainly not idiosyncratic[4]—Sartre's first novel goes from certain initial questions (what is nausea? how will I transcend it?) to certain final answers ("it is Existence revealing itself"; I will become an artist). It begins at the beginning ("something has happened" is at the origin of any and all telling) and it ends at the end (the hero having rejected everything but the artistic vocation that he decides to pursue), an end which, according to Roquentin himself, provides an illuminating and unifying frame for what has preceded: "And I too wanted to *be*. That is even all I wanted; this is the very last word of the story. I see clearly in the seeming disorder of my life: at the bottom of all these attempts which seemed without bonds, I find the same desire again: to drive existence out of me, to empty the passing moments of their fat, to twist them, dry them, purify myself, harden myself, in order to emit at last the sharp and precise sound of a saxophone note. That could even make an apologue . . ." (206). *La Nausée* is thus closed from the hermeneutic and proairetic points of view. It is also closed from a tonal point of view, anxiety (I feel sick. Am I crazy?) giving way to peace (earlier in the novel, rain has been identified as that which dissipates the threatening fog and reinstates boundaries). Besides, it is a *finished* work, with its finish to be seen on every page, in the subtle and complicated network of rhymes and echoes established among its various constituents.[5] So finished is it, in fact, that it can be taken to constitute the very work—"beautiful and hard as steel" (210)—which Roquentin decides to write.[6]

This closing account of *La Nausée*, however, might not be close enough. Take the beginning, for example (Sartre's novel warns us about narrative, on 49: "You seem to start with the beginning. . . . And in reality you have started with the end"). First, there is a series of signs through which the work opens and shuts: the title (a "false" title, since *La Nausée* was to be called *Melancholia*), the dedication to "the Beaver"

---

4. It follows the *prière d'insérer* fairly closely. See *Oeuvres romanesques, 1694–95*.

5. On this network, see Geneviève Idt, *La Nausée: analyse critique* (Paris: Hatier, 1971) and Georges Raillard, *La Nausée de J.-P. Sartre* (Paris: Hachette, 1972).

6. Cf. Hazel Barnes, *The Literature of Possibility. A Study in Humanistic Existentialism* (Lincoln: University of Nebraska Press, 1959), 203.

(Simone de Beauvoir), the epigraph from Céline ("He is a guy without collective importance, he is just an individual"). But, after all, this is the case with (many) works of fiction. Next, there is the Editor's Note which, from the chronological point of view, comes at the end; which proves to be redundant (most of the information it provides is provided again by Roquentin's diary); and which, rather than illuminating the fate of the protagonist and his artistic project, causes confusion. What has happened to Roquentin if the notebooks we read "were *found* among his papers" (3; emphasis mine)? Moreover, if he has no collective importance—if he did not become a novelist, say—why publish them? and if he did, why not mention it? But perhaps the Note is only supposed to function parodically. . . . The "undated pages" follow. They do not constitute a "real" beginning since their origin (their date) is unclear. They are sapped by hesitations or blanks ("For instance, here is a cardboard box holding my bottle of ink. I should try to tell how I saw it *before* and now how I       "[5]) and some of their content is, literally, under erasure: "I must never [here, according to the editors, "one word is crossed out (perhaps 'force' or 'forge'), another one, added above, is illegible"] but note carefully and in the greatest detail everything that happens" (5). Besides, the incident of the stone—the first one, it seems, to provoke the protagonist's nausea (6)—turns out not to be the first: a few years earlier, Roquentin had had a similarly unpleasant sensation in front of a little Khmer statuette ("I really don't know what it was, but it sickened me so much that I couldn't look at it"[10]). Finally (but after what!), there comes the beginning of the diary itself—"something has happened"—a beginning taking its place in the series of "revolutions" that have marked Roquentin's life and given it "such a jerky, incoherent aspect" (9).

The end of *La Nausée* is also problematic. I have already pointed out that, chronologically speaking, it comes before the Editor's Note. Moreover, it designates itself as a beginning ("It's on that day, at that hour, that everything began" [210]) and closes with a future ("tomorrow it will rain on Bouville"). Above all, perhaps, it is difficult to consider it as totalizing or finalizing. On the one hand, the solution proposed may well be impossible, given that art did not save Anny, that Sartre's novel repeatedly parodies Proust's *Recherche*, and that, at the very point Roquentin decides to write a book thoroughly cut off from the Referential and the Communicative, he suggests that one cannot rid texts of all reference to an existent ("one should have to guess, behind the printed words, behind the pages, at something [only at something!] that would not exist, that would be above existence" [210]) and he evokes his future readers: "A book. A novel. And there would be people who would read this novel and say: 'It's Antoine Roquentin who wrote it; he was a redhead who hung around cafés; and they would think of my life as I think of that of the Negress: as of something precious and half legendary" (210).[7] It seems that art cannot save us from existence and the end of the novel represents perhaps still another attempt that is doomed to failure. On the other hand, should art actually save (after all, the last pages are neither identical to nor interchangeable with the first; Anny is not Roquentin; and the same conclusion might be reached by novelists as different as Proust and Sartre), the consequences would be troubling, to say the least. During his visit to the Bouville museum, the protagonist had severely criticized Parrottin, who led his listeners along the most perilous paths, made them reject the most sacred values, went far, so far that they could barely follow him. . . . Yet, "one more step and, suddenly, everything was reestablished, marvelously founded on solid reasons, like in the old days" (104). Now, the success of Roquentin's final project, his redemption, would make of him (of Sartre too) a Parrottin and neutralize the force of what has preceded, the very experience of nausea. No wonder that the last pages of the diary are so hesitant, with the conditional playing a major role and the diarist multiplying the signs of his indecision: "Couldn't I try . . . couldn't I . . . I don't know . . . I don't dare make a decision . . . perhaps . . . perhaps . . . perhaps. . ." (209–10).

From uncertain beginning to hesitant end, in fact, Roquentin's diary abounds in paradoxes and contradictions. Like the stone that is "dry on one whole side, damp and muddy on the other" (6), the hands with silvery backs and fleshy naked palms, or the alternately hard and tender crabs, the diary becomes a two-faced object and it is difficult to know which one of the faces to focus on.[8] The protagonist spurns the very positions he stands on and adopts the ones he has abandoned. For example, he criticizes those who "explain the new through the old" and "think that there is nothing new under the sun" (83); but he says himself that, in life, "everything is the same" (49) and he can only agree with Anny who wonders "how people got the idea of inventing names, of making distinctions" (177). In the public garden, he laughs at the morons to whom the root of a chestnut tree looks like a ravenous claw; but,

7. Cf. Gerald Prince, "Roquentin et le langage naturel" in *Sartre et la mise en signe*, ed. Michael Issacharoff & Jean-Claude Vilquin (Lexington: French Forum Publishers, 1982), 103–13.

8. See Jean Pellegrin, "L'Objet à deux faces dans *La Nausée*," *Revue des Sciences Humaines*, no. 113 (janvier–mars 1964), 87–97.

on two earlier occasions, he himself had compared the root to such a claw (152, 154, 158). When it seems to him that "everything can happen," he excludes "the kind of horror invented by men; Impetraz was not going to start dancing on his pedestal: it would be something else" (92); yet, this "something else," when he describes it, is "a side of rotten meat . . . dragging itself along by crawling" (187) or again "items of clothing that have become living things" (188). And if, according to him, realism fails to represent reality, perhaps it also succeeds, which would explain his strange fascination with *Eugénie Grandet.*[9]

Even the fundamental categories that Roquentin attempts to comprehend and define, the key moments in his itinerary, the most striking elements in his diary are not free from ambiguity. Consider, for instance, his epiphany in the public garden or the jazz melody he so appreciates. It is in the midst of an anti-Eden, next to the root of a chestnut tree, that Roquentin, the anti-Adam, feels thoroughly present to existence and sees it: "suddenly, all at once, the veil is torn away, I have understood, I have *seen*" (150). But has he really seen? The text is not so sure. Perhaps it was an idle fancy, a mirage, a dream: "then I shouted and I found myself with my eyes wide open. Did I dream it up, this enormous presence? It was there, hanging over the garden, tumbling down the trees, altogether soft, making everything sticky, altogether thick, a jelly. And I was inside, I, with the whole garden?" (159). Roquentin's illumination begins to look like an illusion, that of absolute presence to absolutely present existence: "the world disappeared as it had come, or else I woke up. . . . I stood up, I got out. When I reached the iron gate, I turned around. Then the garden smiled at me. I leaned against the iron gate and watched for a long time. The smile of the trees, of the laurel clump, it *meant* something; that was the real secret of existence" (159–60). The protagonist has understood everything but perhaps he has understood nothing. Is the existence evoked above only an ideal limit, a fiction? Or are we witnessing the return of imaging consciousness? It is difficult to know and the ambiguity will never be wholly resolved: "It bothered me, that little meaning: I *could not* understand it, even if I had stayed leaning against the iron gate for one hundred and seven years; I had learned all I could know about existence" (160).

If the experience in the garden constitutes a false apocalypse (it does not quite answer Roquentin's questions about existence; it brings nothing—and certainly not the diary—to an end), the jazz melody at the

---

9. On this subject, see Gerald Prince, "Roquentin et la lecture," *Obliques,* nos. 18–19 (1979), 67–73.

"Railwaymen's Rendezvous," given the novelistic context, is equivocal too. Like adventure, narrative, or the other two popular songs mentioned by the protagonist,[10] it functions as the opposite of existence. Dry, hard, compact, rhythmical, invulnerable, it neither represents nor communicates; it is strictly concerned with itself, asking for nothing, addressing no one, referring to no existent. Except that this is not quite the case. "Some of these days/You'll miss me honey." The words carry a lesson for the protagonist (do not neglect me or you'll be sorry) and, at the same time, express what he wants to be (irreplaceable, necessary).

Here, then, is another account of La Nausée. The novel does not quite begin and it does not quite end. Through its affinity for puzzles, imperfect revelations, and inadequate solutions, through its diary form (which multiplies beginnings and ends and favors successiveness as opposed to hierarchy, interruption rather than continuity, fragmentariness and not composition); through the diversity of its styles also (with it, Sartre rewrites or parodies realism and formalism, Balzac and Mallarmé, Flaubert, Hugo, Proust, Malraux, Michelet); and through the very name of its protagonist ('Roquentin' means, among other things, "a song made up of fragments of other songs . . . in such a way as to produce strange effects"),[11] La Nausée constitutes a scene for incompletion and irregularity. It does not quite answer all of the questions it raises (what is existence? what is being? how can one escape the former and inhabit the latter?). It refuses progress, going from one livre à venir (the biography of Rollebon) to another (the story envisioned toward the end). It features a modern Robinson (Sartre had, at one point, wanted to call his novel Les Aventures extraordinaires d'Antoine Roquentin) for whom uncertainty and lack of mastery slowly become the rule. It is never definitive and, if it is articulated in terms of what has no meaning—existence—it produces what is ambiguous, that is, what has too much meaning.

Now, this account, by insisting on the paradoxes, ambiguities, inconsistencies, and even contradictions in the fabric of the text, stresses the open nature of La Nausée. But it is not necessarily more satisfactory (more "true" to Sartre's novel) than my first account. At any rate, it is not wholly satisfactory. After all, something does happen (a "revolution," leading Roquentin to keep a diary which in turn leads him to think of writing a novel and to abandon his diary); the protagonist does

10. Blue Sky (sic) which Roquentin hears in La Grotte Bleue (49) and The Man I Love ("When the mellow moon begins to beam / Every night I dream a little dream" [122])!

11. See Oeuvres romanesques, 1674–75.

learn something (about the meaning of adventure, say); and, however, discontinuous, heterogeneous, or disorderly a diary might be, Roquentin's does have a signifying order (suppose, for example, that he would think of writing a story "beautiful and hard as steel" before his meeting with Anny). Furthermore, this account also institutes a closure, one we might call a closure of uncertainty (making sense of or exploiting inconclusiveness, hesitation, and contradiction) as opposed to the earlier closure of certainty. Indeed, any account of *La Nausée* (and there are many possible accounts, including the one consisting in a word for word repetition, à la Pierre Ménard), any account taking the novel to represent a unit of some sort must institute a closure, even if (as) it tries to evade it and valorize openness.

In order to give an account of a particular text (in order to say that it is about such and such, that it means so-and-so, that it illustrates this subject or that truth, that it makes this point or that one, that it can be paraphrased and/or summarized as x, y, or z), we assign meaning to the units constituting that text and taken to be relevant to our task, in terms of certain codes and subcodes (linguistic, pragmatic, cultural, etc.). The nature, number, and size of the units—like the nature, number, and size of the codes—may vary from one "accountant" to another and, for the "same" accountant, from one point in the text to another. The unit might, for instance, consist of a single word, a phrase, a sentence, a group of sentences, any one of their features or any one of their relations with other units, and so on and so forth. Thus, given *La Nausée,* I might (I did much of the time!) choose the sentence as a unit and select those sentences I think pertinent. Of course, not all of the sentences making up Sartre's novel would necessarily be retained. In my first account, for example, I eliminated from consideration sentences (or features) that make the work inconsistent (what is the name of the *patronne,* Françoise or Jeanne? how long has it been since Roquentin last saw Anny? and was it in Hanoi, Saigon, or Shanghai that he decided to go back to France?); I also ignored various ambiguities undermining Roquentin's progress toward the project of writing a novel; and I regarded as irrelevant to my purpose some of the lines describing the protagonist's physical attributes or evoking his psychosexual reactions. In my second account, I did not set aside inconsistencies and contradictions; but I did not consider all of Roquentin's unequivocal tirades (against humanism; against the *salauds* of Bouville) and, again, I did not pay attention to his appearance or to his psychosexual behavior. In other words, the textual basis of an account is not necessarily identical to the "text itself."[12]

12. I take this notion to constitute a valuable heuristic horizon.

But how is the relevance or irrelevance of a unit determined? As an accountant (or interpreter!), I construct a frame (subsuming an indefinite number of frames) in which various units can find a place, through which they can acquire additional significance, and in terms of which they can be connected with other units. This frame is based on models derived from an extra- or intratextual reality (and is conditioned by my knowledge, interests, and goals). Thus, for my first account, I basically adopted the frame proposed by Sartre in his *prière d'insérer* (and by Roquentin in the last summary of his experiences) and, among many other operations, I complemented/modified it with much of what I know about the hermeneutic and proairetic dimensions of narrative and much of what I have read about Sartre and his first novel. For my second account, on the other hand, I rejected the *prière d'insérer* (and the protagonist's final summary), kept in mind what Roquentin writes about the beginning and end of stories, had a different Sartre and other critics as references,[13] and used a frame whereby *La Nausée* constitutes an apprenticeship in uncertainty. In both cases (and, more generally, in every case), units that could not fit the frame and/or that would not acquire (much) additional significance through it, units that could not, depending on circumstances, appropriately cohere or clash with other units would be judged irrelevant.

Note that, although certain units in a given text are eliminated from consideration, the textual basis of an account is by no means a subset of that text: if I reduce the work in order to give an account of it, I also expand it. In the first place, fitting units into a frame and linking them to other units entails and/or allows for the specification of what the work does not make explicit (I have to fill the "gaps" between the units involved), the derivation of logical and pragmatic implications from the union of any two (sets of) units, and the addition of evaluative commentary indicating the status of the units in the economy of the frame. Moreover, as I indicated in passing, the frame I use is itself made up in part of constituents derived from my experience and these constituents combine with the units selected. In other words, the account of a text always includes the context of the accountant and there are, therefore, an indefinite number of possible accounts. In the case of *La Nausée*, for example, I could have used a psychoanalytic frame (showing the sexual ambiguity of Roquentin to be the motor of the novel);[14] or a sociocritical frame (one that would not attempt to explain the pro-

13. For example, Dominick La Capra, *A Preface to Sartre* (Ithaca: Cornell University Press, 1978).

14. See Serge Doubrovsky, "Le Neuf de coeur. Fragment d'une psycholecture de *La Nausée*," *Obliques*, nos. 18–19 (1979), 67–73.

tagonist through references to business conditions in Normandy around 1930!);[15] or still many others. Every one of these frames institutes a closure (but a different kind of closure: *La Nausée* is x; *La Nausée* is y; it is x and y; it is neither x nor y; it is x, y, and always something else) and the meaning of a text is the untotalizable sum of its closures.

The quality of an account (the efficiency of a closure) is clearly relative. It depends on the perceived acceptability of the frame and codes invoked, the number and kinds of units selected, the nature, diversity, and complexity of operations performed to link the units and make them yield meaning, the character of this meaning, not to mention the type of summaries and paraphrases effected by the accountant in reaching a finished account. If *La Nausée* is exemplary, and I believe it is, it may be partly due to the fact that it lends itself very well to many different kinds of closure.

15. See *Oeuvres romanesques*, 1800.

GABRIELE SCHWAB

# On the Dialectic of Closing and Opening in Samuel Beckett's *End-game*[1]

In his critique of discursive totalization, Jacques Derrida has defined the concept of "closure" with respect to two poles: finitude and play. His exposition of Lévi-Strauss points up two possibilities for "conceiving the limit of totalization"[2]: against the "classical" insight into the limitation of a finite discourse, which strives in vain to master an infinite richness, Derrida sets the "modern" understanding which no longer anchors the impossibility of totalization in the concept of finitude, but rather in that of play. Within language's field of play totalization would be meaningless since the closure of a finite whole that lacks either a center or an origin allows for infinite substitutions.[3]

Applied to another context, this analysis can be taken to interpret the inner dynamic of Samuel Beckett's *Endgame*. Conversely, however, it is also possible to develop a reading of *Endgame* which challenges Derrida's theory of closure from a new perspective. Closure is in two ways central in *Endgame:* as an interpretive gesture, it forms both an implicit theme and a nucleus for the strategies guiding aesthetic response.

*Endgame* is commonly ascribed to the theater of the absurd. This categorization has tended to determine the nature of interpretation by suggesting an understanding of the play as a symbolic representation of

---

1. This article takes up arguments fundamental to my book, *Samuel Becketts Endspiel mit der Subjektivität. Entwurf einer Wirkungsästhetik des modernen Theaters* (Stuttgart: 1981).
2. See Jacques Derrida, "La Structure, le signe et le jeu dans le discours des sciences humaines," in *L'Ecriture et la différence* (Paris: Seuil, 1967), 409–28, [423]. English translation in *The Structuralist Controversy*, ed. Richard Macksey and Eugenio Donato (Baltimore: The Johns Hopkins University Press, 1972), 247–65 [260].
3. Ibid., 423 [Trans., 260].

an absurd world. Thus we have been brought to see its characters as reduced subjects living in an alienated world of decay and awaiting death or an apocalypse with sick bodies and black humor. As a consequence, both the particularity and the peculiarity of the aesthetic presentation disappear from view and, accordingly, the crucial aesthetic experience as well: interpretation functions as closure. The "absurd" becomes an ethnocentric category of remainders capable of accounting for everything which eludes either the familiar or the already understood.

What is it, then, in *Endgame* which seems so absurd? First impressions actually generate the suggestive fascination of an alien or exotic world. In a gloomy room, suffused with grey light, we meet the two main characters: Hamm in his wheelchair and Clov acting out a strange pantomime by trying to climb a ladder in order to look out the window. But why are the windows in this barren room so high? Did a taller race of men live here once? Or have the characters been shrinking? A picture also hangs in the room, but it is turned towards the wall. Does it symbolize the "world upside-down?" In front we see two dustbins in which Hamm's parents, Nagg and Nell, vegetate. Is this more than a wicked metaphor for the generation gap?

The characters' most striking attribute is their advanced state of bodily deteriorization. Clov is the only one who is still able to move, albeit with stiff knees. Nagg and Nell lost their legs in the famous bicycle accident in the Ardennes. Hamm is lame, blind, and bleeding, needs tranquilizers, and suffers from a chronic cough. All this is so highly suggestive of symbolic meaning that one can hardly evade the atmosphere of finality, decay, and apocalypse. The characters themselves suggest that they might be the last survivors of a great disaster, and the lifelessness of the world outside supports this view. Nothing seems more evident than to see this scene as anticipating the advancing decay of our culture or an imminent global catastrophe.

Yet these interpretive closures lead us directly into the communicative dilemma in which *Endgame* quite openly and intentionally wants us to *be.* Those who limit themselves to such a reading miss the peculiar quality of the play which presents aesthetic strategies aimed at forestalling that gesture of closure which would construe the play as the symbolic representation of a deteriorating world. Whereas Samuel Beckett's own verdict, "Beware of symbols!" is more than just a rhetorical warning against interpretive closures, the play's very atmosphere, its sensual imagery, and its mutilated plot lend themselves to such symbolic interpretations. What we find, in fact, is that the very invitation to "misreadings" is one of the main communicative strategies. One cannot but be affected by the play's suggestive symbolism, especially when responding spontaneously. This conflict is crucial in the aesthetic response to Beckett's *Endgame*. We *ought* not to see any symbols, but find it impossible to see *none*. This communicative dilemma is responsible for the fact that the central (aesthetic) experience of the play is not anchored in referential meaning, but in the strategies guiding aesthetic response.

This displacement becomes most evident when one tries to hold on to one's notions of "identity." An audience whose expectations are still geared to characters having a circumscribed identity will be bitterly disappointed. The main characters, Hamm and Clov, don't seem to commit themselves to any psychic continuity as a basis for identity. To be sure, they display forms of behavior and speech which resemble certain manifestations of an inner life. However, as soon as one attempts to assemble these manifestations into some coherent notion of personality, the characters shift to a different level of self-presentation.

If nothing else, it is at least possible to grasp the basic lines of kinship and relation: Hamm and Clov live their relationship on the model of master and slave. Nagg and Nell are Hamm's parents, and there are vague hints that Hamm might have adopted Clov as his son. But thinking in these terms becomes unreliable as soon as one realizes that not only acting out but also playing with these roles proves to be Hamm and Clov's favorite preoccupation, if not obsession. In these games they relegate even the few palpable traits of identity to an iridescent half-light. The very notion of identity is revealed as a socially induced closure. In Hamm and Clov's playing with such roles the closure inherent in representations of identity is opened through never ending and continually variable substitutions. If *Endgame* brings to light the limits of totalization, then it collapses the "classical" relation to finitude with the modern one to "play."[4] This collapse is possible because the characters' discourse lacks a center which would be able to check and ground the play of substitutions[5] and thus to facilitate the representation of a centered subjectivity.

Doesn't Hamm himself, with his allusion to Zeno's heap of grain, play ironically with the viewer's search for an identity in the characters?[6] Hamm's ironic self-parody, his waiting for a heap to materialize

4. Of course, only in the sense of Derrida's critique of the closure characteristic of totalizing discourses.

5. Derrida, loc. cit.

6. "Moment upon moment, pattering down, like the millet grains of . . . *(he hesitates)* . . . that Old Greek, and all life long you wait for that to mount up to a life." S. Beckett, *Endgame, followed by Act Without Words* (New York: Grove Press, 1958), 70.

out of the accumulation of discrete moments, a new quality that one might call life, resembles the spectator who attempts to compile an "identity" for the characters out of ever new sequential repetitions and recursive speech. The audience might well take Hamm's grain paradigm as a hint that neither the identity of the characters nor the meaning of the play can be discovered by assembling fragments of identity or meaning. Perhaps, then, the audience could give up its search for neatly circumscribed wholes and instead, try to illuminate the iridescent plasticity of characters and play. This would also mean abandoning an interpretative gesture of closure in order to become involved in a decentering language-game of endless substitutions, that is, a game in which fragmented units of speech appear to be randomly substituted for each other. The play's language-game with the audience is reflected and mediated by the equally unfamiliar language-game of the characters. The latter contradicts not only all the expectations of dramatic dialogue, but also the very conditions for the functioning of dialogue. Neither is the dialogue situated in any intelligible context, nor does it derive from any representative function of speech or even a minimal amount of coherence. Moreover, it is full of contingencies, and these would be a stumbling block for any successful communication—at least according to systems theory.

Considering these disturbing qualities, one may be struck nonetheless by the easy flow of the dialogue. Most striking is the constant introduction of new topics, accompanied by the recurrence of nearly identical sequences of dialogue, though sometimes with the roles of the speakers reversed. The characters seem to be involved in a language-game, in which speech units can be moved around like chess pieces. There are not only identical but also unexpectedly abrupt moves in a game which functions according to rules unknown to the audience. An endless substitution of basic existential or anthropological problems seems to control the subject of conversation. The game, as it progresses with its preordained repetition of speech units, allows these themes to circle back on themselves. The content freezes into paradigmatic formulas belonging to an empty speech which the characters toss to and fro between them like a ball. One might think of it as a private use of language, which no longer requires one to mean what one says, but which gives one the freedom to play with the familiarity of old and empty rules. Or, from the perspective of the Derridean theory of closure: Hamm and Clov play with the superabundance of floating signifiers over and above all their possible signifieds in order to thematize the character of this surplus itself.

Yet this language game is also an end-game which focuses on ending and non-ending. Clov knows how to gain the advantage by threatening to violate the rules and terminate what is in principle an endless game. Or does even the threat of breaking the rules belong to the game? The nature of playing this game makes it impossible to identify the characters with their speech. By alternately exchanging slightly varied sequences of stereotyped dialogue in this game of substitution, the characters undermine any conceivable self-differentiation through their speech. So, for example, Clov's question, "Why this farce, day after day?" has already been asked before by Nell; Hamm's "Don't we laugh?" will in turn be taken up later by Clov.[7] Such a play with the substitution and repetition of speech units undercuts any notion of speech as reliable self-presentation.

To aggravate matters, the characters continually vacillate between different levels of play. Thus the boundaries between the "endgame" and the "games within the endgame" remain fluid. Moreover, Hamm caricatures our expectation that dramatic characters display some presentation of self. He parodies this function of self-presentation and self-ironically unmasks the seduction of the other through self-stylization. By playfully enclosing himself in the role of a narcissistic artist, he discloses self-presentation as a mock fight for recognition. His dependence on Clov as spectator caricatures, in addition, self-presentation as a way of performing for the internalized Other. Such a self-presentation can only portray a fictional self. One need only think of the scenes in which Hamm repeatedly urges Clov to ask him for his story, whereupon Clov immediately stages himself as a character who complies with this request.

How can a spectator react to these language games if they are not played by conventional rules and defy all our interpretive closures? As the characters refuse self-presentation and even caricature the latent function of self-presentation inherent in our speech, we become unsure of our relation to them. Where are the characters in their own speech? They don't seem to share our norms of communication. Their dialogue lacks representative qualities and hardly makes "sense" to us. Whatever has the appearance of identity, representation, or meaning is counteracted or contradicted in the course of the play. *The pervasive structure of negation and contradiction frustrates all partial investments of meaning and thereby fundamentally impedes every gesture of interpretation which strives for closure.*

7. S. Beckett, *Endgame,* 32 and 14; 11 and 29.

Hamm and Clov present their dialogue as an imaginary game, replete with suggestive symbolism, yet without pretensions to any latent
meaning. Thus they hedge themselves against any interpretation bent
on deciphering a truth or centering the decentered play.[8] This strategy
lures the audience into a type of double bind[9]: highly connotative "symbols" suggest a latent dimension and invite ever newer constructions of
meaning—apparently only to dismantle them as soon as they tend to
stabilize. *Each invitation to closure is followed by new openings which
prove that closure to be reductive.* It seems as if *Endgame* doesn't allow
for the construction of latent meaning or as if the invitations to closure
are intentionally set up as traps. The dilemma becomes inescapable: in
order to "understand" the characters, the audience must construe the
symbolic meaning which the characters seem to suggest but, in fact,
later reject. Should the audience do so, it is sanctioned, for the characters deride this meaning as a conventional projection of preconceived
ideas:

HAMM: Clov?
CLOV:(*impatiently*): What is it?
HAMM: We're not beginning to . . . to . . . mean something?
CLOV: Mean something! You and I, mean something! (*Brief laugh.*) Ah
    that's a good one!
HAMM: I wonder. (*Pause*). Imagine if a rational being came back to earth,
    wouldn't he be liable to get ideas into his head if he observed us
    long enough. (*Voice of rational being.*) Ah, good, now I see what
    it is, yes, now I understand what they're at! (*Clov starts, drops
    the telescope and begins to scratch his belly with both
    hands.*)[10]

The dynamic outlined here between a continual invitation to
closure and renewed opening can be seen as one of the play's central
strategic devices. It is anchored not only in what the characters say but
also in the structure of the play and the dramatic language. The very act
of symbolic interpretation, then, is being rejected as an unacceptable
closure of the play's open structure.

At first glance we seem to be offered a play decidedly rich in con-

8. Cf. Derrida, op. cit., 427 [264]: "The one seeks to decipher, dreams of deciphering, a truth or an origin. . ."
9. This is not to be understood metaphorically, but rather in the sense of concrete,
irreconcilable directives which force the audience into a paradoxical situation: (1) You
must construe meaning, (2) This is possible only by means of projection, (3) You must
not project. Compare, C. E. Sluzki and D. C. Ransom, ed., *Double-Bind: The Foundation
of the Communicational Approach to the Family* (New York: Grune and Stratton, 1976).
10. Beckett, *Endgame*, 32.

notation. Literary criticism has worked out allusions to literary and cultural history which are sufficiently broad in scope: Hamm as Hamlet, as "ham" actor; his sheet as Christ's sudarium or a stage curtain, and so forth. Nevertheless, such connotations cannot be woven into the pattern of a coherent structure. The continual fluctuation between offers of connotation and their withdrawal prevents closure.

And yet, understanding that not even specific offers of connotation refer to a hidden meaning already presupposes an involvement in the play. Where closure is continually forestalled and connotations fail to provide meaning, the audience will be excluded from its familiar relation to language.

The different strategies enticing the audience into closures which are subsequently rejected and reopened by the play lead to one significant effect: they challenge language's "structure of double meaning."[11] *Endgame* plays with the "superabundance of signifier, in relation to the signifieds"[12] in order, finally, to exaggerate altogether the line[13] between signifier and signified. This structure of double meaning is, of course, fundamental to language in general. Its effect is revealed as soon as a manifest meaning explicitly refers to a latent one. Yet, if a play such as *Endgame* no longer carries an evident manifest meaning, then we automatically suspect a latent one. While this suspicion can be said to characterize our reaction to poetic language in general, the challenge of *Endgame* consists in undermining this conventional receptive disposition. The failure of our efforts to "make sense" out of what we see by interpreting symbolically is—from this point of view—the basic initial aesthetic experience of the play. Thus both symbolic closure and its failure are the results of textual strategies.

If we accept this, then the significance of the play can be found neither in the manifest nor in the latent dimension of dramatic speech. What I mean here is that significance is produced by dramatic speech but can no longer be bound to its meaning. It even tends towards an asemantic quality. Only when we forego our "need for semantic succour"[14] in our construction of meaning can we grasp what the play is trying to convey and thus avoid projecting preconceived conventional

11. This term is used here in the way Paul Ricoeur uses "La structure du double sens" ["The structure of double meaning"] in his book on Freud. Cf. P. Ricoeur, *De l'interprétation. Essai sur Freud* (Paris: Seuil, 1965), 13–63 (Livre Premier).

12. Lévi-Strauss quoted by Derrida, op. cit., 424 [261].

13. In the sense of Lacan's "barre." ["bar"] See J. Lacan, "L'instance de la lettre dans l'inconscient," in: *Ecrits* 1 (Paris: Seuil, "Coll. Points," 1970), 253.

14. See Beckett, *Watt* (London: 1963), 79.

"meanings" and closures. Due to this shift in the reception process the main aesthetic potential of *Endgame* lies rather in the effect of that process than the substance of its imaginary stage world. The corresponding aesthetic strategy which consists in the rejection of the structure of double meaning, and the denial of closure produces very complex effects. It not only challenges the familiar relation between manifest and latent meaning, but also unsettles the audience's habits and conventions of communication. In the reception process we have to follow the play's strategy to let us shift between invitations to closure and required reopenings. Thus we may experience the extent to which our need for meaning induces us to close the gaps of the play by projecting our imaginations into them. This offers us some insight into our need for projective closures, as well as into the defensive qualities of our own communicative behavior.

One main consequence of those strategies guiding audience response is that in the process of reception they shift our attention from the subjectivity of the fictional characters to our own subjectivity. What we then experience is our own decenteredness. Since the structure of double meaning is the linguistic basis of decentered subjectivity, it is entirely appropriate that the play challenge this structure. The double meaning structure, i.e., a form of expression that can simultaneously show and hide meaning, gives us a chance not only to express, but also to react to, decentered subjectivity. Equally appropriate is the peculiar presentation of characters in *Endgame*. Decentered subjectivity is not conveyed by presenting "decentered characters," but by challenging all familiar notions of subjectivity. To effect this challenge one cannot present so-called "realistic" characters, but only highly stylized ones. Hamm and Clov are condensed and overdetermined characters. Similar to the figures who people our dreams, they have absorbed meanings, signs, and properties from other characters as well as pure psychological or aesthetic functions. This complex and allusive overdetermination has occasioned numerous speculative interpretations.

Hamm and Clov have been seen as mythical characters in a mythical place or set within the tradition of the cosmological dialogue of the gods. They have been likened to Chronos and Mercury, to the sons of Noah after the flood, to Shakespeare's Hamlet, and also to Gloucester and Edgar in *King Lear*. Others have explicated the numerous echoes of other Beckett characters, Pozzo and Lucky in particular, as well as the Unnamable. On the other hand, *Endgame* has also been interpreted as an aesthetic differentiation of what is otherwise conceived of as a unity. Here the characters appear as components of a unified self or their room as a human brain whose various functions are divided up among the characters.

What is common to all of these interpretations is the desire to reduce the condensed form of the characters to a latent meaning. The symbolic connotations are, of course, the indisputable guides for a spontaneous response to the play. They ground the strategy of invitation to closure. The continual openings, however, prove those symbols to be irreducible. They resist any reduction to a latent meaning. Peter Brook characterizes Beckett's peculiar way of using symbols: "A true symbol is like Beckett's *Endgame*. The entire work is one *symbol* enclosing numerous others, though none of them are of the type which stand for something else; we get no further when we ask what they are supposed to mean, since here a symbol has become an object."[15]

The condensation of characters constitutes still another device used to affect the audience's subjectivity. Condensations are gestalt formations unconsciously produced and invested with meaning. By appealing to our unconscious, then, the condensed characters of *Endgame* allow a different function of the communicative strategy to come into play: the transgression of the boundaries between consciousness and the unconscious. But in order to make the audience transgress these boundaries *Endgame* must pursue a double strategy. It takes into account decenteredness by appealing on different levels and by different means to both conscious and unconscious domains of response.[16] Those aspects of the play which allow for immediate access are also those which invite interpretive closures. The central devices here are condensation and diffusion of meaning, both of which produce highly ambivalent appeals. Conscious annoyances are often counterbalanced by unconscious fascination. The latter becomes evident if we consider that the dissolution of the conventional symbolic functioning of language, which renders the process of understanding so difficult, also allows for effects which are normally absent or remain unconscious. Thus the strongest appeal and the most far-reaching effect of *Endgame* issue from what cannot be integrated into the symbolic order or cannot be centered: for example, speech acts violating the symbolic order of language, dramatic elements which cannot be integrated into the plot, behaviors which cannot be centered in the characters. In turn, this

15. P. Brook, "Mit Beckett leben," in: *Materialien zu Becketts "Endspiel"* (Frankfurt: Deutsche Erstansg, 1968), 32. The quotation has been translated from the original, which was in German.

16. The complexity of this double strategy has to be somewhat simplified here. For a more detailed analysis see G. Schwab, op. cit., 105–25.

decentering affects the audience. The relative security of our status as audience allows us to be drawn into the game Beckett's characters are playing. But in so doing, we become temporarily infected by their decentered condition. Hamm and Clov play their identity games above all with the audience's identity, making it experience both its own decenteredness and its need for centering interpretations and closures.

The strongest impulse for the reflective side of the aesthetic experience of *Endgame* comes from the strategy of continual opening by means of rejection and frustration. However fascinating these openings may unconsciously be, they must nonetheless be coped with consciously, for they are responsible for the continual failure of our attempts at interpretation. The history of Beckett criticism proves how difficult such an experience is even in terms of aesthetics. Thus it could also be viewed as the history of a collective defense against this failure, which in turn has given rise to a Beckett industry virtually addicted to symbolic interpretation.

Coping positively rather than negatively with the continual rejection of interpretations and the opening up of closure leads the audience to reflect upon the character of such interpretive acts themselves. For as long as the audience does not bale out of the communicative situation which arises in the immediate experience of the text and its dialectic of closing and opening or attraction and frustration, it remains trapped in an aesthetic double bind. There are, however, a number of clues in the play indicating that the way to get out of the trap is by shifting to a metalevel and reflecting on one's own interpretive acts. This strategy involves implicit references to the audience's situation—references which, like the above quoted passage, explicitly deal with projection and closure. *The aesthetic devices are thus targeted to a self-reflection which is both a mastery of the frustrated spontaneous response as well as an insight into one's own acts in interpretation.* In addition to the emotive and unconscious effects on the audience, self-reflection, then, can also be considered one of the basic elements in the overall response to *Endgame*.

I would now like to summarize some of the main points concerning the strategies guiding aesthetic response. As we have seen, the dynamic between closures and openings in *Endgame* entangles the audience both in the game the characters are playing and in a network made up of its own projections of meaning. This dynamic, however, is only one of the dis-illusioning strategies, which aim at a type of meta-understanding or, better yet, metaexperience of one's own communicative acts. The effect is to make the audience conscious of how it projects meaning. This allows it to experience its projections as an attempt to close and center something inherently open and decentered. We might also call this effort a defense against the experience of otherness. At the same time the dis-illusioning strategies aim at altering our need for centering and closing open structures.

The subtlest and most far-reaching of these strategies is the "withdrawal of double meaning," i.e., the play's insistence on rejecting latent meaning, which interestingly enough itself operates as a double strategy. The separation of conscious from unconscious appeals accounts for the fact that the spectators themselves are decentered subjects. The importance of this double strategy lies in allowing them to transgress the border between consciousness and the unconscious. As our decentered subjectivity depends on polarizing these domains, transgressing the boundaries between them also affects our decentered condition. Seen in this way, *Fin de partie*—the *Endgame*—*becomes a game involving the limits of our own subjectivity*. In the reception process, the conventions characterizing our subjectivity are temporarily suspended. It is little wonder that so many react to the play as if a taboo were being violated.

Ambivalence, then, is also an important aspect of the aesthetic experience of *Endgame*. Transgressing the line between consciousness and the unconscious is always fraught with ambivalence. It releases anxieties of disintegration, emptiness, or inundation by the unconscious. Simultaneously, however, it can become a source of delight. We derive pleasure from our positive investment in that original, undifferentiated mode of being which has been forced by the reality principle to survive in the reserves set aside for alternative states of consciousness.

This transgressive quality of *Endgame* is perhaps best documented by the isolated laughter so typical during the performance of Beckett's plays. I see this laughter as an expression of unconscious understanding or reaction. The spectator signals by his laughter that the strangeness of *Endgame* is not so foreign to him after all. This laughter arises spontaneously at the threshold of an unconscious understanding of something which our consciousness does not allow to be understood. However impenetrable or uninterpretable the dramatic action may seem, the laughter indicates that there is indeed a hidden understanding beyond consciousness. This laughter itself subverts the boundaries of our subjectivity in a specific way, since it involves, like laughter in general, a temporary abandoning of our ego-limits. And this is, of course, precisely one of the effects which *Endgame* had set as its goal.

The seemingly insignificant spontaneous laughter physically anticipates a type of transgression which has become one of the hallmarks of aesthetic response to contemporary art. The conscious experience of a shift in, or an expansion of, the limits of our subjectivity is more painful and has provoked extremely defensive responses towards modern art. *Endgame* makes us aware that not only the open rejection of a work of art but also its "centering" by interpretive closures can be such a defense. In order to be able to derive benefit from the play's potential transgressions, we must learn to renounce interpretive closures. *Endgame* challenges them in three ways: it rejects them, it activates our unconscious desire for dissolutions, and it counterbalances its own transgressive tendencies by making us shift to a metalevel. Thus it aims at expanding the boundaries of our consciousness in two directions: towards the unconscious and towards self-reflection. Simultaneously, however, our need for closure emerges, in the aesthetic experience of *Endgame,* as a function of our need for meaning. One historical function of Beckett's strategy guiding aesthetic response resides in the objective not simply to supplant this need with another, but instead to work on it and, in so doing, to activate our latent desire for openings. By its dialectical rendering of closure, *Endgame* marks a historically significant threshold beyond which we experience an important change in our dispositions and in the nature of our aesthetic response. Hence, this is really the main reason *Endgame* has become so successful as an "endgame" which plays with the limits of our subjectivity.

Translated by D. L. Selden

JOAN BRANDT

# The Theory and Practice of a "Revolutionary" Text: Denis Roche's "Le mécrit"

As a self-proclaimed adversary of the "poetic establishment in all its forms," the poet, Denis Roche, launched a series of deliberate and sustained attacks on traditional poetic conventions beginning in 1964 with *Les Idées centésimales de Miss Elanize* and culminating in what was to be his last work of poetry, "Le mécrit," in 1971.[1] This desire to negate traditional standards of aesthetics, which can also be found to a certain extent in his earlier poems, developed forcefully in Roche's work in the course of his association with the French journal *Tel Quel*, evolving at the time of his membership on the editorial board and when the journal itself was in its most radically political phase. Founded in 1960 by Philippe Sollers as a primarily literary venture, the journal and its various contributors, including not only Roche and Sollers but Julia Kristeva and poet-theoretician Marcelin Pleynet, became increasingly interested in Marxist theory and began to see language and the literary text as a means to further the cause of social revolution. Claiming that communicative language is a principal vehicle in the preservation of the ideological structures that dominate Western culture, the group attempted to formulate and put into practice a revolutionary materialist theory of language in an effort to work against the traditional concept of the literary text and of language itself as predominantly meaningful

1. See the notice on the back cover of the book in which this particular text appears and which also bears the same title: *Le mécrit* (Paris: Editions du Seuil, 1972). Here Roche gives a brief outline of his project. *Le mécrit* was first published in *Tel Quel* in the fall of 1971 and later reprinted apart in book form. "Le mécrit," a neologism formed by combining the term "écrit" (writing or written) with the privative prefix "mé" (un-, mis-, non-), it conveys the idea of wrong writing or "miswriting." Roche's text is characterized by this kind of play with verbal form, particularly with the visual and sonorous properties of language, which can easily be lost in translation. Consequently, some of my translations of Roche's text will be accompanied by the original French.

structures and thus to help achieve, by indirection, a transformation of the social order and its repressive laws as well.[2]

At this particular period in *Tel Quel's* history, then, the idea of a subversive "practice of collective writing" emerges.[3] Indeed, much of Roche's later poetry, and "Le mécrit" in particular, can be viewed as an outgrowth of the theoretical investigations of language conducted by the *Tel Quel* writers and theorists at that time. Discussing his association with *Tel Quel* in an interview that appears in Serge Gavronsky's *Poems & Texts*,[4] Roche sees himself (until 1973 at least when he resigned from the editorial board of *Tel Quel*) participating in a "community of experience" in which new developments in poetry and the *nouveau roman* are to occur in conjunction with certain advances in critical theory.

Given, then, this exchange of ideas between the *Tel Quel* poets and theorists, the writings of the principal theoreticians of the *Tel Quel* group should not be ignored when considering certain of Roche's texts, for it is their theory of a revolutionary "poetic" language, particularly as it is formulated by Julia Kristeva in her earlier work, Σημειωτικὴ, that provides the framework for the literary activity of the poets who belonged to the *Tel Quel* circle at that time. And it means that Roche's last work of poetry, "Le mécrit," which was published before his departure from the *Tel Quel* group, represents far more than a purely personal attack on linguistic and literary conventions; it incorporates many of the *Tel Quel* aims and objectives, attempting to bring about a radical

2. Since that time, the thinking at *Tel Quel* has undergone a series of changes, leading first to a break with what Sollers called the "dogmatico-revisionism" of the French Communist Party in 1971, followed by a strong commitment to Maoism. Later, disillusioned by the effects of the Cultural Revolution and recognizing that the followers of Mao, like those of Marx, betrayed his revolutionary spirit by transforming his principles into dogma, the group's interests turned once again to the literary. While the emphasis, currently, is still on the possibilities for subversion that lie within language, there is a recognition that such subversive activity is less easily translated to the socio-political realm. For an interesting discussion of the various changes that have occurred at *Tel Quel* over the years, see Shuhsi Kao's interview with Sollers in *Sub-Stance*, no. 30 (1981) where he openly criticizes the "romantic vision" that prevailed during this highly political period of the late sixties and early seventies.

3. Sollers later repudiates this idea of a collective effort, however, claiming that the collectivity itself could be just as oppressive as the social order it opposed: "A collectivity consists of people who get together because they are rebelling against an established order. But as soon as this collectivity takes over, then it is no longer an interesting collectivity. *Tel Quel* was collective up to the time when the movement threatened to become affirmative. If "Telquelism" were to prevail, it would have to be contested right away; I would even be the first to take command of a Liberation Front against Telquelism." *Sub-Stance*, no. 30, 40.

4. Serge Gavronsky, *Poems and Texts* (New York: October House Inc., 1969).

transformation not only of the poetic text but of what Roche has called the "retrograde, obscurantist ideology" dominating the entire structure of Western culture and thought.

Roche's critique of the Western literary tradition is thus to have not just aesthetic but also social and political ramifications, and it stems from the view that continues to prevail at *Tel Quel* that the Western concept of the text as a closed and basically meaningful literary "object," whose communicative language effectively safeguards the objective status of the reality it portrays, ultimately works to preserve the closed and oppressive political structures that have dominated Western society from the feudal era to the bourgeois social system of the present day. Related to what is described by Kristeva in particular as the traditionally "positivist" epistemology at the core of Western thought, the structure and function of the traditional literary text are seen to perpetuate an objectivist view of the world, one that has consistently refused to recognize that its belief in an ordered and objectifiable universe is not due to something inherent in the nature of things, but is a function of the predominant ideology which seeks to reduce the multifarious nature of the real to comprehensible and, therefore, controllable limits. Communicative language and traditional aesthetics, whose logic of meaning must posit a fixed and representable universe, thus serve, according to Kristeva, the needs of an essentially totalitarian and repressive social order, a society dominated by what she calls the "Law of One" which dictates that all diversity, all that poses a threat to the cohesiveness of the total social organization be either eliminated or enclosed within the system. The unified structure of the literary text, which, according to Kristeva, must itself repress all that interferes with the production of the author's intended meaning, thus helps to constitute and preserve the closed structures that a cohesive and basically totalitarian social system requires.

This means, then, that for Kristeva, the various operations of the traditional literary text, like the society of which it is a part, are strictly controlled. This is, in fact, one of the principle ideas of her essay on "Le Texte Clos," which first appeared in Σημειωτικὴ (1969) and was later translated in *Desire in Language* as "The Bounded Text."[5] Here, she uses Antoine de La Sale's fifteenth-century novel *Jehan de Saintré* to demonstrate the "structural closure" which she claims characterizes not only the traditional novel but all of Western literature before the

5. Julia Kristeva, *Desire in Language*, ed. Leon S. Roudiez (New York: Columbia University Press, 1980).

"epistemological break" of the late nineteenth century when writers like Mallarmé and Lautréamont attempted to challenge traditional aesthetics. She argues that the entire trajectory of La Sale's text is controlled and directed by what is announced at the outset: "The text opens with an introduction that shapes (shows) the entire itinerary of the novel. . . . We thus already know how the story will end: the end of the narration is given before the narrative itself even begins."[6] The trajectory of the novel is programmed, according to Kristeva, both by the intentions of its author and by the "non-disjunctive" operations of the text's discursive language which ultimately resolves all conflict and contradiction and assures the production of a unified and immediately appropriable meaning. The reader's response will be carefully programmed as well. Cast as a mere recipient of the author's message, the reader is placed in a purely passive role with the freedom of his interpretive activity drastically limited by the meaning he is required to extract from the structure of the work.

It is by challenging, therefore, this concept of the text as a perfectly controlled, communicative object, whose operations are carefully regulated to ensure the production and ultimate consumption of a fixed and unified sense, that Kristeva and the other members of the *Tel Quel* group seek to undermine the objectivist precepts that structure the totality of Western discourse and, in so doing, to shake the foundations of the prevailing social structure with its static and reified vision of the world. The literary text is to become the laboratory for a radically new discourse, one that attempts to move beyond the traditional subject-object polarity by exploding the boundaries that separate the literary "object" from its reading and writing subjects, by revealing what Western culture has consistently denied—that the language of the text does not simply mirror from a position of exteriority a preexistent psychological or social reality, but is actually constitutive of the reality it purports to describe, and that the reader, in turn, does not merely lift out or extract the meaning implicit within the work itself, but, in fact, participates in the production of that meaning through his own interpretive activity. To question the objective status of the literary text and of the reality it portrays is thus to undermine a whole system of interpretive conventions, for the text can no longer be reduced to or enclosed within a single and finite meaning, but requires instead a recognition of the processes that go into the production of that meaning, processes that serve, in effect, to "open up" the text, to break down the boundaries so

6. Ibid., 42.

necessary not only to the traditional concept of literature, but to the entire structure of Western positivist thought.

A concept of the "open" text, which focuses on the process of textual production rather than on the finished product (i.e., on the supposedly unique meaning that the text produces), is thus what emerges in the course of the *Tel Quel* critique. Implicated in this concept is a necessarily open-ended theory of reading, for the text cannot be viewed as a fixed object of analysis with specifiable properties and determinable boundaries; its open-ended structure instead resolutely resists all attempts at total comprehension and thus forces the reader constantly to question the validity of his own interpretive assumptions and, ultimately, to become critical of his tendency to systematize, to reduce the complexity of the text to a simple and comprehensible structure.

The problem of reading is thus central to the *Tel Quel* theory of the "open" text and will serve as a major focus for my own analysis of Denis Roche's "Le mécrit," for it raises one of the most fundamental questions of the entire enterprise, that of finding a way to read the revolutionary text in terms of the theory, in terms of its opposition to the concept of the closed, literary object without granting a certain specificity to the former, without establishing the kinds of distinctions that, in effect, restore many of the objectivist assumptions that the group so vigorously attacks. In the course of the analysis that follows, I plan to show that *Tel Quel* theory does not succeed entirely in finding a satisfactory solution to this problem, for the notion of the text as a revolutionary *praxis* contains within it certain assumptions about the nature of the text and the act of reading that, in fact, reinstate many of the premises it is meant to oppose. Indeed, to construct a theory of the text on the basis of its revolutionary character is already to impose certain limits, to close off its supposedly open-ended structure by defining the text in terms of its difference from its more traditional counterpart. Not only that, but it requires that the reader respond to the text in a very particular way and implies a structuring principle of some kind, a controlling force governing the operations of the literary work.

Kristeva's conception of the revolutionary text thus accentuates the very paradoxical nature of her own and the *Tel Quel* position, for it involves the formulation of a revolutionary "program" to undermine the precepts of the traditionally "programmed" text, an intentional strategy to contest the notion of a preexistent authorial intention. An examination of the practical implications of this particular conception of the text both in terms of its effect on the formal configuration of the work and on the mechanics of reading will thus provide the basis for the

following analysis of "Le mécrit." It will become clear after a preliminary reading of the work as an "open" text that questions of intentionality and textual comprehensibility are raised by the work itself
that are not ultimately raised by the theory. A closer look at the theory
will indeed reveal that, in certain respects, it does not challenge the
interpretive norm to the extent that the *Tel Quel* group would like, but,
in fact, permits a very different reading of "Le mécrit," one that restores
many of the precepts of the closed, programmed literary work it is
meant to oppose.

Let us turn, then, to "Le mécrit," a work made up of six texts and
two inscriptions. Here the effort to exploit the unlimited possibilities of
the open text is most immediately apparent in the poem's fractured
poetic structure. Preceded by a discursive theoretical preface which
appears enclosed in a well-defined, rectangular frame, the six texts that
follow seem to be breaking through the structural boundaries that the
frame imposes, their margins either eliminated, opened or displaced,
with the words often spilling over the edges, appearing unrestricted by
the confines of the poetic text. This impression of openness and incompletion is accentuated by the lack of finality in the concluding lines.
Often ending in midsentence (if it is possible to call this chaotic juxtaposition of words a "sentence") or with a dash instead of a period, the
operations of each poem appear to progress interminably from one text
to another with each successive text both transforming and ultimately
bringing about the disintegration of the initial enclosure. It is almost as
if the closed, discursive space of the preface is actually exploded into
little fragments, with bits and pieces scattered throughout the work; as
an example, "m'y enfoncer" ["thrust myself into it"] in the preface
becomes "jl'enfonc" ["I thrus i"] in text 2 and "J'enfonce" ["I thrust"] in
text 5; "dans les limites très étroites" ["within the very narrow limits"]
becomes "l'&enflant étroit" ["the narrow & swelling"] in text 4, "dans
l'&troit moi" ["within the n&rrow me"] in text 5, and "à l'étroit dans"
["to the narrow within"] in text 6. And although "meaning" as such has
not been completely eliminated (for instance, the expression "forte
tour" ["fortified tower"] which appears repeatedly throughout the texts,
carries over semantically the idea of enclosed, limited space), the possibility of communication, the allegorical function of the traditional
poem, is essentially obstructed; the ordered discursivity of the preface
becomes an anarchic jumble of words and typographical symbols.

The disruption of syntax and signification, then, can also be seen as
an "anticlosural" strategy, one that works in conjunction with the
structural derangement of the text to prevent the traditional, discursive

progression toward a meaningful conclusion.[7] This attack upon the finality of meaning and the effort to undermine all closural effects occurs on the most fundamental level, that of the word itself, whose unity is broken by the omission of letters, by the splitting of a word in two so that it appears on two different lines within the poem, or by the appearance of an unnecessary and misplaced capital letter. The linguistic operations of the poem, then, become manifestly self-destructive, waging war on the prevailing rules of grammar and punctuation by "pulverizing" the very structure of the word, producing a system of shocks and tensions that upset the regular rhythms of the traditional poem.

Thus, in almost every possible instance, the traditional qualities of closure (i.e., unified meaning and structure) are contested by "Le mécrit," with the spatial configuration of each text all but obliterating the framed introduction and undermining, as a consequence, the teleological character of the traditional literary form. No longer following the pattern of the conventionally "programmed" text, as defined by Kristeva, the trajectory of "Le mécrit" does not simply repeat the introductory preface but engages that preface in a series of transformations and permutations that proceed toward no point of culmination but are inscribed in an ultimately unresolvable, open-ended process. Not even the margins of the pages succeed in imposing limits, for the texts flow into one another, each one repeating and transforming the various components of the preceding structure: "la ferme" ["the farm"] in text 1 is either repeated in text 2 or reemerges as "la fermièR" ["the femaL farmer"] in text 3, or "le fermier" ["the farmer"] in text 6; "2 pourceaux" ["2 swine"] in text 2, which reappears in text 3, becomes "Pour ces 2-ci" ["For these 2 swine here"] in text 5, or "2 doux pourceaux" ["2 sweet swine"] in text 6. All of this is, of course, not for the purpose of evoking some idyllic, pastoral vision but rather to accentuate the movement from text to text, with the semantic and typographical variations of the preface also appearing to reverberate throughout.

This emphasis on the mutual interaction between texts whereby the structure of each is constructed on the basis of its relationship to other textual surfaces once again serves to open the text by showing that each individual poem is structured not only as a permutation of texts within "Le mécrit" itself, but as an expression and contradiction of an entire body of literature whose traditional aspects are called to mind even as they are being transformed. As Roche states in the preface to

7. See Barbara Herrnstein Smith's *Poetic Closure* (Chicago: The University of Chicago Press, 1968) for an analysis of the apparent tendency in much contemporary poetry toward "anticlosure" and for an outline of a number of anticlosural techniques.

*Eros énergumène:* "To de-figure the convention of writing is to bear constant witness that poetry is a convention (of genre) within a convention (of communication)."[8] Moreover, in conjuring up the literary conventions it sets out to negate, the work inevitably implicates the cultural beliefs and presuppositions with which it remains inextricably intertwined. Consequently, the operations of "Le mécrit" do not simply attempt to negate the rigid stanza arrangements and the closed communicative patterns of the traditional poem but are directed at an entire culture; the text's antipoetic, antidiscursive writing ("mécriture") is to lead, as the words in the preface to "Le mécrit" seem to indicate, "poetic production toward its most extreme *miscultural* point (*mécriture*), the zero point, clearly, of poeticity."[9]

Underscoring this effort to move beyond cultural constraints are the Etruscan and Mongolian inscriptions which, from the point of view of *Tel Quel* theorists, provide a means of breaking out of the bonds of Western ethnocentrism by introducing other civilizations and other forms of language, most particularly the languages of the Orient whose emphasis on tonality and rhythm is seen by *Tel Quel* as disrupting the ordered and logical system of Western discourse and thus contesting the rigid constraints imposed by Western rationalist thought. In addition, the basic incomprehensibility of the inscriptions (to the average Western reader, at least) serves to counter to the most extreme degree traditional interpretive approaches by confounding the reader's search for meaning, leaving him with little more than the formal arrangement of symbols on the page. The inscriptions then whose "system of functioning," Roche writes at the end of the work, is closely related to that of his own poetic texts, become in certain respects, "models" for the other texts within "Le mécrit" where the attempt to emphasize the mechanisms of language and textual formation is meant to dissolve all totalizing meaning. Thus, just as the theoretical preface participates in the structuring of "Le mécrit" through the negation of its closed discursivity, so too do the inscriptions, which must be confronted as a complex system of writing and not simply in terms of their content, exercise a certain influence on the formation of each text.

8. Denis Roche, *Eros énergumène* (Paris: Editions du Seuil, 1968), 11.
9. See Carlos Lynes's article "Ecrire/Mécrire (Poétique et Antipoétique chez Denis Roche)," *French Forum*, 2, no. 1 (January, 1977), 70–89, for an interesting discussion of the struggle for cultural revolution that structures "Le mécrit." Sarah N. Lawall also examines "Le mécrit" from this point of view, underlining the "utopian ideal of social perfectibility" that informs the poetry of both Roche and Marcelin Pleynet: "The Poem as Utopia," *French Forum*, 1, no. 2 (May, 1976), 153–76.

This emphasis, however, upon the materiality of language should not, according to *Tel Quel* theory, be interpreted as a purely formalist position, as an attempt to constitute an exclusively verbal universe separated from all social, historical or even psychological considerations, for it is precisely this exclusivity, the limitations imposed by those who consider language as a strictly formal and basically analyzable system that is to be countered by the revolutionary text. And, although we shall see that the *Tel Quel* theory of the text remains in some respects within the formalist enclosure, Formalism, as far as the *Tel Quel* group is concerned, is just as closed and repressive as the aesthetic idealism it is meant to replace. The operations of "Le mécrit," then, are to be viewed as more than a simple verbal exercise. Structured by a multiplicity of written and unwritten influences (viz., the literary conventions and the philosophical assumptions of the tradition it attempts to negate; the rhythmical antidiscursive practices of the extra-European cultures it seeks to affirm; the interweaving of the texts within "Le mécrit" itself; the intentions of its author; and as we shall see, the interpretive activity of the reader), the text emerges as an open, dynamic interweaving of linguistic and nonlinguistic practices which complicates the formalist model by moving beyond the confines of a static linguistic system. As a consequence, the reader's attempt to analyze the text, to reduce it to a monolithic structure is frustrated.

The reader, then, is also caught up in the dynamics of the "open" text; his effort to establish consistent patterns is both stimulated and frustrated by its complex operations.[10] The various gaps that appear within its structure, the broken words, the omitted letters, in fact, play upon the reader's tendency to link things together, to marshall all elements into a single and finite meaning, by inviting him to participate actively in the reconstruction of the text. The reader finds, however, that his attempts at reconstruction fail abominably. The rejoined words convey no unified image; the various patterns offer no point of convergence. This is particularly evident in the substitution of the abbreviation "&" for what the reader assumes could be either "e" or "u" (as in "dans l'&troit moi" or in "&n"), and yet, the reader immediately discovers that his process of decoding uncovers no underlying system, for his conclusions are countered by the appearance of the symbol in other

10. See Wolfgang Iser's *The Implied Reader* (Baltimore: The Johns Hopkins University Press, 1974) for a very explicit and informative discussion of this tendency within the modern text both to encourage and frustrate the reader's attempts at "consistency building." His analysis of the reading process, particularly as it relates to the modern literary work, proved very useful to the following analysis of "Le mécrit."

contexts where its existence has no apparent justification (for example in "&u&cs").[11]

The text, then, while continually provoking the reader into establishing his own connections, at the same time interferes with his ability to do so, for the reader discovers that every meaning he attempts to impose upon the work is countered by a conflicting possibility. Turning to the introductory preface in his search for consistency where, on the basis of his experience with traditional textual analysis, he expects to find certain directives that will guide his interpretation, he finds that far from leading him to a "correct" reading of the text, the preface only adds to his uncertainty, first heightening his expectations and then preventing their complete fulfillment. Each of the succeeding texts within "Le mécrit," whose operations challenge the conventions of genre and communication by undermining referentiality and poetic principles of structure and versification, appear initially to be working in conformity with the stated aims of the preface: "As for what they call *poetry*, as far as I am concerned I must always try to thrust myself into it more deeply, carrying into it the poetic material in order to bring it to the point where it figures only *reductively* (afin de l'amener à ne plus figurer qu'*en moins*) and that within the very narrow limits of the only landscape in which I still move about." The traditional poem is transformed into a multiplicity of "textes" whose chaotic juxtaposition of words and pulsional rhythms counter the traditional conceptions of poetic structure and meaning. Thus, in response to the indications set forth in the preface (and rendered all the more "authentic," the reader assumes, by the dated signature which closes the statement), the reader abandons his habitual search for the thematic or symbolic content of the work and looks for consistency on the formal level alone where, here again, the introductory preface provides certain guidelines: "So it is necessary, in order to better dispose of the spectacle of writing, through the expedients which enable our signs to carry on, to bring poetic production back to its most extreme *miscultural* point, the zero point, clearly, of poeticity." The reader is thus led to assume that the visible play with form and language becomes the unifying force within the work, a view that is initially and briefly reinforced by the spatial configuration of each text whose heavy concentration of words at the center of the page gives the

11. This pattern of changing substitutions for "&" was pointed out by Sarah Lawall in her essay on Bonnefoy and Roche in *About French Poetry from Dada to "Tel Quel,"* ed. Mary Ann Caws (Detroit: Wayne State University Press, 1974), 69–95. I would disagree, however, with her implication that the pattern remains consistent throughout the texts.

poems a closed, hermetic appearance which appears to encourage a purely visual appropriation.

Once the reader decides, however, that the formal unity of writing as "spectacle" replaces the semantic unity of the traditional poem, he finds that certain discrepancies arise. He discovers that the succeeding texts also appear to be working against the notion of spectacle by dissolving the borders of the frame and by bringing the reader *into* the text, forcing him to become involved in the process of textual construction rather than remain outside in a mere spectator's role. The reader, then, at this point, becomes increasingly uneasy about his interpretation of the text as a purely formal construct, for he comes to realize, on the one hand, that the work could not in this case be viewed as completely devoid of "message" or content (for the content becomes the form itself) and, on the other hand, that his enclosure of the work within the bounds of a single and determinate "meaning" is exactly what the succeeding texts appear to be contesting. The closed configuration of the preface with its well-defined frame, the finality and conclusiveness that the author's signature implies, the rigid discursivity and the idea of closure and limitation that its language conveys ("within the very narrow limits") is fractured by the work's open-ended, intertextual structure. In this regard, even semantics has a role to play, for throughout the texts words or images appear that evoke open, unlimited space ("une por-tE/*ouve*/ṛ te" ["an *op*/ęn/doo R"], "la mer" ["the sea"], "le vent" ["the wind"], "les nuages" ["the clouds"], etc.) or indicate an attempt to break through or to expand all boundaries either in the form of erotic or obscene images or in expressions such as "me voletant autoU/r *de.* cette forte tour" ["fluttering aroU/*nd.* this fortified tower"], "cette forte tour gonfle poUr/r rire" ["this tower blows tO/o laugh"], "J'enfonce le/s 2. qui sortent tous—Les fortes tours" ["I thrust th/e 2. who all leave—The fortified towers"].

Given the texts' contradiction of the preface in all other areas, the reader begins to assume that the unifying principle resides in this deliberate negation of the prefatory statement and that the author actually intended a reversal not only of its well-defined structure, but also of its explicitly stated intentions. And yet, the reader finds that his attempt to find a consistent pattern of negation is also undermined, for the texts, as we have seen, often attempt to carry out the dictates of the initial statement and actually repeat, or so he assumes, many of its elements (images of closure appear that contradict those signifying openness and the idea of the solitary voyage in the last two lines in the preface is expressed in texts 2, 4, and 5—although, here again, he can never be sure whether the coarse language in the last two lines in text 4 are meant to confirm that idea or to disparage it, or even, taking it one step further, whether it is possible to state with absolute certainty that the two lines are related to the preface at all). The language of the text, then, and its structure as well do not permit the reader to find consistency either in the affirmation of the preface or in its negation, for the texts appear both to accentuate the visible manifestation of form and to contest it at the same time, not only structurally but semantically as well; (the eye sees: "leurs cils errant son R" ["their eyelashes wandering its (his/her) R"] and it does not see: "sans avoir vu écrit" ["without having seen written"], "pas rien qui confie qui voit" ["not nothing that entrusts that sees"]). The reader's attempt to focus on content is thus countered by the prominently formal aspects of the work, and yet his accentuation of form only makes him more acutely aware of the content.

The text thus arouses continual conflicts within the reader, making him increasingly uncertain about his attempt to interpret it in accordance with the preface as a pure "spectacle" of writing and yet preventing him from declaring with absolute certainty that the texts are engaged in a deliberate reversal of the "author's" introductory statement. The reader thus comes to realize that the introductory preface provides no real guidelines for his interpretation of the work and that its insertion, in fact, raises more questions than it answers. Finding that the succeeding texts represent not just a simple confirmation but also a denial of the prefatory "intentions" and yet never certain that a complete reversal of the preface was in itself "intended" by the author of the text, the reader begins to reexamine the problem of intentionality itself, to question not only his preconceptions about the role of the preface in programming both the text and the reader's response to it as well, but also his assumption that the prefatory statement expresses the actual intentions of an empirical author and, more importantly, that those intentions could ever truly be ascertained. Thus, in this case as in all others, the text resists appropriation and subverts the teleological operations of traditional literary form by offering a multiplicity of conflicting perspectives over which the author, his introductory preface and the reader no longer have total control.

The process of reading, then, no longer directed and guided by the traditionally programmed text, requires a continual change of viewpoint, a constant modification of the reader's preconceptions. Deprived of a specific frame of reference, which in the traditional text the preface might provide, and supplied with no precise indications within the texts themselves as to how they should be interpreted, the reader becomes increasingly disoriented, both entangled in the operations of the text in his effort to piece things together and alienated at the same time, compelled to either reject or to question the meanings he himself proposes. This discovery of the basically provisional nature of any and all projections of meaning heightens the reader's awareness of his own interpretive activity, an awareness that is, in fact, elicited the moment he approaches one of the texts. Finding the margins in some instances *within* the texts rather than outside, the reader immediately becomes concerned about the appropriate method of reading, asking himself whether the divided parts should be read vertically, as separate columns, or from left to right in the traditional horizontal fashion. The process of reading itself, then, becomes a prominent feature within the work. The reader "reads" his own activity, his attempts at reconstruction, and comes to recognize that he is himself a productive force within the text, that the meaning he uncovers is not necessarily due to something inherent in the work itself but is the result of his own interpretive projections. The reader, as a consequence, becomes increasingly self-critical, constantly scrutinizing and revising the expectations underlying his search for textual comprehensibility and ultimately realizing that his own interpretive capacities are limited, that he can never fully dominate the operations of the text.

It is here, then, within the reader through the modification of his usual modes of perceiving and interpreting a work that, according to *Tel Quel* theory, the revolutionary possibilities of the "open" text lie. By presenting itself as a constantly changing object that involves the reader in the endless production and cancellation of meaning, the revolutionary text deprives the reader of a central focus, prevents him from attaining the distance he needs to formulate an all-encompassing perspective. The text comes to be viewed not as a product to be consumed, analyzed or dissected from a position outside its perimeters but as an open process of textual production which the reader apprehends not by means of a purely visual appropriation but "dynamically," by becoming directly involved in the dynamics of the open text. The operations of the revolutionary text thus constitute, according to *Tel Quel* theory, a radical transformation of the conventions of reading. As Sollers writes in an article entitled "Programme" in which he outlines the *Tel Quel* position in 1968: "This textual rupture . . . is the crisis itself, the violent revolution, the leap, of readability."[12] The reader, who moves interminably from meaning to the dissolution of meaning, is unable to arrest

12. Philippe Sollers, *Logiques* (Paris: Editions du Seuil, 1968), 10. My translation.

the movement of the text, to place it within an interpretive enclosure. The text, as a consequence, becomes "unreadable" in the traditional sense, an "undefined-defined space," as Kristeva calls it, "which has *nothing to do* with closure."[13]

That this rather categorical opposition, however, between the closed and essentially readable literary product and the open, "unreadable" process of textual production might in itself undermine the theory of the open text is a possibility that is never seriously considered by the members of the *Tel Quel* group, and yet, it appears that such a distinction and the apparent politicization of the literary text, which stems from the unquestioned belief in its revolutionary capacities, raise a number of difficulties for *Tel Quel* theory and in many instances actually undermine the revolutionary project as a whole. For, as we shall see, implicit in the concept of the text as a revolutionary *praxis* is the idea of a certain complicity between the reader and the written text that in a number of ways reinstates the communicative model of interpretation by restoring many of the assumptions governing the traditional relationship between author, reader and text. For if the practice of writing is to be used as a revolutionary weapon, as a means of fulfilling certain goals and objectives, then the operations of the modern literary work must be strictly controlled in order to produce the desired "effect" on both the reader and the society of which he is a part. And the reader in turn must be carefully programmed as well, guided and directed toward the "correct" and appropriate response.

In this context, a second reading of "Le mécrit" produces quite different conclusions. Referring to the author's theoretical pronouncements in an effort to interpret the work, the reader discovers that very explicitly stated intentions underlie the structure of the text itself and are to inform the reading of it as well. Outlining his position in the notice on the back cover of *Le mécrit*, Roche writes:

> *Le mécrit* marks the end of a search . . . which wants to be, through the *denatured, materialized* utilization of every aspect of the poetic process whether it be traditional or not, a progressive annullment of both the retrograde, obscurantist, in a word, inane ideology, which is embraced by those who "write poetry," and of the practices in which they habitually engage . . .

And responding to a question in his later "novel," *Louve basse*, about his apparent renunciation of poetry after writing *Le mécrit*, he states:

13. Julia Kristeva, Σημειωτιχὴ Recherches pour une sémanalyse (Paris: Editions du Seuil, 1969), 283. My translation.

. . . I never used the word "renounce." In fact, *Le mécrit* is only the
result of an enterprise, of a demonstration inaugurated at the time of
the publication of *The Centesimal Ideas of Miss Elanize*. When I gave
*Le mécrit* to my editor, I had the impression that I had arrived at the end
of this demonstration, that it was closed.[14]

That this demonstration is in itself dependent upon the existence of
certain structuring principles and controls does not seem to be a matter
of concern for Roche, and yet his apparent affirmation of the ultimate
success of his venture only serves to confirm rather than to subvert the
closed, teleological structure of the traditional text by positing the fulfillment of certain goals and objectives and indicating, as a consequence, that specific principles and intentions continue to program the
operations of the text.

The problems inherent in Roche's comments on *Le mécrit* thus
bring into particularly sharp focus the difficulties that plague the *Tel
Quel* theory as a whole, for to view the text as a demonstration or an
application of a revolutionary theory of textual practice, one that is
meant to undermine the sovereignty of a preexistent authorial intention, is not to do away with the problem of intentionality but simply to
transfer the problem to another level where the intentions of an individual author become those of the revolutionary group or project with
which that author identifies and whose precepts serve as the primary
motivating force behind the literary work. This identification by Roche
with the *Tel Quel* project is thus what leads him, as we shall see, to
counter his own position in certain respects. While attacking the traditional concept of the poem as a perfectly controlled, communicative
object whose signification emanates from a single structuring source,
he at the same time, by virtue of his endorsement of a revolutionary
theory or program, posits a certain capacity to control the operations of
the text. In his interview with Serge Gavronsky where he discusses his
association with *Tel Quel*, Roche's comments reveal the deliberateness
and sense of purpose that underlie his own and the *Tel Quel* position:

This poetry of *Tel Quel* . . . can be characterized by a desire, a very
determined desire, to negate or deny completely everything that could
be said to belong, strictly speaking, to poetry. . . . Let us say that we are
moving further and further away from the metaphor, or from a well-
turned poetry. . . . We are trying to do something being fully conscious
of it, and doing it voluntarily and naturally in order to succeed at it.[15]

14. Denis Roche, *Louve basse* (Paris: Editions du Seuil, 1976), 55–56. My translation.

15. Gavronsky, *Poems and Texts*, 176–77.

This presumably deliberate effort to contest prevailing poetic conventions thus provides the organizational principle that programs both the language of the text and, as Roche's comments will clearly indicate, the reader's reactions as well. Discussing his own works of poetry and the role that they play in shaping the reader's response, Roche states:

> all of my poems are always of the same length in order not to distract the reader by extensions or retractions or things like that. They are always of the same form, the speed of narration, so that the reader will be solely preoccupied about what is going on inside the poem itself and with the language itself, continuously folding back upon itself.[16]

An examination of "Le mécrit," then, with these comments in mind would produce a completely different conception of the work. Confronted, first of all, by the introductory preface, which outlines the revolutionary principles and intentions that lie behind the work and which, according to Roche himself, was inserted "as a prefatory note to my friends,"[17] the reader comes to realize that his interpretive effort is not to be countered and contested at every turn but is to be carefully guided and directed by its theoretical precepts. By constantly referring to the introductory preface in his effort to make sense out of the text's distorted syntax, he discovers that a certain comprehension of the work becomes once again possible, provided, of course, that he abandon his search for meaning on a purely referential or representational level and attempt to view the text in accordance with the preface, as a "spectacle of writing," as an infinite process of poetic production which, drawing both the author and reader into its unlimited movement, is meant to undermine the conventional relationship between author, reader and text.

What occurs, however, is that rather than undermining this relationship between the "author," the text and its reader, the introductory preface, which functions as a kind of revolutionary manifesto in miniature form, becomes the means by which that relationship is ultimately reinstated. A structuring intention or theoretical precept is given command over the text and is presumed to organize the subsequent operations in such a way as to assure total control over the reader's reactions. This means that the uncertainty that the reader felt upon first approaching the text, when he found himself continually invalidating his own interpretive constructs, gives way to the certainty that each of the suc-

---

16. Gavronsky, Ibid., 178–79.
17. Denis Roche, *Notre antéfixe* (Paris: Flammarion, 1978), 31–32.

ceeding texts works in support of the prefatory intentions and in fact imposes certain constraints on the reader in order to assure the appropriate response. The disruption of the normally referential or mimetic function of language within each of the individual poems comes to be seen as part of a deliberate effort to prevent the reader from viewing the work as a simple representation so that he will be forced to look elsewhere for a common element or unifying principle. And, turning to the preface to guide him in his search for consistency, he finds that unifying principle not in the relationship between the text and some concrete and well-defined image of reality but rather in the relationship of text to text where the mechanism of language, the process of textual production, is to become the one interpretive construct that is not to be blocked but is in fact to be facilitated, not only by the guidelines and directives that the preface provides but by the emphasis within the text on primarily formal considerations. The reader, in this case, perceiving certain structural similarities as he moves from text to text, ceases to direct his attention outside the perimeters of the work but becomes conscious of the inner workings of the text itself. Thus, reading the text on the most literal level, he sees the repetition of images such as "le champ" ["the field"] which first appears in the preface and is then repeated in text 6 or becomes "le pré" ["the meadow"] or "les prés" ["the meadows"] in texts 2 and 4. He notices the emphasis on the visual which is accomplished both semantically, with words such as "oeil" ["eye"], "vue" ["sight"], and "regard" ["look"] appearing in various places throughout, and formally, through the graphic and phonic disposition of words or letters on the page. He finds himself caught up in the irregular rhythms that this movement from word to word and sound to sound produces, and he becomes aware of the succession of the pages as well as the movement of his own reading as he passes from text to text. Thus, reading the text comparatively rather than referentially, he comes to the conclusion, with the aid of the preface, that it is this system of intertextual relationships that is to become the single principle of construction governing the organization of the work, that continuity can be found in the uninterrupted flow of writing itself.

Read in accordance with the theory, then, the text becomes a purely formal construction. The network of intertextual relationships comes to be perceived not as a means of opening the text, of rendering it multidimensional and plural, but as a rule or law governing the system of textual production, a formal principle of generation that is to be rendered visible and apprehended by the reader at the expense of its content. And yet, as we have seen before, by providing a principle of ordering, a fixed center around which all else is organized, the content or sense of the work has not been eliminated but is in fact reinstated. The incompatibilities and contradictions that the reader finds on a simple referential level become, as Michael Riffaterre has pointed out in his analysis of various poetic texts, logical and comprehensible once they are perceived by the reader as part of another system of relationships. And it is consequently by learning to read the text on a primarily structural level, by focusing on the mutual interaction between texts, that the reader comes to a new understanding of the literary work, performing what Riffaterre has called a "semantic" or "semiotic transfer" whereby the "ungrammaticalities" that the reader finds with regard to the mimetic function of language are "eventually integrated into another system."[18] Here, it is the system of writing, the process of textual generation that determines the specificity, or what Riffaterre calls the "significance," of the literary work, replacing the semantic unity that referential meaning provides with a formal, intertextual unity that becomes, in effect, its "content."

In this context, the "ungrammaticalities" within "Le mécrit" become once again "grammatical." The repetition of sounds, the various permutations of a particular word, of the verb "monter" ["to climb"], for example (which becomes at various points: "montant," "montons," "monte," "remonte," and "remontant") are not seen as a haphazard occurrence but are viewed as part of the organizational plan or design of the text and are to provide the reader with a concrete manifestation of the engendering process, of words generating other words and sounds generating other sounds. Thus, everything within the text acquires meaning as it relates to the ideas expressed in the preface; that is, as it signifies the generating process. And while the syntactical and grammatical distortion in text 5, for example, of the concluding lines of the preface may be viewed as a negation of the coherent and logical structure of its language, the idea of an endless and solitary voyage remains. The "nous nous dirigeons" ["we make our way toward"] in the preface, becomes "nos 2 voix remontant" ["our 2 voices climbing up again"] in text 5; they both designate the involvement of the reader and writer in the movement of language itself. The "nous" ["we"], in this case, is not to represent the traditional fusion of two unified subjects, but is to be viewed, as Kristeva's analysis of Sollers' *Nombres* would seem to indicate, as a dissolution of the subject: " 'We' inclusive . . . marks the

---

18. Michael Riffaterre, *Semiotics of Poetry* (Bloomington: Indiana University Press, 1978), 4.

impossible place—axial, sacrificial—of the non-person in the uniden-
tified, a-personal multiplicity. Pronoun of the a-person, pronoun of en-
genderment . . . "[19] The "we" designates "process," "production," and
the absence of closure in the final line of text 5 following the reference to
the Greek port "Itéa," which is both a destination and a point of departure; thus it reinforces this sense of irresolution and open-endedness
that is to characterize the modern poem.

The conclusions one can draw from this particular reading of the
text thus become rather obvious. The attempt to interpret the work in
conformity with the dictates of the preface as an infinite "spectacle of
writing," as a "formalism" of process, which is to be perceived at the
expense of the product, does little to preserve the sense of openness and
incompletion that the texts are meant to convey but produces a conception of the work that is limiting and constrictive and actually reinstates
the precepts of meaning it is meant to exclude. The open and dispersed
intertextual space of the modern literary work, which is meant to call
into question traditional modes of interpretation, becomes enveloped in
the closed, theoretical space of the preface where the notion of intertextuality, which is also the notion of process, the unlimited movement of
writing itself, becomes a restrictive theoretical construct by becoming
the only acceptable interpretation of the work.

This, then, is one of the major drawbacks of the *Tel Quel* theory of
the revolutionary text, for if the notion of intertextuality, or the process
of textual production, is to become the single mode of interpretation,
the only structuring principle at work within the text, then the concept
of intertextuality may actually foster the kind of reading it was initially
supposed to contest by giving the work an inner coherence and logic
that merely repeat, by means of a simple inversion, the ordered unifor-
mity of the traditionally programmed text. Structured by a theoretical
intention, the implied author of the work, and interpreted by the reader
in accordance with those intentions, the text becomes part of a meaningful circularity, forming a closed circuit of communication in which
the "author" as producer and the reader as consumer come together and
function as one: "That toward which we make our way, henceforth
assured of our solitude, and without it being possible for anyone to
follow us." For Kristeva, the "we" designating process also belongs to
"the revolutionary masses," designating communication, a fraternal
solidarity between "author" and reader that may ultimately serve
rather than contest the tradition by reinstating the "Law of One."

19. Julia Kristeva, Σημειωτικὴ, 359–60.

*The Literary Palimpsest*

RICHARD GOODKIN

# A Choice of Andromache's

"Ich kann nicht wählen!"
—W. Styron, *Sophie's Choice*

## I. "DEUX FOIS VEUVE, ET DEUX FOIS L'ESCLAVE DE LA GRÈCE . . . "[1]

Such are the words by which Andromaque describes herself at the close of the first version (1667) of Racine's play, and they are words which instantly pose the question of the valence of Andromaque's relation to Greece: lover or captive, the widow of Pyrrhus or his slave, these are the poles between which readings of Andromaque have vacillated. Is this a character who is irrevocably closed upon her past, who is inattentive and even resistant to the demands and the possibilities of the present, who lives the present as an unwanted intrusion? Or one whose dwelling upon the past gives way to an almost imperceptible movement of openness to the present, so that the bereavement she feels as Hector's widow yields to the grief of being the widow of his killer's son, Pyrrhus? In this, Andromaque's final appearance in Racine's first version of the play, her paradoxical nature—the nature of a woman who claims to live only in and for the past, whose raison d'être would seem to be to mourn the past—is in a sense resolved, for in spite of the ambiguity of her final speech, she shows herself to be capable of finding fresh sources of bereavement in the present. Her mourning of Pyrrhus thus subsumes and effaces her mourning of the Trojan past, even though she herself continues to cling to her perpetual widowhood as proof of her fidelity.

Indeed, although Andromaque's words here seem to suggest that the present is repeating the past, the repetitions they seem to hearken to ("Deux fois . . . deux fois") are not simple repetitions. Andromaque's first widowhood is at the hands of Greece, but the second is a bereavement of Greece itself. In the first case Greece is her oppressor, in the

1. "Twice a widow, and twice the slave of Greece." Jean Racine, *Oeuvres complètes*, ed. Raymond Picard, Bibliothèque de la Pléiade (Paris: Gallimard, 1950), 1, 1088 (note to 296). All quotations of the play, including variants, are cited from this edition; all translations mine.

second it is the very thing she is deprived of. Likewise, her first enslavement is at the hands of Pyrrhus, her first master, and her second enslavement, while literally referring to Oreste standing at her side as her new captor, also figuratively refers to the not simply literal nature of her enslavement to Greece: because Greece has moved from the status of master to that of marital partner, Andromaque is no longer simply a slave to her Greek masters; she is also, and more fundamentally, a slave of her nonenslavement, that is, a slave to her own (long resisted) attachment to her captor. As a simple slave to Greece and as a widow at the hands of Greece, Andromaque had the freedom of non-choice, the freedom of being able to say that she had no responsibility for her present situation and condition. But it is because, in spite of herself and her efforts to remain closed upon the past, she goes beyond the relationship of literal enslavement and oppression to Greece that she is enslaved by another tyrant: her own sense of responsibility once she begins to live again in the present, as if her life had not drawn to a close on the day Troy fell.

If this brief and powerful self-description—one which signals the end of the balancing act Andromaque has been performing throughout the play, teetering between total devotion to the past and a dawning interest in the present—is suppressed by Racine in the edition of 1673, it is that Andromaque's characterization of herself as twice "esclave de la Grèce" describes not only her own relation to the Greeks, but also that of Racine to Euripides, a fact which is supported by Racine's rewriting of his preface to *Andromaque* shortly after having suppressed Andromaque's final appearance and speech. In his first preface to *Andromaque*, Racine claims utter and total faithfulness to the models of antiquity:

> But truly my characters are so famous in ancient times that one need only be acquainted with antiquity to see how I've portrayed them just as the ancient poets gave them to us. And so I haven't thought that I was allowed to change any of their values. [*Oeuvres complètes*, 1, 241.]

Racine is here making a claim for enslavement, for a kind of closure onto the past, for the very sort of complete fidelity which is one of the hallmarks of his Trojan heroine. He says that his play, like Andromaque's game of closure against the present, wishes to deny the passage of time and as if magically, reproduce a past model in the present. To this extent his aim here, one which attempts to link past and present as fully as possible given the various cultural and historical differences, is a form of representation, for he wishes the present to be a copy of the past.

And yet it is in the early version of the play, the version for which the first preface is written, that Racine goes beyond the Euripides play by allowing Andromaque to come onstage in act V and open her heart instead of leaving the stage well before the end (at line 765 out of 1288 in the Euripides play),[2] her attitude toward her captor unresolved. It is in Racine's second version (1673) that Andromaque leaves the stage early (IV, i) and is not seen again, thus conforming to Euripides' model, and it is in his second preface (1676) that Racine makes a claim for his own liberty, the non-closure that is the rightful benefit of any artist:

> [Hermione's personality] is almost the only thing which I am borrow-ing here from that author [Euripides]. For although my tragedy bears the same name as his, its subject is nonetheless quite different. . . . [*Oeuvres complètes*, 1, 243.]

Same name, different meaning: is this not an indication of a non-simple representation? That a single name should cover up a divergence of sense puts the relations of Racine to his predecessor in the domain not of representation, but of interpretation.

And in fact, interpretation is precisely what simple representation is not; for while the desire to represent antiquity is an indication of a form of closure-as-fidelity, the desire to interpret it suggests a freedom and an openness which Racine emphasizes in this preface, the very freedom of France to diverge from Greece: "I am writing in a country where that liberty [changing an inherited myth] could not be ill re-ceived" (*Oeuvres complètes*, 1, 243), he says first, before going on to speak of the tradition by which the French kings are descendants of the son of Andromache by Hector, the very son whose existence he "saves" from the cruel death imposed upon him by Euripides (among others). What links Racine to Greece would then not be a simple inheritance to be used as is, but a lineage, a tradition of transformations, of openings effected by each generation.

Indeed, Racine even goes so far as to praise Euripides himself for feeling free enough to transform the inherited elements of myth: "How much bolder Euripides was in his tragedy of *Helen!* In it he openly shocks (*choque ouvertement*) the common belief of all of Greece" (*Oeuvres complètes*, 1, 244). We may wonder why Racine writes an apologia of literary freedom as a preface to the revision of his play which

---

2. All references to Euripides' *Andromache* are to the text established by Louis Méridier in Euripide, Collection Budé (Paris: Belles Lettres, 1973), vol. 2.

reconforms to the Euripidean model from which the original Racinian version diverged. Why should Racine conform to a model of the past, a gesture which seems symptomatic of a kind of respect for closure-as-fidelity, all the while he is lauding innovation and non-closure ("choque ouvertement")?

The answer to this question, or at least its formulation, can already be found in germ in Euripides' *Andromache,* which furnishes a number of examples of what I would like to call "andromachism": andromachism is not simply closure to the present and utter faithfulness to the past (closure-as-representation of the past); it is rather the unrealized conflict between fidelity to the past and the inevitable assertion of the needs and choices of the present. And indeed, although the present may be felt in the case of Andromache as an opening up, or a destruction of the ideal of closure-as-fidelity to the past, it is itself also a movement of closure, for in eliminating the possibility of a simple enslavement to the past, it brings forth the possibility of being trapped in the bonds of present responsibility. Andromachism is in fact a confusion between two forms of closure: between closure-as-representation of the past and non-presence, a guarantor of non-responsibility and thus of innocence, and closure as a stable identity, capable of making choices and of living with the constraints of responsibility and the possibility of guilt.

Andromachism can be described by no image more memorable than that of Andromache clutching the altar of Thetis throughout most of her presence onstage in Euripides' play: for she is clutching not only her own closure into the past, her pose of non-presence and non-responsibility as a protection against their unwanted partner, guilt; she is also, perhaps in spite of herself, clutching an image of the family of her captor, Neoptolemos, since Thetis is his grandmother. Attempting to take refuge in the past, Andromache finds herself reaching for the present nonetheless; her arms, closed about the goddess as if the divine realm were the only possible source of help in her present position of danger, also close about an image of the present, Neoptolemos, who can be of help to her only if he compromises her fidelity to Hector and the past.

That the opening up of Andromache's closure-as-fidelity leads to another form of closure is nowhere more apparent than in the scene of her choice. When Andromache chooses to leave the altar, described earlier as the "holy enclosure of the goddess" (253), that is, her stance of closure against the present and against the mortal realm, she is instantly subject to the closure of responsibility: "Here I go, sent down to Hades, my bloody hands enclosed [κεκλημένα , cognate with "close"] in chains."[3]

It is in fact the largely surreptitious movement between Andromache's initial stance of non-presence and non-responsibility and her final position as the active maker of a decision which is the essence of andromachism, as we can see in examining several of the play's key moments. Following close upon Andromache's first description of her attitude as a complete rejection of the present and an absolute longing for the past (closure into the past) comes a compromising utterance which seems to betray Andromache's ambiguous position toward the present, and particularly toward her captor:

> My master married the Spartan Hermione, and pushed my slave's bed aside . . . Hermione claims that . . . I'm trying to force her out of his bed; out of a bed which I at first unwillingly accepted, but now have abandoned [29–37]

The quick and almost imperceptible reversal here leaves us with the question: who abandoned whom? Andromache here gives two conflicting versions of the termination of her conjugal relations with Neoptolemos: she first says that her master deserted her when he married a Greek princess, Hermione; but she then says that it is she that abandoned Neoptolemos's bed. By claiming herself as the source of the abandonment, Andromache is undoubtedly trying to minimize her feelings of guilt at sharing her master's bed at all; but it is by attempting to make the present "correct" the past that Andromache unwittingly claims the responsibility necessary for guilt itself, that is to say, admits implicitly that her moral sense is still functioning. Even if, as a slave, she has had no "choice" but to share Neoptolemos's bed, her affirmation of self-determination here ("a bed which I have now abandoned") is a prefiguration of her ultimate closure-as-choice.

When, in what may be the play's most telling example of andromachism, Andromache tries to deflect responsibility for her present distressing situation onto Menelaos, she finds that her attempt at irony backfires:

> Why are you killing me? For what? What city have I betrayed? What child of yours have I killed? What house have I burnt? [ll. 388–90]

Andromache defends herself on the basis of her past innocence; she attempts to close herself into the safety of passivity. Thus, while Men-

---

3. *Andromache*, 501–3; this and all translations of Euripides are mine.

elaos and the Greeks have killed her first child, Astyanax, and burnt her house, she had done nothing of the sort to them: the first round goes to Andromache. And yet the single most general accusation that she makes here, "What city have I betrayed," is one which resists the reversal she wishes to confer upon it and which zeroes in on her in an accusation of closure-as-responsibility. Does Andromache really mean to suggest that Menelaos has betrayed his own city, or even Troy? He can hardly have betrayed his own city, since the Greeks won the war, and he cannot have betrayed ("προύδωϰα," gave up) Troy, for while one can damage or destroy any city, native or foreign, one can betray only one's own city. If Troy has been betrayed, none present in Andromache's company can have betrayed it except her.

It is this moment, the moment at which Andromache's closure-as-representation of the past is betrayed by the reversal that refuses to reverse, or perhaps that reverses twice and boomerangs back onto her as both accuser and accused, which brings out at last the real reason for her clinging to the first form of closure: guilt. Andromache is guilty of the worst of crimes in her situation: survival, her very presence, a necessary and in this case perhaps a sufficient condition for self-condemnation. Andromache's words, directed to Menelaos but returning to their source, tell her that the non-property she has been inhabiting as a refuge against the present cannot itself persist, that Menelaos, by foreclosing the "mortgage" on that (non-) property and threatening the safety of Andromache's son, Molossos, is also forcing closure-as-responsibility upon her, and that in a double negation parallel to the double reversal of her words, she is going to be forced to admit that she is still alive and capable of action.

Faced with a choice between choice and non-choice, Andromache not only chooses choice, she also well chooses her words: "Look, I am abandoning [προλείπω] the altar" (l. 411). This climactic statement made at the moment of choice echoes the first example of andromachism discussed above, but whereas Andromache's "abandonment" ("ekleloipa" ἐϰλέλοιπα at l. 37 is also a compound of the verb *leipō*, λείπω, to leave) of Neoptolemos's bed was in fact a case of andromachism, a false statement of closure-as-responsibility made by a woman still clinging to the altar of closure-as-fidelity to the past, Andromache's abandonment of the altar of Thetis is a genuine transformation of closure-as-fidelity into closure-as-responsibility. Andromache chooses, the past loses.

If we now turn back to Racine's first version of *Andromaque*, we can read the composition of the play and its preface as yet another example of andromachism. In the preface to the first version, Racine makes a claim for closure-as-representation ("I have portrayed them just as the ancient poets gave them to us"), and this claim is a form of protection: *Andromaque* is widely considered Racine's first masterpiece,[4] and Racine's claim to have followed Euripides and Virgil with a slavish form of fidelity only thinly disguises the fact that the power of his own play is built not only on the extraordinary beauty of his emerging mature style, but also on a considerable degree of innovation.[5] A seeming slave to Greece, Racine, like Andromache, does nothing but hide his emerging personality under the names of his masters.

For in fact Racine, also like Andromache, is not only a slave to Greece, but also a widower of it, and in order to be a widower of it he must first allow it to pass from the status of simple oppressor to that of a complex partner whose death will be a genuine source of bereavement and not simply a release. Even in this first version of Racine's first unqualified success, there is closure of the second kind: Racine gives a stunningly perceptive reading of Euripides' play by making Andromaque give explicit voice to her feelings for Pyrrhus, feelings which remain essentially implicit in Euripides' play[6] and are among the greatest sources of its power. Racine does not merely copy Andromache's choice from Euripides' play; in effect, he chooses that choice by taking it further than Euripides, by portraying an Andromache even more shockingly open to the present at the play's end than Euripides' heroine. All the while Racine is naming himself an imitator of Euripides, he is in fact an interpreter of him.

Thus, we might expect that the moment of reckoning, the moment of choice forced upon Euripides' heroine, has come for Racine. Just as the vacillation inherent in andromachism is brought to an end in Eu-

4. See, for example, R. C. Knight and H. T. Barnwell, *Andromaque* (Genève: Droz, 1977), 7–8.

5. For an excellent discussion of the sources, ancient and modern, of the play, see Roy C. Knight, *Racine et la Grèce* (1951; rpt. Paris: Nizet, 1974), 266–85.

6. Pyrrhus is of course the Latin equivalent of the Greek Neoptolemos. Andromache's vacillation in her attitude toward her captor, although it is never definitively resolved, is clear in the various ways in which she speaks of Neoptolemos in Euripides' play, e.g., " For his father [Neoptolemos] is not beside me to help me" (49–50); "Troy does not repute him to be so cowardly [as to let his son be put to death]; he will go where he must; for he will show by his actions that he is worthy of his father Achilles" (ll. 341–43); "I was violently forced to bed down with my master" (ll. 390–91); "When I arrived in Phthia, I was joined to the murderers of Hector" (ll. 402–03; the discreet plural, "phoneusin," murderers, associates Neoptolemos with the actual murderer of Hector, his father, Achilles); and finally, her compromising instructions to her son by Neoptolemos, Molossos, to be carried out presumably after her death: "Kiss your father and weep and embrace him and tell him what I've done" (ll. 416–18).

ripides' play by Andromache's abandonment of the altar of fidelity and her acceptance of the chains of responsibility, that same vacillation, applicable to the mixture of "fidelity" and "choice" in Racine's first version, would seem to come to a close with Andromaque's final appearance, a signal of Racine's choice of Andromache's.

And yet, this is not Racine's final version of the story. The "opening up" of the character of Andromache at the close of Racine's first version—a questioning of her fidelity to the past which coincides with her being pinned down by present choice—does not correspond to the moment at which Racine closes his own text. The conflict underlying andromachism, seemingly settled by the first play's ending, is called back into question by its revision. And indeed, whereas Euripides' play, like Racine's first version, leaves us with a sort of resolution of the paradox of Andromache, Racine's imposition of a second ending leaves us with nothing but questions.

## II. A TWICE-TOLD TALE: RACINE'S *ANDROMAQUE*

The very fact of having two endings is but one of the many ways in which Racine's final choice in his treatment of Andromache is not to choose: two widowhoods; two enslavements; two endings. The play of Andromache seems to encourage the act of doubling, as Georges Poulet points out: "Thus the whole drama is only an immense and infinitely complex repetition of a more ancient drama. It is a drama played for the second time."[7] Like the plaintive Christian in his Third *Cantique*, the Racine who in rewriting the ending of his play faces a choice of Andromache's might well describe himself as two men, one faithful, one rebellious,[8] for Racine, in a situation analogous to that of his heroine, has the choice between fidelity and freedom, or between closure-as-representation and closure-as-interpretation. In the end, will Racine choose an Andromache who has the freedom to choose or one who is too "faithful" to choose?

As we approach the question of Racine's choice, it will be useful to give ourselves the choice of two critical positions which essentially deal

7.  George Poulet, *Studies in Human Time*, tr. Elliott Coleman (Baltimore: The Johns Hopkins Press, 1956), 120, hereafter quoted in the text.

8.  "Mon Dieu, quelle guerre cruelle! / Je trouve deux hommes en moi: / L'un veut que plein d'amour pour toi / Mon coeur te soit toujours fidèle. / L'autre à tes volontés rebelle / Me révolte contre ta loi," *Oeuvres complètes*, 1, 999. ["My God, what a cruel war!/I find two men in myself:/One wants my heart, full of love for you/To be always faithful to you./The other rebellious to your wishes/Makes me rebel against your law."]

with the two forms of closure that make up andromachism. Georges Poulet emphasizes the importance of closure-as-fidelity:

> The Racinian tragedy is an action *in the past* . . . it seems that we are witnessing the process by which things in the last analysis become "fatal" in our eyes and force us to recognize that indeed they could not have happened otherwise. . . . Racinian fatality . . . has the nature of irreversibility. [123]

In sum Poulet sees *Andromaque* as a play about the inevitable intrusion of the past into the present: "It is impossible to escape from this *representation* of the past in the present" (120). For Poulet, any attempt by the hero to effect closure-as-choice is undermined when he—or at least the audience—learns that the present is effectively closed to choice by its debts to the past; the lesson of *Andromaque* is the lesson of closure-as-representation of the past.

And yet we might point out that for the character of Andromaque, closure-as-representation is not the end point of the play but rather its starting point. What Andromaque needs to learn is not the inevitable intrusion of the past into the present, but rather the inevitable intrusion of the present into the past. This is essentially the position taken by Lucien Goldmann:

> Over against a world with its own laws, in which we can only live by choosing (Andromaque can save the life of Astyanax if only she will marry Pyrrhus; or she can save her loyalty to Hector if only she will give up Astyanax), a world whose laws force us to choose, . . . tragic man calls for rejection of all compromise and all choice, because choice for him is the essence of evil or sin.[9]

Choice can be made only in the present: and the choice presented to Andromaque, as Goldmann characterizes it here, is a choice based on the enmity between the past (fidelity to Hector) and the present (saving Astyanax). For Goldmann, it is choice itself, seen as a yielding to the blackmail of the present, which undermines Andromaque's potential heroism; her free will as a heroine can manifest itself only as a refusal of choice:

> Andromache is tragic in so far as she refuses the alternatives, and confronts the world with her voluntary refusal of life and her freely accepted choice of death. She ceases to be tragic, however, when she decides to accept marriage with Pyrrhus and then kill herself.[10]

9. "The Structure of Racinian Tragedy" in *Racine: Modern Judgements*, ed. R. C. Knight (Nashville: Aurora, 1970), 105.

10. *The Hidden God*, tr. Philip Thody (London: Routledge and Kegan Paul, 1964), 324.

In Goldmann's view, Andromaque begins with a position of closure against the present and the temptations of its choices; in the course of the play, she yields to those temptations by allowing herself to be forced to choose. The "end" of Andromaque—both her final position and the end of her tragic heroism—is, according to Goldmann, her selling out to closure-as-choice.

I would like to argue that Andromaque, and particularly the Andromaque of the second version of the play, slips between these two readings, and that she leaves the stage early partially in order to do so. Andromaque does not, as Poulet claims, learn about the necessity of fidelity to the past; rather, she begins with that knowledge; if anything, she learns about the unfeasibility of claiming that form of closure as a single principle of life. And yet, any knowledge she might gain about the impossibility of closure-as-representation does not move Andromaque, like her Euripidean counterpart, into the domain of closure-as-choice. Despite Goldmann's belief that Andromaque chooses, and that it is choice itself which makes her fall from tragic stature, I would like to claim not only that Andromaque does not choose, but also that it is her non-choice which makes her tragic.

It is the nature of Racinian reversal, one of the characteristics which Aristotle uses to define tragedy, which determines the status in Racine's play of the two forms of closure which make up andromachism. If Aristotle describes reversal (*peripeteia*) as "a change of situation into its opposite,"[11] then we can identify the reversal of Euripides' play as the movement between closure-as-fidelity—which has the disadvantage of enslavement to the past and the advantage of non-responsibility in the present—and its reverse, closure-as-choice, with the advantage of freedom and the disadvantage of potential guilt. But whereas in Euripides' play, fidelity yields punctually to its reverse, choice, in *Andromaque*, the absence of fidelity for all three of the frustrated lovers, Oreste, Hermione, and Pyrrhus, is matched by the absence of choice: if freedom exists, it exists only as a kind of regulated but unstoppable vacillation or flow, a circuit of futile efforts to make a choice which results only in a seemingly perpetual series of reversals.

It is in this sense that Racinian reversal is not Aristotelian poetic reversal, but rather the principle of non-heroic life, of an existence in search of some unshakable decision which will bring its vacillations to a close, as Roland Barthes points out: "the hero has the feeling that *every-*

11. *Poetics* 1452a in Aristotle, *On Poetry and Style*, tr. G. M. A. Grube (Indianapolis: Bobbs-Merrill, 1958), 21.

*thing* is caught up in this rocking motion: the whole world oscillates, there is no alloy in the minting of Destiny."[12] Racinian reversal is not the principle which precipitates the end of the tragedy, as Aristotle implies,[13] but is rather "a perpetual feature of the whole plot, not simply of its end."[14]

If anything, reversal in Racine is what constitutes the need for an end; it is itself symptomatic of non-closure, a metaphysical rather than a poetic reversal, an uncertainty as to one's most fundamental nature and desires. It is the very reversal—the incapacity to say a definitive "yes" or "no" to life's choices—which Aristotle himself excludes as a principle of knowledge in the *Metaphysics*, as if to preclude the endless questioning implicit in Hamlet's famous soliloquy, emblematic of all tragic vacillation:

> Thus in the first place it is obvious that this at any rate is true: that the term "to be" or "not to be" has a definite meaning. [1006a] It will be impossible for the same thing to be and not to be. [1006b] Nor indeed can there be any intermediate between contrary statements, but of one thing we must either assert or deny one thing, whatever it may be. [1011b][15]

These statements, part of Aristotle's discussion of the law of the excluded middle (a thing may not be both x and not-x), depicts choice in the simplest and most brutal of terms, as a necessary element in any system of knowledge that strives to settle an issue or close a question. In the light of this law, the vacillations of Racine's characters are seen to be made up of everything that does not fit into this binary system of choice, everything human that infringes upon this law and ultimately resists resolution.

If Racine's play offers any possibility of putting an end to the metaphysical crisis of choice, it comes in the character of Andromaque herself, the only character to whom either closure-as-fidelity or closure-as-choice is open. As a captive and a slave the weakest character politically, Andromaque is also the only one of the four main characters to be

12. *On Racine*, tr. Richard Howard (New York: Octagon Books, 1977), 42.

13. See, for example, his discussion of the proper length of a tragedy: "such length as will allow a sequence of events to result in a change from bad to good fortune or from good fortune to bad" (*Poetics* 1451a, 17), which implies that the play should come to a close once reversal has taken place.

14. H. T. Barnwell, *The Tragic Drama of Corneille and Racine* (Oxford: Clarendon Press, 1982), 233.

15. *Metaphysics* in Aristotle, 17, tr. Hugh Tredennick, Loeb Classical Library (1933; rpt. London: Heinemann, 1975), 165, 167, and 199–201, respectively.

loved and not loving, so that in reality she need simply listen to her own desires in order to determine the positions of the other three. Like a domino poised in indecision at the moment of choosing in which direction to fall, Andromaque bears within her the single choice that will determine all of theirs.

During the time that Andromaque takes to make that choice, or rather not to make it, we see in the portrayal of the other three protagonists a perfectly modulated example of Racinian reversal, that is, a model of human existence with neither fidelity nor choice. All three of these characters are unable to affirm or deny their "choice"; they all find themselves in the place of the excluded middle, in a perpetual betweentime, a transitional state between the two poles which could constitute choice if ever one of them were finally chosen. And yet this middle position is precisely the least tolerable one, as Pyrrhus makes clear in speaking of his love for Andromaque: "Oui, mes voeux ont trop loin poussé leur violence/ Pour ne plus s'arrêter que dans l'indifférence." ["Yes, my pledges have pushed their violence too far/ To stop in indifference now" (ll. 365–66).] Stalled between the equally unfeasible alternatives of love and hatred, Pyrrhus can no longer find the enviable norm of neutrality from which his oscillating emotion is a kind of deviation. If the point of indifference would neutralize the middleground between the poles of love and hatred precisely because "indifference" alone can discharge the explosive pressure of choice, itself based on differentiation and therefore on "difference," the problem is that it is a point that cannot be reached, as the eighteenth-century writer Marmontel points out in speaking of tragic choice: "The first rule is that the alternatives have no middle-point."[16]

The best that can be done under these circumstances is to make choice take the form of a mechanism translating unrequited love into the independence brought by hatred. The drawback of such a mechanism is that since, in the absence of a genuine choice, it is reversible, love being translated into hatred by pride and hatred retransformed into love by hope, it cannot effect the closure of fatality which, to recall Poulet's terms, "has the nature of irreversibility." The "transports" which it causes—whether of love or of hatred—are forms of motion as well as emotion, endless transportations between the extremes of love and hatred. The futility of this mechanism, apparent in all three characters who attempt to use it as an agent of choice, reaches its apogee in the character of Pyrrhus, doubly indecisive in his powerlessness either to

16. "De la tragédie" in *Poétique française* (Paris: Lesclapart, 1763), 2, 199.

reject Hermione definitively or to force a decision of acceptance from his own idol, Andromaque:

> Hermione elle-même a vu plus de cent fois
> Cet amant irrité revenir sous ses lois.

"Hermione herself has more than a hundred times seen/ That frustrated lover come back under her sway," (ll. 115–16).

Pyrrhus's love and hatred of Andromaque and his disdain and acceptance of Hermione take the form of a valve, always open to one side if closed to the other and vice versa, a movement which is indicated in a moment of transition between a discussion about the future of Hermione and Oreste and the appearance of Andromaque:

> PYRRHUS: Ah! qu'ils s'aiment, Phoenix: j'y consens. Qu'elle parte.
> Que charmés l'un de l'autre, ils retournent à Sparte:
> Tous nos ports sont ouverts et pour elle et pour lui.
> Qu'elle m'épargnerait de contrainte et d'ennui!
> PHOENIX: Seigneur . . .
> PYRRHUS: Une autre fois je t'ouvrirai mon âme:
> Andromaque paraît.

> PYRRHUS: Oh! let them love each other, Phoenix: I consent. Let her leave. Let them go back to Sparta, entranced with each other. All our ports are open for her and for him. How much bother and constraint she would spare me!
> PHOENIX: Lord . . .
> PYRRHUS: Another time I'll open my soul to you: Andromaque is appearing, 253–58.]

Pyrrhus's first movement in this transitional scene is to free himself from Hermione: "Tous nos ports sont ouverts," "ports" being the geographical equivalent of the spiritual "transports," that is, the transportation of Pyrrhus's emotion swaying from side (Hermione about to be packed off) to side (Andromaque about to be brought back in). "Ouverts," like Pyrrhus's explicit mention of removed constraints, indicates the release of Hermione in an opening up that might prepare the way for a permanent choice: "qu'ils *retournent* à Sparte" emphasizes the fact that Hermione's proper place has always been and always will be in Sparta and that Pyrrhus hopes that this will be the second half of a round trip, a closing of the loop opened with Hermione's arrival in Epirus.

And yet this desire for choice is nothing more than a desire: that

Pyrrhus can in fact do nothing more than "open" his ports to Hermione's departure recalls his own inability to send her away with a permanent "no" that could not be transformed into a "yes" by Andromaque's rejection of Pyrrhus himself. It is Andromaque's arrival alone which represents the only hope of choice: the appearance of Andromaque brings with it the suggestion of closure, or at least an end to openness: "Une autre fois je t'ouvrirai mon âme." That the long-awaited choice of Andromaque becomes a projection of the possibility of choice itself is clear in Pyrrhus's final ultimatum to Andromaque:

> Je vous le dis, il faut ou périr ou régner . . .
> Je meurs si je vous perds, mais je meurs si j'attends.
>
> I tell you, one must either perish or reign . . . I die if I lose you, but I die if I wait, (ll. 968–72).

We may speculate that Pyrrhus's insistence upon the necessity of either reigning or perishing is addressed not only to Andromaque, but also to himself, since he has in effect not reigned since his love for Andromaque made his ultimate decisions contingent upon hers. If Pyrrhus experiences the idea of further postponement as a kind of death, it is that he has reached the moment at which the openendedness of life has taken on the proportions of a crisis and demands the closure of choice as a prefiguration of the stability and irreversibility of death.

Non-closure is thus a model not only for emotion, but also for life itself: so long as there is life, there is the possibility that tomorrow may destroy the "decisions" of today, as is indicated by Hermione's words to an Oreste hesitant to kill Pyrrhus:

> Tant qu'il vivra, craignez que je ne lui pardonne.
> Doutez jusqu'à sa mort d'un courroux incertain:
> S'il ne meurt aujourd'hui, je puis l'aimer demain.
>
> So long as he lives, fear that I may forgive him. Until he's dead doubt my unsure wrath: If he doesn't die today, I may love him tomorrow, (ll. 1198–1200).

It is in this sense that the desire for death, expressed almost explicitly by Oreste himself when he demands a final decision from Hermione,[17] is symptomatic of the value of choice itself: it is as if the desire to have

---

17. "Enfin je viens à vous, et je me vois réduit/ A chercher dans vos yeux une mort qui me fuit," [At last I come to you, and I see myself reduced/ To seeking in your eyes a death that flees from me,"] 495–96.

done with indecision were stronger than the prospect of an unfavorable outcome, the need for irreversibility greater than the illusory advantages of an always unfulfilled hope.

Thus, three characters are in search of a closure. And as for Andromaque herself, she is, unlike her predecessor in Euripides' play, faced less with a choice to be made than with the problem of how not to choose. The problem confronting Euripides' heroine once she has understood the pressing need for choice is what to choose. Once she does choose, there is no need for her to be at the center of our attention, since by the nature of her choice, she has already fully defined herself. In other, more brutal terms, she is interesting only so long as she is concealing something, even if it is only the possibility of choosing. Her story comes to an end precisely because once she has chosen, futilely as it turns out, events proceed more or less without her, swept on by other forces and other agents.

It is not so with Andromaque, whose central question is never simply what to choose but always remains whether to choose. The paradox is that the fact of having a choice between choice and non-choice is itself a choice, and thus closes out non-choice as a viable option. The longer Andromaque stays onstage, the more apparent it becomes that the choice is hers: where the Euripidean character leaves the stage out of superfluity, Andromaque is whisked away because she is too central; not because she knows too much to be able to choose, but rather because she knows too much to be able not to choose. The more Andromaque understands, the more she opens her eyes to what is going on around her, the greater is her vulnerability to choice. If Racine's first Andromaque opened her eyes—and ours as well—once and for all by her final reappearance, his second Andromaque leaves the stage when she is on the threshold of understanding.

It is in this light, the light of barely closed eyes, that we can perceive an incipient movement in the character of Andromaque, a movement cut short by her departure. It is neither a movement of "transport," of an emotion that would betray her stance of indifference to the present, nor a movement of choice. Rather it is a movement of conscious non-choice, a movement brought on by the dawning realization of the imminence of choice and by the refusal to let that realization make its full appearance.

Early in the play, Andromaque is described as having "des yeux toujours ouverts aux larmes," ["eyes always open to tears," (l. 449)] and we may read this depiction of her as a sign of her closure to everything but her mourning, an explanation of her refusal to "see" Pyrrhus in front of her eyes. But in describing what she thinks will be her own imminent death, Andromaque tells her servant, "Céphise, c'est à toi de me fermer les yeux" ["Céphise, it's up to you to close my eyes," (l.1100).] Is Andromaque, like the three characters who look to her for a decision, starting to open her eyes to choice? Are her disappearance from the stage and the death which she is planning for herself a sacrifice to the temptations of choice, a proof of the need to experience directly, as a final and unassailable means of protection against herself, what choice needs to turn to for support, that is, the finality of death?

Andromaque lives in a world of closure-as-representation which is menaced from the start, a world which comes to life at the unit (or "unity") of time during which representation is threatened by choice, but refuses to yield to it in a simple way. Roland Barthes speaks of the play as the struggle between an old and a new order:

> [the old order] is a circle, it is *that from which one cannot escape*, enclosure [*la clôture*] is its adequate definition. Of course this enclosure is ambiguous; it is a prison, but can also be an asylum. [*On Racine*, 72]

The moment of Andromaque's final exit from the stage comes with the realization of the ambivalent nature of closure. When Andromaque sees that closure for her is not only a prison, a role befitting her status as a slave to the past, but also an asylum from the present, she has also understood that life is offering her something which she is at pains to refuse, and this is the moment of her flight. As her last words tell us, Andromaque flees Hermione's "violence" (1129), but in fact, she is also fleeing her "vie," the very life which can exist only as an ill-understood movement between opposites. In a move designed to maintain her difference from her three fellow protagonists endlessly moving between the opposite poles of love and hatred, by leaving the stage Andromaque leaves to the living the unresolved question of closure. Hers is a move which, like that of the ancient Oedipus buried alive in the sacred grove of Colonus, will allow her to refuse to disclose her precise location, a move not of closure, but of foundation, since it does nothing more than perpetuate the dilemma of the nature of her choice even as it "decides" the end of the drama.

Andromaque's flight from life is made in the name of a reconciliation between life and death, between the dead Hector and the living Astyanax; she believes its terms will be made known only as the wishes of a dead woman, as if her "legacy" responded to the question posed by Barthes in speaking of the play: "How can death give birth to life?" (72).

And her choice is in fact the choice of the dead: of Hector "who produces this miracle in your soul" (l.1050) and of Andromaque herself, whose choice is death. The movement between the end of act III and the beginning of act IV, the crucial moment of decision, is a non-movement, since both scenes find Andromaque and Céphise alone onstage, and this "change" of scene with no change of character, unique in all of Racine's theater, is a further indication of the nature of the moment of choice: like Pyrrhus's desperate plea, "Je meurs si je vous perds, mais je meurs si j'attends," Andromaque's non-movement in the most crucial progression of scenes in the entire play—the progression from not knowing to knowing what she will do—further suggests that this is the moment when life must look to death for a decision, when life cannot simply choose itself but must go outside of itself. Andromaque's choice is not her choice, but her escape from the domain of choice.

Andromaque's final scenes onstage are the climax of the play: they depict her ultimate understanding of the relation of past to present, of death to life. The key word in these scenes is "songe": in the accelerating conflict between present and past, "songe"—a word halfway between thought and dream, logic and imagination—marks the perception of the increasingly hostile relationship between the two time periods. The absolute fidelity of present to past—a fidelity which claims to be based on reason and not on emotion, since it is itself a non-motion, a fidelity which has been the keystone of Andromaque's position of closure-as-representation—crumbles under the burden of imminent choice; and "songe" is the emblem of that crumbling:

> Dois-je oublier son père [Priam] à mes pieds renversé,
> Ensanglantant l'autel qu'il tenait embrassé?
> Songe, songe, Céphise, à cette nuit cruelle
> Qui fut pour tout un peuple une nuit éternelle . . .
> Songe aux cris des vainqueurs, songe aux cris des mourants,
> Dans la flamme étouffés, sous le fer expirants.

> ["Must I forget his father [Priam] cut down at my feet,/ Bloodying the altar which he held in his arms?/ Think, think, Céphise, of that cruel night/ Which was for a whole nation an eternal night/ . . . / Think of the victors' screams, think of the screams of the dying,/ Strangled in the flame, dying beneath the iron," (ll. 995–1004).]

The decision to save her child by accepting Pyrrhus would require a corresponding movement of forgetfulness, a turning away from the past. What will not allow that action to take place is the astonishingly vivid description of the night of Troy's destruction, seen in "songe," not a simple memory or recollection of the past but a projection of what the past will look like in the future if it is sacrificed to the needs of the present: these are the scenes which will never cease to haunt Andromaque if she chooses Pyrrhus; this is the past colored by the imminent and terrifying choices of the present. The only solution which will put those scenes to rest in Andromaque's mind is for her to become a character in them:

> Non, je ne serai point complice de ses crimes;
> Qu'il nous prenne, s'il veut, pour dernières victimes.

> ["No, I'll not be an accomplice of his crimes;/ Let him take us, if he wishes, as last victims" (ll.1009–10).]

What Andromaque learns in this confrontation with her conscience is the impossibility of closure as simple representation; the past exists in terms of a language, but that language is not the language of representation, rather it is the language of figure: "Songe, songe, Céphise"; "Figure-toi Pyrrhus"; "Peins-toi dans ces horreurs Andromaque éperdue." ["Think, think, Céphise"; "Imagine Pyrrhus"; "See for yourself Andromaque at a loss in the midst of these horrors," (ll. 3997–1005).] If closure as simple representation were functional, the past would exist in terms of a series of clear-cut orders, of behaviors to follow. But here it is as if the reawakening workings of conscience—deadened by Andromaque's need to survive the guilt of her own survival at Troy and revived by the imminence of choice—prefigured the new role of closure asserting itself upon her: her anticipatory revolt at the thought of marrying Pyrrhus, evoked by the non-neutral nature of the scene of carnage recalled in memory, does nothing more than counter her internal movement toward choice, the choice of Pyrrhus as successor to Hector which Racine avoids revealing by allowing Andromaque to disappear. Andromaque's "refusal" of Pyrrus is not simply an obedience to the orders of the past; it is a resistance to the temptations of the present which are setting the memories of the past into motion, or emotion. Now that the present has begun to refuse its indifferent status, the past must be evoked not so much by thought and reason as by a tortured moral sense, as a series of indelible images. The past can no longer be an indifferent standard, dictating the choices of the present without any movement of emotion, without any responsibility taken in the present.

If we now return to the positions taken by Poulet and Goldmann, we see that this is the moment at which Andromaque slips between their readings. If Andromaque understands that she can do nothing more in the present than pay her debts to the past, it is that she has at last come to the point of recognizing the past as being past, of feeling the inexorable and no longer resistible pull of the present away from the past. The only gesture Andromaque can offer in the face of this understanding is the gesture of her omission, her refusal to participate in the illusory continuities offered by the "transports" of life, and her move offstage, emblematic of the movement between two eras: hers is a sacrifice not simply to the past, but more fundamentally to the future, as the transformation of the word "songe" in Andromaque's final long speech to Céphise demonstrates: "Songe à combien de rois tu deviens nécessaire"; "Mais qu'il [Astyanax] ne songe plus, Céphise, à nous venger." ["Think of how many kings you will become needed by"; "But let him [Astyanax] no longer think, Céphise, of avenging us," (ll.1106 and 1119).] It is a sacrifice which defers the paradox of the relation of past and present, eternally floating between representation and interpretation, an admission that that paradox can never be "solved," the question "closed," but that it must perpetually be re-opened and re-closed.

And yet if tragedy is defined, as Goldmann claims, by a refusal of the alternatives, the moment of Andromaque's sacrifice is not her least tragic, but rather her most tragic moment: "trying to transform her moral victory into a material victory which will live on after her" [*The Hidden God*, 324]—the very action which Goldmann claims puts an end to Andromaque's tragic stature—is no more than trying to show how death can lead to life, just as her sacrifice takes place at the moment when life must turn to death if it is to make a choice.

It is in this sense that the central figure of the close of Andromaque's drama is not so much a human figure as a rhetorical figure, oxymoron, the very figure that predicates the coexistence of life and death. The mechanism of love and hatred which is at the center of the three characters who cannot choose is an oxymoron struggling against itself, a contradiction striving toward the resolution of choice (love *or* hatred). But Andromaque's sacrifice recognizes the irresolvable nature of this opposition: "Voilà de mon amour l'innocent strategème"; "Et pour ce reste [Astyanax] enfin j'ai moi-même en un jour/ Sacrifié mon sang, ma haine et mon amour." ["There is the innocent strategy of my love"; "And for this remnant, finally, I myself in one day/ Have sacrificed my blood, my hatred, and my love," (ll.1097 and 1123–24).] The "innocent strategy" of Andromaque, an oxymoron insofar as any strategy has the potential of bringing with it a charge of guilt, perfectly characterizes the departing Andromaque who refuses to choose between fidelity to the past (innocence) and responsibility in the present (strategy). Similarly, Andromaque's sacrifice of her hatred and her love is not so much a sacrifice of two separate emotions, love for Hector and hatred for Pyrrhus, as one which understands the symbiotic relationship of love and hatred, since her hatred for Pyrrhus is itself a reversible emotion. Andromaque has seen that neither love nor hatred exists without the other as a source of nourishment, guaranteeing the movements of life and precluding the movement of choice, and her understanding of the nature of this reversal is what closes her off from life.

Andromaque's central action, sacrifice itself, is the ultimate oxymoron, since sacrifice is a circumscribed evil in the name of a larger good: like tragedy itself, it says that the suffering it puts into play leads to a catharsis, a beneficial reversal of emotion (fear yielding to relief). To this extent, Andromaque's attempt at sacrifice, while it precipitates the end of the drama of non-choice, is simultaneously a closure and an opening:

> Sacrifice is nothing but one more violence, a violence that is added to other violences, but it is the last violence. . . . The gathering of everyone against one sole victim is the normal resolution on a cultural level, and the properly normative resolution, for it is from this resolution that all cultural rules spring.[18]

These two statements by René Girard pinpoint the double-faced nature of Andromaque's sacrifice, the most Janus-like of all gestures: Andromaque's sacrifice, a flight from the *violence* and the *vie* of the play's other protagonists, is oxymoronic violence, the violence that ends violence, since it is a way of making choice—shown by the play to be consonant with death alone—accessible (even if not acceptable) to life. To this extent, it is not only an ending violence, but also a founding violence, a violence that leads to a new order, indeed without even drawing down upon Andromaque's head the responsibility for that order: for it is Oreste's Greeks who are the cause of Pyrrhus's downfall.

Indeed, one of the most striking gestures made by the end of the play is the movement toward an ill-defined, communal responsibility. Oreste, who upon his arrival in Epirus as the representative of the Greeks had no identity, no capacity for choice, begins the play in a position of closure-as-representation, since he comes to the present with orders from the past, on a purely political mission. This is a posi-

---

18. René Girard, *Des choses cachées depuis la fondation du monde* (Paris: Grasset, 1978), 33 and 36. Translation mine.

tion that must initially have been coveted by Andromaque, who wants nothing more than simply to obey orders from elsewhere, to be able to say that the present is out of her hands; but it is intolerable to Oreste. When Oreste, a convenient homonym of Andromaque's ideal—"au reste" suggesting the dream of existing as a pure vestige—does not manage to carry off an identity in the course of the play, when his plan to win Hermione fails, when, on the edge of madness, he cries out, "suis-je Oreste enfin?" ["Finally am I Oreste?"], his meaning is not so much "Amidst all this confusion, am I still the man I have always been?" as it is "After all these attempts to capture an identity of my own, am I at last Oreste?" "Enfin," the desired closure of identity to which Oreste aspires, is the opposite of "au reste," the status of representative which he wishes to flee. And Oreste's madness comes on with the realization that being a "representative" (closure-as-fidelity) can never be fully compatible with having an identity (closure-as-choice): obeying Hermione's orders has not gotten him what he wanted, that is, a true identity, any more than following the orders of the Greeks.

Andromaque, on the other end of the spectrum, might seem to gain an identity in the course of her abortive sacrifice and her coming to the throne of Epirus. But in fact, Andromaque becomes less a personal agent, capable of future choices, than a figure who is spoken about as belonging to another domain. Andromaque's non-appearance at the end of the play allows her to escape the system of the play's movements: just as her "choice" is what brings death into life, or what points out the oxymoron in life itself, she goes outside of the medium of theater and moves into the domain of an almost impersonal legend, no longer a character making gestures which one might interpret, but a name about which one can only speculate:

Andromaque elle-même, à Pyrrhus si rebelle,
Lui rend tous les devoirs d'une veuve fidèle,
Commande qu'on le venge, et peut-être sur nous
Veut venger Troie encore et son premier époux.

"Andromaque herself so rebellious against Pyrrhus
Is doing all her duties toward him as his faithful widow,
Orders that he be avenged, and perhaps at our expense
Wants still to avenge Troy and her first husband," (ll.1589–92)*

The final word about Andromaque in the play is thus a word which

---

* Cf. the rhyme fidèle/rebelle in the third *Cantique,* for which see note 8.

invents a possible scenario for her, a word not of closure, but of openendedness, a "perhaps" that guesses about other dramas which Andromaque might play out now that she is offstage. And Racine's "return" to an ending which, like that of Euripides' play, keeps Andromaque far away is symptomatic neither of closure-as-fidelity nor of closure-as-choice, but of a third form of closure: closure as tradition, the founding of one's own text. This form of closure is itself an oxymoron, since it is an admission of the antithetical nature of the first two forms of closure; it is a form of non-closure, a closure by the terms of which fidelity to the past—to the text inherited—must take the form of interpretation, choice, and endless speculation and risk. The text will now imitate its own interpretation, will prevent interpretation from becoming a simple, one-time choice but rather will work to prolong that interpretation by leading viewers of *Andromaque* back into the domain of vacillation.

The text as founder of an inheritance will thus complement Andromaque's "sacrifice": its very foundation an implicit recognition of the irresolvable conflict between representation and responsibility, it will base its future existence upon the retelling of that irresolvable paradox, just as Céphise was meant to "represent" Andromaque to her son after her death. Responsibility, unsuccessfully sought by everyone in the play and successfully—or unsuccessfully?—shunned by Andromaque herself, now rests upon the spectator, a fact which reverses the terms of Cléone's description of Oreste vacillating over the murder of Pyrrhus:

> Enfin, il est entré, sans savoir dans son coeur
> S'il en devait sortir coupable ou spectateur.

> Finally he went in, without knowing in his heart
> Whether he was to come out guilty or a spectator. (1471–72).

It is no longer the actors who incur guilt and the spectators who escape it, as Cléone's words suggest and Oreste's hesitations corroborate; it is now the spectator himself, he who "determines" the valence of Andromaque and her cohorts, who also assumes the responsibility that they have tried to entrap and she has tried to elude.

Racine thus leaves us, as Andromaque leaves the stage, less as a way of dodging closure-as-responsibility than as a way of making us stop and dwell on its nature: at the close of this representation we, too, are left with a choice of Andromache's. Racine's reversion to the close of Euripides' play—or at least to Andromache's conspicuous absence—is not a repetition of Euripides but a return to him, since it is a reversion that cannot erase the memory of other versions of Andromache, or of the luxury—and the burden—of Racine's choice of endings.[19] *Andromaque*, in sum, is a text which closes into itself the very question of choice, along with the refusal to answer that question for us. Like the site of the play itself, Epirus, a part of Greece much closer to France than the setting of Euripides' play, Phthia,[20] Racine considerately leaves this Greek tale somewhere between its ancient origins and its present audience, as if to tell them, as the close of any tragedy should, that the next move is theirs.

19. On this point we disagree with Barthes' suggestion that "out of critical scruple one prefers not to take this suppressed scene into account" (81), and with his assessment of the outcome of the play as "unambiguous." This play can certainly be studied independently of the question of the establishment of the text, indeed ought to be studied in that way as well; but since Racine himself problematizes the relation of the setting of the text to its themes, the two questions can justifiably be treated together. A similar case could be made for the text of *Mithridate*, in the preface to which Racine claims to have been faithful to history ("I've followed history with great faithfulness," *Oeuvres complètes*, 1, 601, translation mine), and which opens with the line, "On nous faisait, Arbate, un fidèle rapport" ["We were, Arbate, given a faithful account"].

20. Epirus is on the far western edge of Greece; part of it is in present-day Albania. Racine did not of course invent the setting of his play, since the "second Troy" which Andromache and her second Trojan husband Helenos build in the *Aeneid* (3, 295 ff.) is on the site of the fallen Pyrrhus's kingdom in Epirus. But Euripides' play takes place in Phthia, Achilles' land, even though it takes place long after Achilles' death. And Racine's use of Virgil's setting is perhaps meant to recall the dangers of simply building a "second Troy," as Virgil's Andromache and Helenos do. To this extent, the audience of Racine's play would be in a position analogous to that of Virgil's hero-observer Aeneas, who is witness to the limitations of closure-as-representation of the past when he sees the second Ilium in Epirus, and consequently comes to realize that no new order can be simply a copy from the past, but that every new foundation must be a gesture of present responsibility.

DAVID F. HULT

# Closed Quotations: The Speaking Voice in the *Roman de la Rose*

Bien souvent le sens de la vie est que ce n'est pas la mort.
—Théophile Gautier

Any critical evaluation of literary continuations must in some way deal with the question of a text's relative openness or closure—the extent to which a "first" text can be considered complete and unified in an ideal way or, conversely, in need of further additions. Indeed, as a literary gesture, the continuation tacitly proclaims a work's incompleteness (how else to justify its own existence?) and declares itself in turn to be the missing piece in a newly formed totality which comprises both parts. Gérard Genette has recently argued that continuations should take their place along with other texts (such as parodies or pastiches) whose total structure derives from a previously existing work, to form a category which he names the *hypertext*.[1] But the extraordinary vastness of Genette's corpus, which ends up stressing a typology of derivation, ultimately loses sight of the essentially symbiotic quality of the continuation, an aesthetic construct based on strategies of mimetic supplementarity *and* recombination. Not only can literary continuaton transcend a fixed typology such as that of Genette, potentially conveying parodic and serious intentions at the same time, but its location on the borderline between *hypertext, intertext* and *metatext* (to borrow three of Genette's favorite neologisms) suggests a dialogic semantic structure which perhaps amounts to more than the sum of its parts.[2]

While the continuation can no longer constitute a viable literary enterprise in view of the modern restrictions on artistic property (and propriety), it was a flourishing genre in the Middle Ages and through to

1. *Palimpsestes: La Littérature au deuxième degré* (Paris: Seuil, 1982), 14: "I thus call hypertext any text derived from a previous text through a simple transformation . . . or an indirect transformation, which we shall call *imitation*." Except where otherwise noted, all translations in this article are my own.
2. Genette, 8–14. On dialogism and intertextuality, see Julia Kristeva, "Le mot, le dialogue et le roman," in Σημειωτικὴ: *Recherches pour une sémanalyse* (Paris: Seuil "Coll. Points," 1978), 82–112.

the eighteenth century. One of the most celebrated and remarkable examples in all of Western literature is the *Roman de la Rose,* a narrative allegory undertaken by Guillaume de Lorris around 1235 and completed some forty years later by a second author, Jean de Meun. Jean's two-faced, even contradictory, attitude toward the poem provides a fascinating example of the complexities involved in the work of continuation. For on the one hand, his continuation is seamlessly welded to Guillaume's *Rose* (however irreconcilable, the two parts have always been designated by a single title and thus, more often than not, viewed as two components of one text); on the other, Jean de Meun manages to reveal in the midst of his own work the change in authorship and thus the inauthenticity of the continuation. The paradox is all the more subtly advanced since Jean avoids giving this information in a direct narrative intervention, couching it in the guise of a fictionalized prophecy: Amor, the God of Love, points to the fictional Lover and identifies him with the poet Guillaume de Lorris (a name hitherto unmentioned). He then prophecies two events: the death of Guillaume, which will occur at an unspecified future time when he is in the midst of writing the *Roman de la Rose,* and the subsequent birth of Jean de Meun, who will bring the romance to its proper term:[3]

> Puis vendra Johans Chopinel,
> au cuer jolif, au cors inel . . .
> Cist avra le romanz si chier
> qu'il le voudra tout parfenir,
> se tens et leus l'en peut venir,
> car quant Guillaumes cessera,
> Jehans le continuera,
> enprés sa mort, que je ne mante,
> anz trespassez plus de .XL. . . .                [ll.10535–560]

Then will come Jean Chopinel with gay heart and lively body . . . He will be so fond of the romance that he will want to finish it right to the end, if time and place can be found. For when Guillame shall cease, more than forty years after his death—may I not lie—Jean will continue it . . . [187–88].

The peculiarity of this passage is underscored by the fact that no apparent narrative transformation has occurred such that the reader might

---

3. Guillaume de Lorris and Jean de Meun, *Le Roman de la Rose,* ed. Félix Lecoy, 3 vols., CFMA 92, 95, 98 (Paris: Champion, 1965–70). English translation by Charles Dahlberg (Princeton: Princeton University Press, 1971). All references to these two works (line numbers for Lecoy, page numbers for Dahlberg) will be given in the text.

expect an alteration in the fictional perspective of the "I"-narrator, even though the change of authors is situated some 6000 lines previous to this point in the poem.[4] How is the reader to construe Jean's mimicry of the first-person narrative form in the face of Amor's blatant disclosure of his own authorial otherness? How does this strategy relate to the premises of Guillaume's *Rose* as well as to Jean's own work as a continuator? A stark taxonomy such as that proposed by Genette is far from being able to cope with the radical convolutions which the *Roman de la Rose* imposes on the otherwise simple theoretical models of writing and rewriting, text and commentary.[5] In the following pages, I would like to describe and attempt to characterize by way of specific narrative categories the manner in which Jean de Meun effects the transition with his predecessor's work and, then, manages to encapsulate it.

The narrative frame of Guillaume's poem, the first-person account of a dream experience, presented problems to the continuator which were considerably more delicate than those involved in continuing a third-person narration such as Chrétien de Troyes's *Conte du Graal* or Boiardo's *Orlando Innamorato*. In adopting the narrator's first-person voice, the continuator feigns a solidarity not only with the persona of the first narrator but also with the fictional character who is identified as the narrator's past, or fictional, self. For the *Rose*, this initial factor is complicated by the observation that, as of the final lines written by Guillaume, the Narrator has collapsed the chronological and even spatial coordinates of his tale, approaching a position which closely resembles the disembodied metaphysical realm of the lyric poet. Specifically, what had been the Narrator's retrospective account of his dream-self's adventures in the Garden of Deduit (Diversion), carefully framed in a sequence of past tenses, turns into a personal plaint aimed at a specific addressee and characterized by a consistent use of present, future and optative tenses. Two hitherto separate "selfs," past character and present narrator, have merged.[6] I have argued elsewhere that Guillaume's

4. Within this same speech, Amor obligingly quotes the last six lines of Guillaume's fragment (lines 4023–28, repeated at lines 10525–530) and the first two lines of Jean's continuation (lines 4029–30, repeated at lines 10565–566). Amor's speech thus necessitates a retrospective glance.

5. Genette, in his brief discussion of the *Rose* (op. cit., 214–15), makes no mention of these crucial authorial coordinates and even mistakes a scribal notation for a part of the text. As for the poem's content, he merely repeats the banalities of traditional scholarship, qualifying Jean de Meun's continuation as "an act of hijacking (*détournement*), indeed of treason" (215) and as "an official [!] continuation freed from any stylistic imitation, indeed from any ideological fidelity" (214).

6. Cf. E[velyn] B[irge] Vitz, "The *I* of the *Roman de la Rose*," *Genre*, 6 (1973), 49–

Narrator has painted himself into a corner as far as the narrated action is concerned, but thereby reaches a point of lyric stasis which can be interpreted as the appropriate conclusion to a work predicated upon stereotypes derived from the courtly *chanson*. [7] Be that as it may, such an essentially aesthetic evaluation is largely irrelevant when it comes to questions of how the work could be, or was, continued. For even if one believes that Guillaume managed to close his poem, it must be conceded that none of the fictional expectations prepared for in the poem's prologue are satisfied: the dream never ends and the rose remains unattained. If Guillaume's enterprise involved a subtle strategy of generic manipulation, it will incumb upon any continuator to redirect the tale to its romance presuppositions and thus to reestablish the chronological framework which will permit further events to take place.

A brief (78-line) conclusion to Guillaume's poem (usually referred to as the "anonymous continuation"), undoubtedly written prior to that of Jean de Meun, has been transmitted by seven different manuscripts, including the only extant copy in which Guillaume's *Rose* is not completed by Jean de Meun's continuation. Following is the final complete sentence of Guillaume's work along with the first ten lines of the "anonymous continuation":[8]

---

75, to which we are particularly indebted. Vitz concludes that the revision of perspectives at the end empties the *Rose* of any possible irony and makes it, on the contrary, "intensely harmonious and unified" (69). Vitz seems to contradict these conclusions in a later article ("Inside/Outside: First-Person Narrative in Guillaume de Lorris' *Roman de la Rose*," *Yale French Studies* 58 [1979], 148–64), to the extent that she there stresses the poem's nonsubjective vision, one totally lacking in a "modern" sense of psychological interiority; this fundamental exteriority, she posits, is typical of the theological culture of the Middle Ages, which saw in man an incomplete appendage whose only hope for completeness was to strive for an outward Unity. Aside from the fact that this interpretation is belied by the Narrator's obsessive need to speak in his own voice (and his incapacity to adopt any view but his own), one need only refer to the work of René Girard on modern literary fictions (*Mensonge romantique et vérité romanesque* [Paris: Grasset, 1961]) in order to understand that the ideal of inner psychological fullness is itself a modern illusion and that, moreover, structures of external desire and longing are not simply a limitation imposed by theological structures.

7.   See my forthcoming book, *Self-Fulfilling Prophecies: Readership and Authority in the First Roman de la Rose*. This interpretation has been suggested, somewhat less systematically, by Paul Strohm, "Guillaume as Narrator and Lover in the *Roman de la Rose*," *Romanic Review*, vol. 59, no. 1 (February 1968), 3–9; and Rita Lejeune, "A propos de la structure du *Roman de la Rose* de Guillaume de Lorris," in *Etudes de langue et de littérature offertes à Félix Lecoy* (Paris: Champion, 1973), 315–48.

8.   The text of the "anonymous continuation" is quoted from Ernest Langlois's five-volume edition of the *Roman de la Rose* (Paris: Firmin-Didot/Champion, 1914–24), vol. 2, 330–33. I have underscored the last three lines of Guillaume de Lorris's text (Lecoy, 4026–28; Dahlberg, 88) and bracketed the period which appears in the Lecoy edition.

*Ja mes n'iert rien qui me confort*
*se je pert vostre bienveillance,*
*car je n'ai mes aillors fiance* [.]
Ne reconfort nul qui m'aïst.
Ha! biaus douz cuers, qui vos veïst
Au meins une foiz la semaine,
Assez en fust mendre sa peine;
Mes je ne sai sentier ne voie
Par ou jamais nul jor vos voie.
En ce qu'estoie en tel destrece,
Si vi venir a grant noblece
Devers la tor dame Pitié,
Qui maint cuer triste a fait haitié.

*If I lose your good will, there will never be any comfort for me, since I*
*have no ties of faith elsewhere* [.] nor any consolation which might help
me out. Ah! fair sweet heart, whoever might see you at least once a
week would have his suffering reduced considerably; but I do not know
of any passage or trail by which I might ever again come to see you some
day. While I was in such distress, I saw Lady Pity (who has made many a
sad heart joyous) come from over by the tower with a very noble air.

The continuator exploits the ambiguity of *ne* (which can be a negative
particle, "not," or a coordinating conjunction, "nor") in order to attach
his initial fragment to Guillaume's syntactically complete final clause:
"Ne reconfort" ["nor consolation"] harkens back to the negation contained in line 4028 and thus imposes itself as a second direct object to
the verb "ai" ["I have"]. The text of Guillaume is thus grammatically
opened up to accept an additional line, which in turn effects another
opening, this time of a prosodic nature: the first half of a new rhyming
couplet ("aïst") calls for its completion. In the lines which follow, several of the stylistic features characteristic of the closing passage of
Guillaume's work are mimicked: apostrophe ("Ah! dear sweet heart");
first-person present tense system ("I do not know"); imperfect sub-
junctives with a hypothetical force ("might help"; "might see"; "would
have"); direct address ("you"). However, an outright shift in point of
view can be detected as of the seventh line of the continuation. First,
there is an abrupt transition from the present/optative tense structure
to a retrospective vision, marked by the imperfect "estoie" ["I was"],
followed by the narrative *passé simple* "vi" ["I saw"] in the eighth line.
Not only does the imperfect serve to encapsulate chronologically and
aspectually the situation which precedes it, but this effect is reinforced
by a further evaluative expression, "tel destrece" ["such distress"].
While "distress" provides a semantic recapitulation of a particular in-

ner emotional state, "such" functions typically as a comparative adjective referring to an "explicitly or implicitly mentioned reality."[9] The object of this comparison, the "reality" being referred to, is constituted by the previous lines of the poem, henceforth viewed at a distance, from the exterior: "such distress" describes summarily a previously evoked state of mind, and the previous passage of direct discourse is itself the very sign of that distress to the extent that it is the verbal result of the emotion (in the same way that to speak of one's physical pain involves a descriptive, recapitulative mode, whereas to say "ouch!" is to reveal verbally the feeling itself, or its direct effect).[10] Were a speaker to say, "I *am* in such distress," he would likewise be situating himself at a remove, but as a means of assessing a present situation; the combination of the recapitulative phrase with the shift in verb tense (present-to-past) assures that we have here an example of one of the most common of narrational devices: direct quotation. But before we continue with our discussion, a few words need to be said about the problems of direct quotation in medieval texts.

Those of us whose acquaintance with medieval literature comes exclusively from modern editions or translations (a group which is likely to include most people reading these lines) have been "spoiled" in all senses of the term. This is to say that the careful diacritical marking of direct quotation, as well as the imposition of other forms of punctuation, renders the reader's task easier, but it also in some sense alters the text.[11] For most medieval manuscripts, punctuation of any kind (even including the most basic sentence marker, the period) was virtually nonexistent. And those manuscripts which do include some kind of punctuation, such as Guiot's transcription of Chrétien de Troyes's romances, certainly do not correspond to any modern (or medieval, for

9. Philippe Ménard, *Manuel du français du moyen âge:* v. 1. *Syntaxe de l'ancien français* (Bordeaux: SOBODI, 1973), 48.

10. Cf. Roman Jakobson, "Shifters, Verbal Categories, and the Russian Verb," in *Selected Writings*, vol. 2: Word and Language (The Hague: Mouton, 1971), especially 130–36. We have here an example of one of the "overlapping" language functions (language serving a capacity both as message and as code), which Jakobson terms "autonymous" and specifies as follows: "Any elucidating interpretation of words and sentences—whether intralingual (circumlocutions, synonyms) or interlingual (translation)—is a message referring to the code" (131). This function, directly associated by Jakobson with the use of direct discourse, can be compared to J. L. Austin's distinction between descriptive and performative utterances; cf. his *How to do Things with Words*, ed. J. O. Urmson and Marina Sbisà (Cambridge, Mass.: Harvard University Press, 1962), 78ff.

11. Cf. the brief remarks by Leo Spitzer, *Modern Language Notes*, vol. 58, no. 2 (February 1943), 134–35, reiterated in his "Des Guillemets qui changent le climat poétique," in *Romanische Literaturstudien* (Tübingen: Max Niemeyer Verlag, 1959), 34–48.

that matter) standard: Guiot's markings, haphazard at best, include an occasional comma, which is a marker of exclamation, and a dot, apparently an indication of rhythmic suspension.[12] These marks seem destined to facilitate a reading of the poem aloud, rather than to provide guideposts for a silent reading. The paucity of individual, silent readers provides an explanation for the lack of widespread standardized notation, but it does not imply that the syntactic and discursive units which we take for granted as fundamental (e.g., clause, sentence, quotation) were not so perceived. It merely suggests that the audience for which verse narratives were destined was probably more highly attuned to grammatical and rhythmic factors in grasping the meaning of a passage as it flowed from a sequence of clauses fixed in the mold of the rhyming couplet.[13] This would account for extended periodicity (as, for example, the potentially limitless succession of clauses beginning in "si" ["and so"], "que" ["for"], and "car" ["for"]) which is only artificially punctuated by commas, semi-colons and periods in modern editions: the particles are *themselves* the punctuation. Furthermore, as any textual editor will attest, there are certain passages which, by their ambiguous nature, militate against a clean, simple form of punctuation as required by modern reading standards (cf. the *apo koinou* construction), thus suggesting admissible syntactic structures which have long been excluded from a modern, normalized French idiom.[14]

The question of how to situate quotation marks in a text which does not mark them diacritically leads directly into the domain of discourse analysis—that is, the study of linguistic features as they pertain to, and determine, such transphrastic (i.e., textual) factors as voice, aspect, point of view and so forth. In the most basic terms, direct quotation means the passage of a narrator's voice from words that are manifestly his own to a direct report, or repetition, of words voiced by someone else. The result is an intermingling and interference of discourses, a dialectical situation in which, to adapt the expression of

12. Mario Roques, ed., *Les Romans de Chrétien de Troyes*, vol. 1: *Erec et Enide*, CFMA 80 (Paris: Champion, 1968), xl–xlii; and "Le Manuscrit B. N. fr. 794 et le scribe Guiot," *Romania*, 73 (1952), 177–99.

13. The move toward prose will thus effect numerous stylistic changes in the Old French language. For an illuminating discussion of early prose writing, cf. Bernard Cerquiglini, *La Parole médiévale* (Paris: Minuit, 1981).

14. The *apo koinou* construction, a not uncommon one in Old French texts, involves a single phrase which carries out two distinct grammatical functions, one in the clause which precedes it and another in that which follows it. Alfred Foulet and Mary Blakely Speer (*On Editing Old French Texts* [Lawrence, Ks.: The Regents Press of Kansas, 1979]) persist in calling it a "grammatically illogical double sentence" (65).

Antoine Compagnon, "the two texts work on each other."[15] Indeed, the idea of direct quotation requires that there be two juxtaposed texts or voices, the one nested inside the other. Where there is not the confrontation of two differently attributable speaking voices, we can only talk of indirect types of discourse.[16] Whether the inscribed voice is that of a written, learned authority, or simply the transcription of a vocalized statement is more or less immaterial as far as its linguistic description is concerned; in both cases the circumscribed direct discourse allows for a mimetic "play" on the part of the narrator, who redirects the original meaning of the quoted text and in turn defers his own responsibility.

The significance of direct discourse as a major narrative tool can be traced as far back as Plato (*Republic*, 3, vi–ix [392c–398b]), for whom the repetition of another's words within one's own utterance is a type of *mimesis* which should be avoided insofar as it can give rise to moral baseness. Plato's assertions in the *Republic* might appear to contradict views on *mimesis* which he expresses elsewhere (and, after all, is not the direct report of another's words the most perfect form of imitation in the

---

15. *La Seconde Main ou le travail de la citation* (Paris: Seuil, 1979), 37: "The quotation works on the text; the text works on the quotation."

16. We can only mention in passing the theoretical problems which arise when one attempts to describe free indirect discourse ("discours indirect libre") in medieval texts, where quotation itself is not always clearly demarcated; the narrator's access to "borrowed" voices is freer and on occasion more sophisticated than one would suspect. We must in any event take exception to Ann Banfield's somewhat faulty assertion that "represented speech and thought [i.e., free indirect discourse] in medieval literature is not a deliberately exploited and fully developed stylistic form," based on "the consensus of scholarly opinion and the scarcity of examples produced" ("Where Epistemology, Style, and Grammar Meet Literary History: The Development of Represented Speech and Thought," *New Literary History*, Vol. 9, no. 3 [Spring 1978], 443). Those who represent "scholarly opinion" seem to have little acquaintance with early French texts and come up with the same examples only because they depend on each other for the knowledge they do have. For a different view, cf. Spitzer (Note 11, above). A brief search turned up the following clear example from Marie de France's *Chevrefoil* (ed. Jean Rychner, CFMA 93 [Paris: Champion, 1968]), lines 83–86:

Les chevaliers ki la [Iseut] menoent
E ki ensemble od li erroent
Cumanda tuz a arester:
Descendre voet e resposer.

She [Iseut] ordered all the knights who were leading her and riding along with her to come to a halt: she wishes to dismount and take a rest.

The reader knows that Iseut has a secret rendez-vous with Tristan, and so the last line is the narrator's report of the excuse she gave her men—obviously at some distance from the truth. Can we not consider this a "deliberately exploited . . . stylistic form"? In any event, a full study of the various types of discourse in medieval narrative has yet to be done.

verbal mode?), but, as Compagnon persuasively argues, Plato's condem-
nation of direct discourse in this context is not to be construed as part of
a general campaign against *mimesis* in all of its possible manifestations;
on the contrary, his uneasiness is symptomatic of a general disaffection
from words which merely repeat other words since such a usage suggests a potentially closed verbal circuit independent of meaning or ideas
and, ultimately, the possibility of a "discourse lacking denotation."[17]
For good reason, Plato avoids expressing his reservations in these terms
and, instead, takes advantage of a facile (and specious) equation between
quotation and performance. A narrator's role may be analogous to that
of an oral storyteller, and this may be realized when a text such as that of
Homer is delivered before an audience, but this does not mean that
vocal *mimesis* written in the form of direct discourse can be reduced to
the status of an actor's mimicry. Plato's subtle use of the dialogue form
itself offers abundant proof of persuasive capacities which differ essentially from the theatrics of the oral performer.[18] Plato finds an easy basis
upon which to condemn a large portion of literary fictions in the potentially immoral social act of the verbal mimic. However, the stakes are
much higher, and the furthest extension of what is implied by verbal
repetition—the rhetorical dimension of language, the "turning" of
words away from an "original" meaning through contextual play—
should be eliminated from a society where meaning must remain carefully controlled. The deviousness of Plato's argument is in part substantiated by the observation that he scarcely admits the possibility of a
discourse freed from such *mimesis*, implying that this might be a universal and not simply accidental stylistic factor of spoken and written
discourses.[19]

Medieval fictions shed light upon Plato's discussion not simply
because they were frequently performed, but because the traits of vocal
mimicry have been mapped onto the written text; the narrator occupies
such a wide range of positions, from distanced viewer to enlightened
critic to active participant, that even his own voice is susceptible to
being framed or contextualized. The subtle possibilities of a slippage

17. Compagnon, 117. This reading is confirmed by Richard McKeon's seminal
study of Plato's varied use of the term *mimesis*, "Literary Criticism and the Concept of
Imitation in Antiquity," in *Critics and Criticism*, ed. R. S. Crane (abridged edition)
(Chicago/London: University of Chicago Press, 1957), 117–45.
18. Compagnon, 109–27. Plato gives a fuller description of the performer's art in
the *Ion*.
19. Although he proposes alterations to Homer's text in order to remove examples of
*mimesis*, he does not conceive of epic poetry in a purely diegetic mode; only one example
of the latter, marginal at that, is proposed—the dithyramb.

from inside to outside, from self-expression to exterior mimicry, hint at the danger and titillation of quotation: through the opaque filter of writing, it questions *any* voice's authenticity as a pure and unimpeachable medium of expression.

But insofar as the *detection* of quotation is concerned, it should be clear that the change of perspective implicit in the transition from one speaking subject to another will leave its marks both within the framed and the framing discourse. Harald Weinrich's groundbreaking work on verb tense as a discursive marker which performs functions well beyond its primarily grammatical one (that of indicating temporal relations) provides a number of criteria for detecting such transitions.[20] Weinrich's initial distinction between "commentative" (present, future) and "narrative" (past, conditional) verb tenses forms the blueprint for a variety of textual coordinates including attitude, perspective, and aspectual relief. In his discussion of temporal transitions within a given text and their linguistic markers, Weinrich cites four criteria which make apparent the presence of direct discourse within a narrated text: (a) a passage from a third-person to a first- or second-person account; (b) a temporal transition of the sort past-to-present; (c) presence of an introductory verb of communication (such as "he said" or "she replied"); and (d) a redundancy of character names, which seems to occur in the environment of a quotation. These features do not of course apply uniformly to every text; in the case of the *Rose,* as of any quasi-autobiographical text, the passage from third- to first-person will not be applicable. As far as (d) is concerned, the redundancy of character names will be of help in detecting *other* speakers, but not the direct speech of the Narrator's past self, the Lover, who is unnamed and designated only by the ambiguous pronoun *je* ["I"]. Two other criteria could, however, be added to Weinrich's list: (e) a noticeable shift in reference or point of view with respect to the narrative situation, which could take the form of demonstrative adjectives, adverbs of place or time, or, as we saw above, metatextual commentary; and (f) the use of apostrophe (which would of course coincide with second-person and/or imperative verb forms and thus denote a dialogue situation). Especially in a text where quotations are not set off beforehand, these six criteria will become essential markers. It should further be stressed that in a first-person, autobiographical narrative account, where the shift in grammatical person is largely unimportant, certain of the other factors will acquire a

20. *Le Temps: Le Récit et le commentaire,* trans. Michèle Lacoste (Paris: Seuil, 1973), especially 205–208. The original text, more directly oriented toward tense usage in German, appeared in 1964 under the title *Tempus.*

higher functional load, particularly the temporal transition marked by verb tense, and of course the most obvious and basic of all, the introduction by a verb of communication (which, as an explicity verbal form of bracketing, is the closest medieval equivalent to the diacritical quotation mark).

Inasmuch as the inclusion of quotation becomes an affair of style, the variation among authors is great. The *jongleuresque* affinities of the narrator of the *Chanson de Roland* explain perhaps why direct discourse is frequent and especially well-marked.[21] Chrétien de Troyes usually marks direct discourse with introductory verbs of communication, but his own ironic narrative voice frequently mixes in with those of his characters and on occasion creates within itself a factitious dialogue, as in the following passage from the *Chevalier de la Charrete* where he attempts to account for Guenevere's absence at the moment of Lancelot's triumphant return to court:[22]

> Et la reïne n'i est ele
> a cele joie qu'an demainne?
> Oïl voir, tote premerainne.
> Comant? Dex, ou fust ele donques?
> Ele n'ot mes si grant joie onques
> com or a de sa bien venue
> et ele a lui ne fust venue?
> Si est voir . . .
> Ou est donc li cuers? Il beisoit
> et conjoïssoit Lancelot.
> Et li cors, por coi se celot?
> N'estoit bien la joie anterine?
> A y donc corroz ne haïne?
> Nenil certes . . .

And is the queen not there, at this joyous scene which is going on? Yes indeed, right in front. What? By God, where else might she be? Never did she experience such great joy as she now does upon his safe return: is it possible that she might not have come out to him? It is indeed true . . . Where then is her heart? It was kissing and rejoicing with Lancelot. And her body, why did it remain in hiding? Was the joy not quite complete? Does that mean there is anger or hatred? Certainly not . . .

It is clear that Chrétien has split his voice in two in order to play the

---

21. Eugene Vance, "Roland and the Poetics of Memory," in *Textual Strategies*, ed. Josué V. Harari (Ithaca, N.Y.: Cornell University Press, 1979), 374–403.

22. Ed. Mario Roques, CFMA 86 (Paris: Champion, 1981), lines 6820–35.

facetious role of curious spectator and thus to defer an omniscient voice which is also his but which he chooses here not to deploy.

An author such as Jean Renart, on the other hand, who often creates abrupt shifts in scene and in speaker without any warning, tends to obscure the presence and/or limits of quotation. The latter's own *Roman de la Rose* provides several instances of inscrutable quotation, of which we present here one example:[23]

> Il li respont mout sagement:
> "Frere, dit il, l'empereor
> doint Diex grant joie et grant honor
> autant com mes cuers en desire.
> Et, por Deu, que fet il, mis sire?
> Mout a grant tens que ge nel vi.
> —Gel lessai tot sain, Deu merci.

> He [Guillaume de Dole] replies to him [the messenger] most wisely: "Brother, says he, may God grant the Emperor great joy and honor, as much as my own heart could desire. And, by God, what is my lord up to? I have not seen him for a long time.—I left him in good health, thank God.

This short passage brings into focus a couple of the characteristics discussed above. The situation is one in which a messenger of the Emperor has arrived at the court of his lord's vassal, Guillaume de Dole, in order to present greetings and a written invitation on the Emperor's behalf. The opening of the above quotation, which follows immediately upon a short address by the messenger, is carefully introduced by "il respont" ["he replies"] on line 980 and reiterated by "dit il" ["says he"] on line 981. The transition is further marked by the apostrophe "Frere" ["Brother"] on line 981 and the possessive adjective "mes" ["my"] in line 983. A distinct problem arises, however, with respect to line 985: even though it is clear that the question in line 984 is attributable to Guillaume de Dole, and that the answer in line 986 belongs to the direct speech of the messenger, it is uncertain to whom we must attribute the declarative statement of line 985 ("I have not seen him for a long time"). The editor has chosen to situate the line within Guillaume's speech (for reasons which are included in a note), but it is not totally excluded that the messenger is qualifying an otherwise affirmative response by underscoring the great distance he has traversed in coming to Guillaume's

23. *Le Roman de la Rose ou de Guillaume de Dole*, ed. Félix Lecoy, CFMA 91 (Paris: Champion, 1970), lines 980–86.

court and thus possible developments that might have happened in the meantime. While this isolated ambiguity is not of overriding importance for an interpretation of the romance, a later quotation (lines 1137–39) attributable either to Guillaume or to his sister Lïenor could affect the way in which we perceive the two characters. One might ultimately draw a connection between these stylistic ambiguities of speaking voice among Jean Renart's characters and the insertion of dozens of lyric pieces in the romance, which allows for a similar extension of speaking voices and a fictional intersection between lyric intonation and romance events.[24]

The medieval scribe was not totally insensitive to the need for differentiation among speaking voices in the face of authorial ambiguities. For instance, the dissolution of narrative levels at the end of Guillaume de Lorris's *Rose* is matched by an attempt on the part of scribes to ascertain the identity of the speaking voice at strategic points. A large number of *Rose* manuscripts contain rubrications which provide episodic summaries of the plot and which also designate speakers. A clear example of the latter can be found in the discussion between Reason and the Lover in Jean de Meun's continuation: there, the exchange of speeches is neatly demarcated and the interspersed rubrications of the type "dist l'amant" ["the Lover said"] make the episode look like a theatrical text. A certain confusion is to be found, however, when the scribes attempt to designate the Lover/Narrator in the last half of Guillaume de Lorris's poem. The two possibilities are *l'aucteur/l'acteur* ["the Author"] and *l'amant* ["the Lover"], and in some manuscripts a random interchange of the two reflects the scribes' indecision as to how to identify the speaking voice. To give one quite typical example, on a single folio of B.N. ms. fr. 378, at the moment of the Lover's first encounter with the God of Love, the following rubrics are to be found:

Ci devise *li aucteurs* comment li diex D'amours navra *l'amant* des saietes
"Here *the author* explains how the God of Love wounded *the lover* with his arrows"
[fol. 18r°, preceding Lecoy's line 1679]

24. Cf. Michel Zink, *Roman rose et rose rouge* (Paris: Nizet, 1979).

Ci raconte *l'aucteur* comment li diex d'amours vint a *l'amant*
  pour lui prendre
"Here *the author* tells how the God of Love came to *the lover* in
  order to capture him"
                    [fol. 18v°, preceding line 1879]


Ci respont *l'aucteur* au dieu d'amours
"Here *the author* replies to the God of Love"
                    [fol. 18v°, preceding line 1896]


Ci endroit parole li diex d'amours a *l'amant*
"At this point the God of Love speaks to *the lover*"
                    [fol. 18v°, at line 1926]


If it was in theory clear to the *rubricator* that the Author tells the story
and that the Lover acts in it, the distinction was harder to maintain as
their roles grew closer and closer. In the first two examples above, the
level of narration is clearly distanced from that of the action, but in the
final two the difference is muddled as the God of Love ends up interact-
ing with both Lover and Author. One might infer from these last examples that the Author simply takes the active role of speaker in any
context and that the Lover is the passive addressee, but in this same
manuscript there are later examples where the Lover himself speaks:
"Ci parole li amans" ["Here speaks the lover"]. In one manuscript, at
this same point in the narrative (B.N. ms. fr. 1559, fol. 17v°), the original
rubric designating the speaker as *l'aucteur* has been crossed out by a
later hand and replaced by *l'amant*. Far from betraying an indifference to
the question of speaking voice, the poem's scribal reception suggests a
desire for clarification and rectification which does not tolerate the
fundamental narrative ambiguities in Guillaume's poem. It is not surprising, then, that we should find continuators also working toward the
effacement of such ambiguity, and thus effecting a clean break with
Guillaume's problematical final lament.
    Turning to Jean de Meun's continuation, we find a strategy which is
strikingly similar to that of the anonymous continuator, but on a much
grander scale. The first lines attach themselves to the final lines of
Guillaume in a slightly different, but no less definitive way:

*Ja mes n'iert rien qui me confort*
*se je pert vostre bienveillance,*
*car je n'ai mes aillors fiance* [.]
Et si l'ai je perdue, espoir,
a poi que ne m'an desespoir.                    [ll. 4026–30]

*If I lose your good will, there will never be any comfort for me, since I*
*have no ties of faith elsewhere* [.] And perhaps I have lost it; I am ready
to despair of it. [88–91]

Rather than taking up the previous grammatical construction, Jean uses
a reinforced conjunction ("et si" ["and indeed"]) and repeats the verb
and direct object of Guillaume's penultimate line, replacing the latter
by a pronoun which makes the reference backward even more imperative.[25] Jean de Meun judiciously continues the monologue for over 150
lines, making use of a high proportion of commentative verb tenses
(present, future) along with frequent apostrophes and rhetorical questions.[26] The following passage occurs at the end of the lengthy lament:

a vos, Amors, ainz que je muire,
des que ne puis porter son fes,
sanz repentir me faz confés
si com font li leal amant,
et veill fere mon testament:
au departir mon queur li les,
ja ne seront autre mi les.
Tant com ainsinc me dementoie
des grans douleurs que je sentoie
ne ne savoie ou querre mire
de ma tristece ne de m'ire,
lors vi droit a moi revenant
Reson, la bele, l'avenant . . .                    (ll. 4184–96)

---

25. Paul Zumthor, "De Guillaume de Lorris à Jean de Meung" (in *Etudes . . . Félix
Lecoy* [Note 7], pp. 609–20), remarks that the shift from present in line 4027 ("je pert" [I
lose"]) to *passé composé* in line 4029 ("ai je perdue" ["I have lost"]) betrays already a
shift in point of view. This is true to some extent, but since the speaker's mood is clearly
one of uncertainty and vacillation, it is quite possible to interpret this transition as a
symptom of an incapacity to reach a decision.

26. In the 162 lines of this section (lines 4029–4190), I count 80 instances of the
present tense, 21 of the future, 15 of the present subjunctive and 6 of the *passé composé*.
This may be contrasted with 20 instances of the *passé simple* and only 5 of the imperfect. Thirteen of the twenty *passé simple* verbs are concentrated in a section of 23 lines
(4100–22) which consists almost exclusively of a recapitulation of the events in
Guillaume's poem.

> I make my confession to you before I die, O Love, as do all loyal lovers, and I wish to make my testament here: at my departure I leave my heart to Fair Welcoming; I have no other goods to bequeath. While I raved thus about the great sorrows I was suffering, not knowing where to seek a remedy for my grief and wrath, I saw fair Reason coming straight back to me . . . [93]

At line 4191, in a transition which might lead one to suspect that Jean knew the anonymous continuation, he shifts to an encapsulating imperfect: "Tant com ainsinc me *dementoie*" ["While I raved thus . . ."]. Parallel to the transition we looked at above, the shift in tense is reinforced by semantic markers of exterior summarization: "ainsinc" ["thus"]; "des grans douleurs que je sentoie" ["about the great sorrows I was suffering"]. As before, these stylistic markers in combination dictate our perception of a movement from one speaking voice to another and thus the closing of a quotation. The careful continuation of verb tenses after the first imperfect leads to the characteristic *passé simple* indicating a narrative progression: "vi" ["I saw"]. It might be mentioned that while some twenty instances of the *passe' simple* occur within the Lover's speech, they refer without exception to events which have already been recounted in the poem: the "past" has become the written text of the first *Rose* and is no longer the dream event. In the work of the continuator, this retrospection suggests a need to bring the poem up to date by familiarizing the reader with the events which have already taken place. The "vi" of line 4195, on the contrary, designates a new event which is to occur chronologically subsequent to the Lover's suspended monologue, now circumscribed as a quotation.

The linguistic closure of quotation on the part of both *Rose* continuators is not solely an external imposition. At a couple of moments within Guillaume's tale, similar temporal transitions can be found, as for instance in the following section immediately following Amor's departure:

> Ensi com je me porpensoie
> s'outre la haie passeroie,
> je vi vers moi tot droit venant
> un vallet bel et avenant . . .                    [ll. 2771–74]

> As I thus thought over the possibility of passing to the other side of the hedge, I saw, coming straight toward me, a handsome and personable youth . . . [69]

Here we see a similar resumptive construction, "ensi com" ["just as"] + imperfect, followed by the same *passé simple* "vi" ["I saw"], but there is no abrupt transition in verb tense (present-to-past) such as in the continuators' examples. A change of perspective is indeed being marked, but not between two speaking voices; in this context, we are dealing with a type of background relief made possible by the tense modeling of imperfect and *passé simple*.[27] A few hundred lines later, we find still another such transitional moment:[28]

> Par poi que li cuers ne me part
> quant de la rose me sovient
> que si esloignier me covient.
> *En cest point* ai grant piece esté,
> tant que me *vit ensi* maté
> la dame de la haute engarde . . .          [ll. 2952–57; emphasis mine]

My heart almost leaves me when I remember the rose from which I am thus obliged to distance myself. I was *in this state* for a long time, until the lady of the observation point *saw* me downcast *in this way*. [72–73]

Here we have a clearer sense of relief, inasmuch as a transition from present to past is more in evidence, but it is equally clear that the first speaking voice (lines 2939–54) is that of the Narrator and not of the Lover, underscored by a distinct sense of memory or looking back: "De ma folie me recors" (l. 2939) ["I recall my folly"]; "quant de la rose me sovient" (l. 2953) ["when I remember the rose"]. Here the transition merely marks a modulation within the Narrator's own voice (from an elegiac to a descriptive stance) and not a disruption of voices. Up to this point, one still cannot say that the Lover speaks.

A final transition of this kind occurs at line 3231, after the arrival of Dangier ["Resistance"]:

> Si com j'estoie en ceste poine,
> atant e voz que Dex m'amoine
> Franchise, et avec li Pitié . . .          [ll. 3231–33]

Just as I was in this distress, God leads Openness to me, and Pity with her. [77]

Here we are much closer to a quotational transition, insofar as the previously expressed thoughts in the present (lines 3204–30) seem to

27. Weinrich, op. cit., 107–30.
28. I have had to alter Dahlberg's translation in the following three quotations: he has regularized the tense confusion in order to conform to "normal" narrative patterns. This is especially inappropriate in the last 300 lines, which are all told in the present by Guillaume (cf. *infra*; Dahlberg will only shift to a present tense structure at line 3950.

indicate a point of view simultaneous with the events which are occurring (that is, a sense that the Lover, and not the Narrator, is the source of the words we are reading). However, the possible vocal relief is undermined initially by the use of the present tense "amoine" ["leads"] to represent the disruptive action, followed by a helter-skelter mix of past and present tenses to describe the arrival of the allegorical assistants:

| | |
|---|---|
| N'i *ot* onques plus respitié, | [*passé simple*] |
| a Dangier *vont* endeus tot droit, | [*present*] |
| car l'une et l'autre me *voudroit* | [*conditional*] |
| aidier, s'eus *pueent*, volentiers, | [*present*] |
| qu'eus *voient* qu'il en *est* mestiers. | [*present*] |
| La parole *a* premiere *mise*, | [*passé composé*] |
| seue merci, dame Franchise, | |
| et *dist* . . . | [*passé simple*] |

[ll. 3234–41; emphasis mine]

There *was* no more delay. The two of them *go* straight to Resistance, for the one and the other *would like* to help me willing, if they *are able*, since they *see* that there *is* need. Lady Openness—my thanks to her— *spoke* first and *said* . . .[77]

It is easy to see that the primary function of these stylistic mechanisms is that of setting the action back into motion after an introspective interlude which risks invalidating totally the narrative action. The only way to return to the action is to insert some kind of perceptual relief and introduce a new narrated element. This explains the frequent recourse to *passé simple* forms of the verb *veoir* ["to see"], which introduce literally unfore*seen* events and thus interrupt the various modalities of the Narrator's lament. The intensity of the transition, the extent to which we may speak of a juxtaposition of voices, depends of course heavily upon the context which is established. We regularly identify the commentative lamenting voice as one aspect of the otherwise objective, retrospective Narrator's voice. He is affected by, perhaps involved in, the story he is telling. The question brought up by these curious maneuvers, however, and which becomes increasingly intense as one progresses, is the following: is the lamentation, which intrudes more and more, a direct expression of the Narrator or is it a borrowed voice, the quotation of a past self which the Narrator is dutifully recording for us? To what extent can we interpret the Narrator's voice as genuinely objective? I would suggest that the above specious transitions and the tense confusion of the last passage are all failed attempts to assure the distinctness of voices and thus the continuation of the narrative progression. These attempts are abetted by the reader's narrative expectations which have been programmed at the start of the dream account. However, at the moment of Dangier's violent fury (line 3737), which leads directly to the seizure of the rose and the building of Jealousy's castle, an overwhelmingly lyric, plaintive voice intercedes and, while continuing from that of the Narrator, situates itself chronologically *within* the narrated action. From this point, once the "situation, or verse, has changed" (line 3743: "Des or est changiez mout li vers"), no Narrator can return without cutting off and encapsulating this plaintive voice.

The inability to get out of the situation other than by a circumscribing quotation, which means in effect the imposition of an exterior, uninvolved narrator, is in part substantiated by the fact that it is impossible to locate an *opening* for Guillaume's quotation (what we have referred to on occasion as the Narrator's "monologue") even though its closure in both of the continuations, as we have seen, is so neatly demarcated. Paul Zumthor isolates a passage of some 272 lines (3920–4191) straddling the two poems and qualifies it as a "narrative unit" consisting of the "*I*-monologue".[29] The purported monologue opens with the following lines: "Mes je, qui sui dehors le mur,/sui livrez a duel et a poine . . ." (ll. 3920–21) ["But I, who am outside the wall, am given over to sorrow and woe" (87).] The *I* does indeed begin to speak of himself at this point, but his self-depiction is totally integrated into the preceding descriptive passages. From line 3779, the Narrator had undertaken his narrative account of the building of the castle, but the reader is never quite sure from what temporal perspective it is being viewed, contemporaneously or retrospectively. Because of the apparently arbitrary mixing in of the *passé simple* within a framework provided by the present tense, one has the feeling that the Narrator wants the account to seem contemporaneous (he is watching it being built) but is hindered by the constraints of committing one's experiences to paper (almost necessarily implying a retrospective point of view). In the course of this 150-line segment, one feels that the castle is at the same time *being* built and *already* built, demonstrating the awkwardness inherent in prolonging a narrative in the present tense. Once the building of the castle is complete, however (essentially as of line 3830), the Narrator's position is clearly established outside the already-built structure and the rest of the castle's accoutrements can either be *described* in the present tense, or their establishment can be *recounted* in the past (as having occurred before the castle's completion).

29. Op. cit., 610.

In any event, the "Mes je" of line 3920 is only an illusory marker of transition. In a very orderly fashion, the preceding narrative segment covers Jealousy's building of the castle (ll. 3780–3848); an enumeration of the castle guardians (3849–97); the imprisonment of Fair Welcoming (3898–3908); and Jealousy's renewed feelings of security (3909–19). The only element left to describe in this "scene" is of course the Lover outside the wall, the very focal point of all these elaborate preparations. The switch in pronoun to "I" could designate the move to a quoted voice, except that in this case it is accompanied by no other transitional marker (and, in fact, the coordinating conjunction "but" suggests continuity at the same narrative level); it becomes a coy way for the Narrator to insert himself into the dream story, making use of the initial ambiguity inherent in the pronoun itself.[30]

The "monologue" thus cannot simply include the final few hundred lines of Guillaume's poem: for lack of an appropriate opening of quotation marks, attributable to a profound narrative instability which is latent in Guillaume's poem from the start, one must consider that in closing the quotation Jean de Meun has circumscribed not only a small portion of his predecessor's narration, but the totality of Guillaume's poem. The "monologue" is constituted by the entire first *Roman de la Rose*. In so doing, Jean has invested the narrative first-person pronoun with still another identity: his own. If the differentiation between present Narrator and past Lover was already a feature of Guillaume's text (but ultimately unfeasible as a concluding possibility), Jean has installed a "new" narrator whose past "self" becomes identified with the irresolvable existential difficulty of the courtly Guillaume. At once "I am" refers to the author Jean de Meun and "I was" continues to designate the poet Guillaume. But has the "I" merely become an empty convention, a fraudulent use of a self-referential pronoun which now has no meaning? Is this "I" simply a cover for the impersonal third-person pronoun?[31]

The answer must be negative, for to deny the self-referentiality of Jean's first-person narration would invalidate his brilliant poetic strategy while leaving unexplained the urge to *continue* rather than to *criticize* from a distance this poem which must be considered a culmina-

30. The fact that many manuscripts have "fui" ["I was"] in place of "sui" ["I am"] (a reading which was incorporated into Clément Marot's sixteenth-century modernization of the *Rose*) further suggests that this passage was not typically thought by medieval readers to be an opening of the Lover's direct speech.

31. Cf. Emile Benveniste, "La Nature des pronoms," in *Problèmes de linguistique générale*, 1 (Paris: Gallimard, 1966), 251–57.

tion of the courtly literary tradition. Jean meant to reveal his own identity, his exteriority, and simultaneously to maintain a personal identification with the narrative account. Whereas we are not accustomed to interpret the first-person pronoun as multireferential, it must be admitted that in this case it has a personal *and* an impersonal identification: impersonal insofar as Guillaume-the-poet is a separate individual, but personal to the extent that Guillaume represents for the present narrator a type of creative urge which he perhaps shares but which he cannot simply repeat or imitate as if it were his own. Thanks to the multireferential "I," the distinction between Guillaume and Jean becomes thematized (or, more specifically, allegorized) as that which separates direct erotic experience from the mediated work of the writer. Quotation of another's words becomes a narrative figure for such verbal mediation. Jean's continuation is not a prolongation in the simple narrative sense of the word, as when the quests of Perceval and Gauvain are pursued along further paths by Chrétien's continuators, but rather a reassessment and abstraction of a poetic principle which is henceforth viewed from an external, but not necessarily antagonistic perspective. It is not a coincidence that Amor enumerates a lineage of love poets (e.g., Ovid, Tibullus, Catullus) into which he inserts Guillaume and at the culmination of which is to be found Jean de Meun, who will sing the praises of the God of Love "in the language of France" (l.10613). Perhaps the erotic experience is itself denied to Jean (whereas Guillaume loves "the rose," Jean will love "the romance" [l.10554]), but he is able to perceive in the poetic plaint of desire at once a reflection of the writer's own emptiness *and* a possibility of accomplishment through the encapsulated text. A further substantiation of this duality is to be found in the varying preoccupations expressed in the two parts of the monologue around which the two texts are (con)fused: Guillaume (lines 3977–88) makes repeated appeals to the *heart* of the Other, Fair Welcoming; Jean, in stark contrast, points the monologue toward the Lover's impending death and the *testament* which he will leave as a legacy (lines 4184–90, quoted above).[32] The difference between Jean and Guillaume, writer and lover, narrator and speaker, is here crystallized as the difference between written testament and immaterial heart.

To quote, as Compagnon suggests, is not to judge the content of another's speech, but to utilize conflicting notions of authority in order

32. Zumthor, 614, points out that whereas Guillaume's concluding lines evoke a "dialogue situation" and an implicit "double level of enunciation," Jean's continuation of the monologue presents all the discursive features of a "speech regarding the world, and not an exchange between individuals."

to relativize our conception of the truth. Jean's poetic strategy involves a reabsorption of a *type* of discourse and not a simple critique of courtly ideology; in this way, the voice of Guillaume-the-poet, thus circumscribed, differs little from those of Reason and Nature. And even if we cannot ascribe a single point of view to the encyclopedic vision of Jean de Meun, we can interpret his approach as a comprehension, a revision, and perhaps a transcendence of what had become an ossified poetic tradition by the mid-thirteenth century, here typified and personified (author-ized?) by, or in, Guillaume. The long-standing vision of Jean as a poetic, or ideological, adversary of the courtly Guillaume de Lorris is largely insufficient to account for the texts' formal logic which, taken as a whole, creates an irreducible duality—that double movement of statement and retort, text and commentary, which is perhaps the true foundation and raison d'être of the literary text.[33]

33. I would like to acknowledge the generous help of the Griswold fund of Yale University which enabled me to carry out research for sections of this article.

# Contributors

WILDA C. ANDERSON teaches eighteenth-century French Literature at The Johns Hopkins University. She has just completed a book entitled *Between the Library and the Laboratory*.

KATHRYN ASCHHEIM is a graduate student in the Department of French, Yale University.

JOAN BRANDT is a visiting lecturer in the Department of French at the University of California, Los Angeles. She recently completed her dissertation on the problem of discontinuity in contemporary French poetry and theory and has published an article on Claude Simon's *Histoire*.

ALICE M. COLBY-HALL teaches medieval French literature at Cornell University. She is the author of *The Portrait in Twelfth-Century French Literature: An Example of the Stylistic Originality of Chrétien de Troyes* and is currently preparing a book on the William cycle epics of the lower Rhône valley.

EUGENIO DONATO has written extensively on topics ranging from modern criticism to eighteenth- and nineteenth-century French and English literature. His book on Flaubert, *The Script of Decadence*, will be published posthumously in 1985.

ROGER DRAGONETTI teaches French literature at the University of Geneva. He has written numerous articles on medieval and modern literature and his books include *La Technique poétique des trouvères dans la chanson courtoise* (1960) and *La Vie de la lettre au moyen âge* (1980).

RICHARD GOODKIN is an assistant professor in the Department of French at Yale University. His forthcoming book, *The Symbolist Home and the Tragic Home*, on Mallarmé and Oedipus, is appearing imminently with John Benjamins.

THOMAS M. GREENE is Frederick Clifford Ford professor of English and Comparative Literature and chairman of the Renaissance Studies Program at Yale University. His most recent book is *The Light in Troy: Imitation and Discovery in Renaissance Poetry.*

JOSUE HARARI teaches French literature and modern criticism at The Johns Hopkins University. He has edited a collection of essays in post-Structuralist criticism, *Textual Strategies,* and is completing a study on eighteenth-century fiction.

RENEE RIESE HUBERT is professor of French and Comparative Literature at the University of California. She has published several volumes of poetry in French and many articles on modern poetry and the relation of literature and the arts. She is completing a book on surrealist illustrations.

DAVID F. HULT teaches medieval literature at The Johns Hopkins University. He has recently completed a book on the *Roman de la Rose* and is currently working on Chrétien de Troyes and the courtly tradition.

JEAN MCGARRY, poet and short story writer, is currently teaching creative writing at The Johns Hopkins University.

KAREN MCPHERSON is a graduate student in the Department of French, Yale University.

D. A. MILLER teaches English and comparative literature at the University of California, Berkeley. He is the author of *Narrative and its Discontents: Problems of Closure in the Traditional Novel* (Princeton, 1981).

GERALD PRINCE is Professor of Romance Languages at the University of Pennsylvania. He has published *Métaphysique et technique dans l'oeuvre romanesque de Sartre, A Grammar of Stories,* and *Narratology,* and is now preparing *A Dictionary of Narratology.*

GABRIELE SCHWAB is a visiting professor in the department of English and Comparative Literature at the University of California, Irvine. Her home university is the University of Constance, West Germany. She is the author of *Samuel Becketts Endspiel mit der Subjektivität* and has a new book, forthcoming in 1984, which is devoted to the study of subjectivity and aesthetic response in modern fiction.

D. L. SELDEN is Assistant Professor of Classics at Barnard College, Columbia University.

PAUL ZUMTHOR, retired from the University of Montréal, has published numerous books and articles on medieval French and Provençal literature, including *Essai de poétique médiévale* (1972) and *Le masque et la lumière* (1978). His most recent book, *Introduction à la poésie orale* (1983), deals with problems related to an anthropology of literature.

The following issues are available through Yale University Press, Customer Service Department, 92A Yale Station, New Haven, CT 06520.

63 The Pedagogical Imperative:
  Teaching as a Literary Genre
  (1982) $11.95
64 Montaigne: Essays in Reading
  (1983) $11.95
65 The Language of Difference:
  Writing in QUEBEC(ois)
  (1983) $11.95
66 The Anxiety of Anticipation
  (1984) $11.95
67 Concepts of Closure $11.95
68 Forthcoming Issue
69 Forthcoming Issue

Special subscription rates are available on a calendar year basis (2 issues per year):

Individual subscriptions $20.00
Institutional subscriptions $23.90

- - - - - - - - - - - - - - - - - - - - - - - - - - - - - - - - - - - - - - - - -

**ORDER FORM** **Yale University Press,** 92A Yale Station, New Haven, CT 06520
Please enter my subscription for the calendar year
☐ 1983 ☐ 1984 ☐ 1985
I would like to purchase the following individual issues:

_____

_____

For individual issues, please add postage and handling:
Single issue, United States $1.00          Single issue, foreign countries $1.50
Each additional issue $ .50                 Each additional issue $ .75
Connecticut residents please add sales tax of 7½%.

Payment of $_____ is enclosed (including sales tax if applicable).

Mastercard no. _____

4-digit bank no. _____ Expiration date _____

VISA no. _____ Expiration date _____

Signature _____

SHIP TO: _____

_____

_____

- - - - - - - - - - - - - - - - - - - - - - - - - - - - - - - - - - - - - - - - -

See the next page for ordering issues 1 – 62. **Yale French Studies** is also available through Xerox University Microfilms, 300 North Zeeb Road, Ann Arbor, MI 48106.

The following issues are still available through the Yale French Studies Office, 315 William L. Harkness Hall, Yale University, New Haven, Conn. 06520.

**Add for postage & handling**

Single issue, United States   $1.00
Each additional issue   $ .50

Single issue, foreign countries   $1.50
Each additional issue   $ .75

- - - - - - - - - - - - - - - - - - - - - - - - - - - - - - - - - - - - - - - - - - - - -

**YALE FRENCH STUDIES**   315 William L. Harkness Hall, Yale University, New Haven, Connecticut 06520

A check made payable to YFS is enclosed. Please send me the following issue(s):

Issue no.          Title                                                                    Price

_____          _____          _____
_____          _____          _____
_____          _____          _____

                          Postage & handling          _____
                                      Total          _____

Name _____

Number/Street _____

City _____ State _____ Zip _____

The following issues are now available through Kraus Reprint Company, Route 100, Millwood, N.Y. 10546.

36/37 Structuralism has been reprinted by Doubleday as an Anchor Book.

55/56 Literature and Psychoanalysis has been reprinted by Johns Hopkins University Press, and can be ordered through Customer Service, Johns Hopkins University Press, Baltimore, MD 21218.

# american journal of
# SEMIOTICS

A Quarterly Journal of the **Semiotic Society of America**

**Editors:** Irene Portis Winner and Thomas G. Winner

**Editorial Board:** Jean Alter, Eugen Baer, Jerome Bruner, Jonathan Culler, Paul Ekman, Irene R. Fairley, Max Fisch, Kenneth Ketner, Shelagh Lindsay, Ladislav Matejka, Leonard Meyer, Daniel Rancour-Laferrière, Donald Preziosi, Irmengard Rauch, Meyer Schapiro, Robert Scholes, Charles Segal, Milton Singer, Edward Stankiewicz, Henri Zerner.

The *American Journal of Semiotics* is a broadly interdisciplinary journal concerned with the nature and role of sign processes — with special attention to human sign systems and the messages they generate.

From the contents of Volume I, (1982)

Eugen Baer
*The Medical Symptom*

Jerome Bruner
*The Formats of Language Acquisition*

Jonathan Culler
*Semiotics of Tourism*

Daniel Patte
*Greimas's Model for the Generative Trajectory of Meaning in Discourse*

David Lidov
*The Allegretto of Beethoven's Seventh*

Jerzy Pelc
*Theoretical Foundations of Semiotics*

Thomas A. Sebeok
*Dialogue about Signs with a Nobel Laureate*

Milton Singer
*On the Semiotic of Indian Identity*

George Steiner
*Narcissus and Echo*

Volume II, Nos. 1-2 (Spring 1983) is a special issue on Peirce's semiotic, edited by Kenneth Ketner (Texas Tech), which addresses a broad range of topics and includes articles by Hanna Buczynska-Garewicz, Carolyn Eisele, Max Fisch, Kenneth Ketner, Roberta Kevelson, and others. This issue will be of special interest to philosophers, logicians, mathematicians, linguists, and aestheticians.

Volume II, No. 3 (Summer 1983) will be devoted to Roman Jakobson's contribution to semiotics.

-----------------------------------------------------------------------------------------------------

Subscription is included in membership in the Semiotic Society of America. Annual dues are $30; Students and emeriti $15, Institutions $40. Foreign membership/subscription: add $5. Joint membership: add $10 to the dues category of the highest paying member to receive Journal. Please enter my membership/subscription to the AJS:

☐ Individuals $30    ☐ Students/emeriti $15    ☐ Institutions $40    ☐ Joint $_____

Name _____

Address _____

City _____ State _____ Zip _____

Please send check made payable to Semiotic Society of America to:

*Subscription Manager, Semiotic Society of America, P.O. Box 10, Bloomington, Indiana 47402*

# representations

"Emerging out of an international intellectual context, *Representations* synthesizes and reenergizes the various currents of 20th-century cultural criticism."

**Leo Lowenthal**
*member of the Frankfurt
School for Social Research*

"An exceptionally valuable forum within which different approaches to the study of cultural history can speak to and against each other . . . a genuinely important new journal."

**Hayden White**
*Chairperson of the History of Consciousness
Program, University of California, Santa Cruz*

## THE UNIVERSITY OF CALIFORNIA PRESS

$5
Available at bookstores
or by subscription for $20 per year.
Journals Department
Berkeley, California 94720

# HUMANITIES IN SOCIETY

HUMANITIES IN SOCIETY is an interdisciplinary journal concerned with the role of ideas in modern society. It aims to situate intellectual endeavors in a social context and to explore the power relations that govern society. How do certain currents of thought gain legitimacy both within the academic community and outside it and how and why do these currents either reinforce the power of particular groups at the expense of others or challenge the domination of hegemonic groups by proposing alternative perspectives on the past, the present, and the future? Recent and forthcoming issues deal with Psychoanalysis and Interpretation, the Politics of Literacy, Militarism and War (double issue), Michel Foucault (double issue). Future issues being compiled include the following. for which submissions are requested. These should be sent by the date indicated to the guest editor, in care of the Center for the Humanities address below.

RELIGION AND POLITICS: What types of roles does religion play in political cultures, in various times and places? How do religious ideology and political practice interact? (Robert Booth Fowler, June 1, 1983)

RACE, CLASS, AND CULTURE: What is the significance of the current racial and class crisis? What perspectives and insights can the humanities offer which might aid in developing a non-racist and democratic society? Do the norms, myths, symbols, and popular culture that humanists study and promote help to eradicate the crisis or deepen it? (Manning Marable, August 1, 1983)

MARXISTS AND THE UNIVERSITY: What are Marxists doing in American universities? Have Marxist critics of society lost their real voices of opposition? Is the university, a workplace that produces cultural commodities, being significantly changed by Marxists—or are they being changed by it? (Robert M. Maniquis, September 1, 1983)

SEXUALITY, VIOLENCE, AND PORNOGRAPHY: What are the relationships between pornography and sexual oppression, freedom of speech, crimes of violence? What is the relationship between sexuality and political awareness and commitment? What forms might a new truly liberated sexuality take? (Marie-Florine Bruneau and Gloria Orenstein. October 1, 1983)

LITERARY EAST-WEST EMIGRATION: What are the effects of emigration to the West by writers of the Soviet Union, Eastern Europe, and East Germany—upon the writers themselves, their home countries, and their adopted countries? (Olga Matich and Arnold Heidsieck, October 1, 1983)

— — — — — — — — — — — — — — — — — — — — — — — — — —

## HUMANITIES IN SOCIETY

☐ $20.00 individual rate for one year     ☐ $32.00 individual rate for two years
☐ $26.00 institution rate for one year     ☐ $ 8.00 single issue (specify)
    (add $4.00 postage outside the U.S.)     ☐ $10.00 double issue (specify)

Name _____

Address _____

City_____ State_____ Zip_____

Make checks payable to: Humanities in Society

Mail to: Department Q, Center for the Humanities, Taper Hall of Humanities 326, University of Southern California, Los Angeles, CA 90089-0350

# REVUE FRANÇAISE D'ETUDES AMERICAINES

10, RUE CHARLES V — 75004 PARIS

A Journal published since 1976 by the French
Association for American Studies (AFEA)
A tri-annual from February 1982

. . . . . . . . . . . . . . . . . . . . . . . . . . . . . . . . . . . . . . . . . . . . . . . . . . . . . . . .

Fill out and send to : RFEA, 10, rue Charles V - 75004 PARIS

Please ● send ....... copies of Nos 2, 3, 4, 5, 6, 7, 8, 9, 10, 11, 12, 13, 14, 15
      ● enter my subscription for 19...

NAME : ..........................

ADDRESS : .....................
...................................
...................................

o Price per issue : 35 FF (air mail)

o One-year subscription for the 1982 issues :
— individuals : 90 FF (105 FF air mail)
— institutions : 105 FF (120 FF air mail)

# PRAXIS

*Praxis #6:* Art and Ideology (Part 2)

*Michel Pecheux,* **Language, Ideology and Discourse Analysis: An Overview**

*Douglas Kellner,* **Television, Mythology and Ritual**

*Nicos Hadjinicolaou,* **On the Ideology of Avant-Gardism**

*Kenneth Coutts-Smith,* **Posthourgeois Ideology and Visual Culture**

*Marc Zimmerman,* **Francois Perus and Latin American Modernism: The Interventions of Althusser**

*Fred Lonidier,* **"The Health and Safety Game"** *(Visual Feature)*

*Forthcoming issues:*

Praxis #7: Antonio Gramsci                    Praxis #8: Weimar and After

*Single copy: $4.95     Subscription (2 issues): $8.00*
*Make checks payable to "the Regents of the University of California"*
Praxis, Dickson Art Center, UCLA, Los Angeles, CA 90024 USA

*An indispensable
review and
reference
grammar text*

# The French
# Correction

## Grammatical Problems for
## Review and Reference

## NORMAN SUSSKIND

"Some parts of French grammar continue to trouble even the best students throughout their advanced courses in the subject — and often well beyond, into real-life use of the language. In this little book I have isolated a dozen of those points and have devoted a full chapter to each, hoping, by thoroughness or cunning, finally to exorcise the demons." —from the Preface

Norman Susskind has written a uniquely helpful and at the same time entertaining book for anyone who knows beginner's French and would like to advance to a more confident and correct handling of the language. Using English for his basic instructions and comments, Susskind enlightens his readers on many of the "intricacies, illogicalities, and irregularities" of French. With abundant examples, he provides clear and detailed explanations of perennial problems as well as advice about mastering them.

This witty and instructive book, comprehensively indexed, will be indispensable as a review and reference grammar for independent study and as a supplementary text for intermediate and advanced classes.

*Contents*
Preface / Articles / Object Pronouns / Relative Pronouns / Passé Composé and Imperfect / Agreement of Participles / Reflexives / Passive / Subjunctive / Interrogation / Certain Effects of Certain Verbs in Certain Tenses and Moods / Faire, Falloir, S'Agir / Time / Index

Available in cloth ($16.00) and paper ($5.95) editions.

## Yale University Press
## New Haven and London